Cemeteries and Gravemarkers
Voices of American Culture

American Material Culture and Folklife

Simon J. Bronner, Series Editor

Professor of Folklore and American Studies
The Pennsylvania State University at Harrisburg

Other Titles in This Series

Cemeteries and Gravemarkers
Voices of American Culture

Edited by
Richard E. Meyer

With a Foreword by
James Deetz

U·M·I Research Press

Ann Arbor / London

Produced and distributed by
UMI Research Press
an imprint of
University Microfilms Inc.
Ann Arbor, Michigan 48106

Library of Congress Cataloging in Publication Data

  Cemeteries and gravemarkers : voices of American culture / edited by
Richard E. Meyer.
    p. cm—(American material culture and folklife)
    Includes bibliographies and index.
    ISBN 0-8357-1903-0 (alk. paper)
    1. Sepulchral monuments—United States.   2. Cemeteries—United
States.   3. Epitaphs—United States.   4. United States—Social life
and customs.   I. Meyer, Richard E., 1939-   . II. Series.
GT3203.C46   1989
393.1'0973—dc19   88-30119
                                                                 CIP

British Library CIP data is available.

In Memory of
Erwin Conrad Meyer (1910–1980)
Ruhe in Frieden

Contents

Ethnicity and Regionalism

Business and Pleasure

Foreword

To write a foreword to this collection of essays on cemeteries and grave markers is rather daunting, since the excellent introduction serves this purpose quite well. On the other hand, the introduction permits a certain freedom which I shall now indulge by touching on several subjects that otherwise, for better or worse, might never have appeared in print. I suppose it is natural that when our careers stretch further behind us than before, we look back on how it all took place, and what, if anything, it all meant. In my case, the period of the early sixties stands out particularly as a time of great excitement and pleasure, for it was then that Ted Dethlefsen and I discovered cemeteries. The four years we spent studying the grave-markers of early New England were for me the most enjoyable time of my professional life, and one of the main reasons for this is the ephemeral, anecdotal context in which the more disciplined research took place. One was always encountering the unexpected; local folks had wonderful tales to tell; and, on occasion, something would happen that defied rational explanation. It is this aspect of gravestone studies that deserves attention, and I hope that my freedom of subject might allow me to indulge in the anecdotal.

It all began for Ted and me one steamy July afternoon in Somerville, Massachusetts, where we were both teaching archaeology at Harvard summer school. Sitting on the porch of Ted's top-floor apartment in a classic Boston tripledecker, we were finding it very hard to keep cool, in spite of the two quarts of Ballantine Ale we had consumed. Prior to coming east from California, I had read an article in *Time* magazine (I think that Muhammad Ali's picture was on the cover) on Neal and Parker's gravestone rubbings, and having lived in Concord, Massachusetts, some years before, I recalled the gravestones along the street by the Catholic church. I suggested that perhaps Concord would be cooler than Somerville, and that we might drive out and take a look at the "quaint" gravestones as well. It wasn't that much cooler, as it turned out, in spite of two more quarts of ale that we consumed while sitting in the cemetery, looking at the stones with no particular purpose in mind. It was then that Ted, his associative powers perhaps somehow enhanced by the Ballantine, said "Look, you don't really have to read the dates to tell roughly how old the stones are, the designs are different at different times." We were sitting in the midst of *orderly stylistic change* (thunderclap, trumpets), so beloved of archaeologists and art historians alike. This realization was so exciting that we spent a couple of hours checking every stone in the cemetery—a rather large one—and when we had finished, we knew that there was immense research potential in these old cemeteries, if all the others worked the same way as the one in Concord. They did. By that evening we had roughed out a proposal to the National Science Foundation, which was subsequently funded, providing support for our first two years of study.

This work took us through hundreds of cemeteries, and since the only significant work on the subject at that time was Harriette Forbes's (Allan Ludwig's *Graven Images* not yet having appeared), it truly was a voyage of discovery. Aware that these stones showed stylistic regularity over space as well as time, it was exciting to encounter the edge of a particular design's distribution, and see it increase as we moved toward the center, and then fade out as another one replaced it. Finding the cemeteries—all of them— was not all that easy, but with USGS maps and my children, whom I paid first five cents and later fifty cents a cemetery as they searched the maps spread out on the living-room floor, we managed to account for them all, and then go into the field and record them. We may or may not have been the first to demonstrate stylistic regularity in such a well-controlled context (I think we were, though), but when we presented a paper on gravestones and seriation at the Society for American Archaeology at Chapel Hill, Jim Ford led me, almost at a run, to the editor of *American Antiquity* to urge publication.

Ford's work on stylistic seriation in the Mississippi Valley was of course a classic, but until then, the basic premise, that of the "battleship" shape of stylistic frequency curves, had never been so explicitly demonstrated using hard data with remarkable chronological control. Radiocarbon dating was hardly called for when the date of each artifact had been so conveniently inscribed upon it. Out of this grew other studies and other papers, including one with the most curious and esoteric title in all of the archeological literature ("The Doppler Effect and Archaeology: A Consideration of the Spatial Aspects of Seriation"), which I think now perhaps should not have been written, since I don't like the idea of cultural behavior being quite that regular and predictable. The Doppler paper also wound up discussed in David Clark's *Analytical Archaeology* in a section entitled "Doppler Models," but it was the only one mentioned. But it was all fun, and I like to think, important work, albeit to a rather limited circle of scholars. In the years since, Ted and I have both followed other interests, but to both of us cemeteries retain their charm and fascination, and I regularly incorporate the material in my teaching at the University of Cape Town, but must confess that a little is lost in the eleven-thousand-mile Atlantic crossing. Not that much, however, because gravestones and their lore have a universal appeal, as the three following accounts show so well. There are many, many others.

A Curious Reversal

Here and there in the cemeteries of Middlesex County, Massachusetts, we find late-eighteenth-century gravestones with strange little cherubs carved on their tops. Looking rather like bumblebees, they are shown in profile, skinny little arms holding a large trumpet from which emerges a banner on which is inscribed a message, most often "Arise ye Dead." The cherub is in the upper-right-hand corner of the stone's arched top, the trumpet extends diagonally downward from upper right to lower left, and the banner crosses the bottom of the design area. These stones are not too common, but most cemeteries will have one or two. There is one in Billerica, Massachusetts, toward the rear of the cemetery. But this one is quite different from all the others. The entire design is reversed, almost as if a stencil had been used, but turned upside down. The head is upper left and the trumpet extends upper left to lower right. But most curious of all, the inscription on the banner is written in mirror image as well: "ɒɒɘᗡ ɘγ ɘƨiɿA." How is one to account for this oddity? Several possibilities suggest themselves, none terribly convincing. It could be that the stone was carved by an illiterate apprentice who simply reversed the entire design, but this is hardly likely, since someone else would have noticed the reversal. A more appealing explanation would be that the carver of these stones decided, for whatever reason, to reverse the design just one time. Well and good, we can say, up to a point. The design reverses perfectly well, but when it came time to place the inscription on the banner, the carver was faced with a slight problem. If in its usual form the design shows the sentence "Arise ye Dead" coming out of the trumpet as it is read, reversing it results in the message going into the trumpet, into the cherub's head. If the message were to emerge from the trumpet in both a literal and graphic sense, then the only way out of the dilemma was to reverse the inscription as well. The third possibility is the most intriguing one. Perhaps the message was to be read from the rear, or more to the point, from within the stone. This possibility suggests that the inscription of name and dates on the stone was intended, as all such inscriptions are, for the passerby, but that the message on the banner, in this one case, was intended for the deceased. We will never know, but this little stone certainly makes one wonder. . . .

Yankee Frugality

As one goes about doing research on old cemeteries, tales emerge from the local folks about certain stones, the people buried there, or about gravestones in general. Old cemeteries capture the popular imagination, as witness the frequent mention of gravestones in *Ripley's Believe It or Not,* including the drawing of a wooden grave rail in South Carolina that, according to local lore, is supposed to be the head of the deceased woman's bedstead, or the three stones in Little Compton, Rhode Island, marking the graves of a man, his wife, and a woman who was "supposed to be his wife." In the course of our work in Massachusetts, we were told a story about a gravestone that never made it to the cemetery. It is not likely true, but too wonderful not to recount. When the Lamont Undergraduate Library was built at Harvard, an old frame house was razed on the construction site. Under the front porch, workers found a slate gravestone with the inscription "Sacred to the memory of Hezikiah Warren." There was no date, only the name. A local history buff heard about the discovery and set about trying to find out how the stone came to be beneath the porch. The story that was unearthed goes as follows. The Warrens had a small daughter named Hepzibah, who tragically fell ill and died. The distraught parents went to the gravestone carver's shop and ordered a stone for little Hepzibah. When they called back a day later, the stone had been carved and the name inscribed, but not the right name. Either the parents had not spoken clearly, or the carver was hard of hearing, but the name on the stone was Hezekiah. Upon a little reflection the parents hit upon an ingenious solution to this little problem. They commissioned a second stone properly inscribed, which was duly placed on their daughter's grave. But they paid for the first stone, took it home, and when their second child, a boy, was born, they named him after the stone, a brilliant example of colonial "pre-need" provision, perhaps the first instance of a practice so common today in the selling of grave plots. However, Hezekiah ran away to sea at an early age and was never heard from again. The stone stayed beneath the porch where it had been stored for Hezekiah's eventual demise, to be found almost two centuries later. This story has some of the earmarks of modern urban legends, and there could well be other versions of it from elsewhere in New England, an area which prides itself in frugal management of worldly assets.

John Stockbridge and His Tree

The iconography of New England colonial gravestones is by now well understood and forms a powerful component in the study of the worldview of those who made and were buried beneath them. The broad stylistic trends shown by the stones give testimony to a complete transformation of attitudes toward this life and the one after death. Our earlier work suggested that the decline in popularity of the death's head motif was a function of the decline in New England Puritan orthodoxy, and while the two occur simultaneously, this explanation now seems a bit too narrow. Rather, as I suggest in my minibook, *In Small Things Forgotten,* both are functions of a major change in worldview that occurred in America during the later eighteenth century. The death's head is a powerful, emotional, and natural motif that finds its structural counterparts in hall and parlor houses, colorful ceramics, and shared objects and spaces.

The wonderful spirit faces that animate so many of the mid-eighteenth-century stones in Plymouth County are slightly more cryptic. Peter Benes's important book, *The Masks of Orthodoxy,* treats the designs in great detail and corresponding competence, and we can see that they represent a slow drifting of the death's head design toward a more human form. But the drift is sufficiently slow to give us almost a freeze-frame sequence of the change. I have always wondered what these faces might have looked like in profile, and if such a thought ever occurred to the men who carved them. Could it be that their two dimensionality is just that, and they were conceived as flat entities, given that they had no counterpart in the real world? This seems to be an aspect of these carvings that will forever remain in question.

Perhaps the most detailed analysis of the symbolism of New England gravestones is Allan Ludwig's *Graven Images,* in which the various elements of the design are discussed in terms of their symbolic significance in a theological context. One such symbol is the tree, chopped down, symbolizing death. Ludwig illustrates this design, and one of the most graphic is the Elizabeth Norton stone in Durham, Connecticut. Here we see not only the felled tree, but also the hand and arm of God emerging from the clouds, holding the axe that did the job. There is no doubt of the symbolism here, it is very explicit and graphic. But, as Freud supposedly said, sometimes a cigar is just a cigar. The John Stockbridge stone in Hanover, Massachusetts, is a case in point. Here, as on the Durham stone, is a felled tree, lying beside a tree still standing. In this case, the axe is on the ground beside the trunk of the felled tree. But under the fallen tree, we see a face peering out at us, not looking particularly distressed. When we read the lengthy epitaph, we learn that the unfortunate Mr. Stockbridge was killed when a tree he was cutting down fell on him. This stone is a quiet cautionary statement to those who might on occasion overinterpret the symbolism that they find on the stones. Were it not for the inscription, a very different reading of the design might have been in order.

Such, then, have been only a few of the many wonderful things one encounters when one undertakes to study cemeteries and their monuments. Certainly all of the contributors to this collection would have similar anecdotes to relate, and even the most detailed, disciplined, and rigorous analysis of cemetery data cannot mask the underlying thrill of discovery that invariably accompanies this work. Reading this volume will make this quite clear; it is an important contribution to gravestone and cemetery studies.

James Deetz

Acknowledgments

The essays in this volume first saw life at a conference sponsored by the "Cemeteries and Gravemarkers" Section of the American Culture Association. I owe a special debt of gratitude to Western Oregon State College for a faculty development grant which assisted me in forming the Section initially, and also to Ray and Pat Browne of Bowling Green State University for providing it a home within the ACA. My sincerest thanks as well to all those who had a part, however small, in this and past endeavors, but most especially to Barre Toelken, Ruth Butler, and the late Richard M. Dorson, three teachers and friends for whom I have the greatest respect and admiration; to this book's contributing authors, for their dedication to scholarship surely, but also for their diligence, patience, and good humor; to Harvard C. Wood III and Gaynell Stone, for reasons which I am sure they will understand; to Simon Bronner, for telling me the things I needed to hear; to Lotte Larsen, whose matchless gifts of love and support are ever my living monuments; and, finally, to all those countless thousands whose lives and deaths upon these shores have shaped the substance of a book on American cemeteries and gravemarkers.

Introduction: "So Witty as to Speak"

Richard E. Meyer

In 1693, inspired by one of his not infrequent visits to a local burial ground, the powerful Puritan clergyman Cotton Mather was moved to comment that "the stones in this wilderness are already grown so witty as to speak...."[1] Though Mather had a most immediate context for his remark—the unrestrainedly laudatory epitaph found upon the gravemarker of the Reverend Urian Oakes—he was also expressing, albeit unknowingly, what has come to be one of the most fundamentally agreed upon principles of modern material culture studies: artifacts, through a variety of complex and often interrelated manifestations, establish patterns of communication (and even dynamic interaction) with those who use or view them.[2] It is, in fact, largely because of these communicative and interactive processes that the concepts of artifact and culture are inextricably linked in the estimation of many contemporary scholars. "Underlying the idea of an artifact," anthropologist Steven Beckow has written, "is the idea of culture. We are all students of human culture, and our source of information is almost exclusively the human artifact."[3]

It is, then, the voices of culture we are hearing when we pause to consider the objects produced by members of that culture. Whether whispering or shouting, plain-dealing or knotted in intentional ambiguity, they are there to be heard and read in material things ranging from Danish woven Christmas hearts to the tombstone of the Reverend Urian Oakes. To heed them, to grapple with their messages, and, ultimately, to unlock their meanings is at once the goal of material culture studies and its most significant contribution to an integrated view of cultural history and area studies.[4] For artifacts, as Simon J. Bronner reminds us, "tell us of the everyday past and the cultural present. Significantly, they lead us to consider, too, the principles and processes that transcend time, that make us the social animals we are."[5]

It has become almost somewhat of a cliché amongst those who advocate the cultural value of cemeteries to refer to them as "museums."[6] Still, the point has considerable validity. Though certainly not created for that purpose, cemeteries—which might, by one set of criteria, be defined as outdoor, spatially delineated repositories of cultural artifacts—do in fact over time come to assume this as one of their many functions. Not the least attractive feature of their role as museums is the fact that there are so many of them: there is hardly a community of any size in America which does not boast one or more examples within or quite near its municipal boundaries. Here may be found, conveniently grouped within carefully defined sacred or secular perimeters, an astoundingly revealing array of material artifacts which serve as tangible intermediaries in the ongoing communicative process leading to a richer understanding of the history and cultural values of community, region, and nation. "Nowhere else," cultural geographer Terry Jordan has maintained, "is it possible to look so deeply into our people's past."[7] It is, indeed, the past which has formed the focus of most serious studies (including many of those found in this volume) of cemeteries and gravemarkers. Still, as a number of investigators, particularly those in the social sciences, have for some time pointed out, cemeteries and their contents are anything but static entities.[8] They exhibit patterns of change over temporal spans corresponding to their individual existences, and they can in many instances yield valuable cultural insights to a number of discrete time periods, including the present.

Taken as a whole, the study of American cemeteries and gravemarkers may legitimately lay claim to having a respectable place within the total fabric of American Studies. This rests, however, upon two essential presuppositions. One is that its ultimate emphasis, irrespective of immediate focus or particular analytical technique, is upon the illumination of the discrete cultural values which interfuse these sites and artifacts. The other is that the perspectives and modes of critical enquiry of a variety of disciplines be pooled in order to achieve a more balanced assessment of the meanings inherent in these values and the objects which project them.[9] The history of American scholarly treatments of cemeteries and gravemarkers, while sometimes extremely productive in its fulfillment of the first of these criteria, has been generally lacking in meeting the second.

The first serious in-depth study of American funerary art appeared in 1927, and in many respects it set a number of the standards against which all subsequent efforts must be measured. Harriette Merrifield Forbes's *Gravestones of Early New England and the Men Who Made Them, 1653–1800,*[10] a book beautifully illustrated with scores of the author's own photographs (many of stones which no longer exist), was no mere guidebook for the idly curious. Rather, it sought to classify and interpret these artifacts of early American society in terms of the dominant religious and other cultural influences which shaped them. Further, as its title indicates, the work placed a great deal of emphasis upon the crafters of the objects, an emphasis which has become increasingly more dominant in material culture studies of the past several decades. To many, it may have seemed as if Forbes's study was the last word on the subject, for it was not until 1966, almost forty years later, that another significant book-length study of American cemeteries and gravemarkers appeared. But what a book it was! Allan I. Ludwig's *Graven Images: New England Stonecarving and Its Symbols, 1650–1815,* while dealing with many of the same materials as Forbes, extended their treatment to provide for more probing analyses of the symbolic force of these artifacts, noting in particular such factors as European antecedents and the relationship of American puritan gravestone art to puritan theology and eschatology. In meeting Forbes's standard, Ludwig in fact surpassed it, and in so doing created another of the seminal works in this field.

The approaches of Forbes and Ludwig to the study of early New England gravemarkers were largely humanistic in their orientation. In 1967, one year after the publication of *Graven Images,* there appeared an article (perhaps the most frequently cited of all works on American cemeteries and gravemarkers) which demonstrated convincingly the validity of applying the research techniques of the social sciences to an analysis of these artifacts. "Death's Head, Cherub, Urn and Willow," by James Deetz and Edwin S. Dethlefsen, charted the evolution and diffusion of certain symbolic motifs (forms) over time and space and correlated the patterns established with known elements of the evolving cultural history of the area. This essentially archaeological approach would have great impact on a number of subsequent studies conducted over the last twenty years (including Deetz's own treatment of colonial gravemarkers in his splendid book, *In Small Things Forgotten: The Archaeology of Early American Life*), and would inspire the work of anthropologists, sociologists, and cultural geographers working on cemeteries and gravemarkers from a diverse array of perspectives.

The decades of the 1970s and 1980s have seen the appearance of a number of fine studies which have continued the work of the "pioneers" discussed in the previous two paragraphs. Of the book-length studies which continue to appear on early New England materials, the best by far has been Dickran and Ann Tashjian's *Memorials for Children of Change: The Art of Early New England Stonecarving* (1974), a humanistically oriented analysis of the correlations between cultural values and artifacts which once again reinforced, and to a certain degree redefined, the standard of excellence originally imposed by Forbes and Ludwig. Other notable New England (or New England influenced) studies include Peter Benes, *The Masks of Orthodoxy: Folk Gravestone Carving in Plymouth County, Massachusetts, 1689–1805* (1977); David H. Watters, *"With Bodilie Eyes": Eschatological Themes in Puritan Literature and Gravestone Art* (1981); Diana Williams Combs, *Early Gravestone Art in Georgia and South Carolina* (1986); and James A. Slater, *The Colonial Burying Grounds of Eastern Connecticut and the Men Who Made Them* (1987). Two volumes issued as proceedings of the Dublin Seminar for New England Folklife—*Puritan Gravestone Art* (1977) and *Puritan Gravestone Art II* (1978)—contain a number of fine articles on this aspect of American cemetery and gravemarker study. Perhaps the only significant regionally oriented study outside of the New England area, and one which will serve in many respects as a model for such studies, has been *Texas Graveyards: A Cultural Legacy* (1982), by cultural geographer Terry G. Jordan.

The founding in 1977 of the Association for Gravestone Studies has proven to be a very important impetus to the serious study of American cemeteries and gravemarkers and their relationship to the understanding of American culture. Through its annual conference, its archives and special exhibits, its publications (including its annual journal, *Markers,* and a splendid quarterly newsletter of almost journallike proportions), and its many activities designed to heighten public awareness of the value of old cemeteries, the association has in its short history accomplished much in furthering the study of and interest in this area by scholars and nonacademics alike.

Despite past efforts, significant as they have been, certain important gaps remain. There has, for one thing, been an enormous emphasis (perhaps, one might argue, an overemphasis) upon New England materials, often to the exclusion of other regions of the country where important resources beg to be examined. Questions of ethnicity, of the interplay between verbal and visual imagery, of the origins of certain forms and practices, and of the whole economic dimension of cemeteries and gravemarkers in American life have not received the attention they deserve. Perhaps most importantly, there has never been a serious attempt to bring to bear in one venue the resources and critical insights of a variety of academic disciplines for the purpose of analyzing these sites and artifacts in terms of their relationship to the evolving nature of American culture. All of these, and more, are factors which the present volume of original essays on American cemeteries and gravemarkers seeks to address. Growing out of the ongoing activities of the Cemeteries and Gravemarkers Section of the American Culture Association, itself an organization devoted to the study of American cultural phenomena from a variety of disciplinary perspectives, each of the essays found herein focuses upon some aspect of past or current American cultural values as illuminated by a particular disciplinary approach to the study of sites and artifacts. Ethnicity, regionalism and subregionalism, family, occupation, religion, and worldview—these are but some of the descriptive labels denoting cultural emphasis which may be applied to the work of the volume's contributors, who themselves represent the varying academic disciplines of Folklore, Art History, Cultural Geography, English, History, and Anthropology.

Readers will note that the book is divided into several sections, corresponding in large part to certain of the issues deserving further attention which were mentioned in the preceding paragraph. I have provided brief introductions to each of these sections in order to indicate both the rationale for the various groupings and the scope of the individual articles found therein. However, it should be emphasized here that any such grouping is by nature arbitrary and imperfect to some degree. My own article on logger gravestones, for instance, placed logically enough within a grouping of essays stressing verbal and visual imagery, could as easily have been included in the category stressing regionalism as one of its distinguishing characteristics. The same might be said for a number of other essays in the collection. Certainly, this should not be viewed as a defect in structural concept, for if anything it may be asserted that most substantially significant examinations of American cemeteries and gravemarkers will be seen to transcend the limits of their primary categorization.

Ultimately, the best and perhaps most truly satisfactory explanation of the book's purpose and scope may be summed up in a somewhat broad question and its essentially simple reply. Why study cemeteries and gravemarkers at all? For the same reasons, in essence, that we value and study all artifacts which embody lasting cultural truths: to help us achieve a better understanding of ourselves—what we are, what we have been, and, perhaps, what we are in the process of becoming. Having read over the years any number of justifications for our interest in these matters (of which the present essay is, of course, but one more example), I find myself returning time and again to the words of one of my former students, who, in attempting to articulate his reactions to a recently completed fieldwork project, may have said it best:

> In choosing gravestones, without knowing it I had opened a whole new world to myself. Graveyards are not just a place of superstition or morbid high school pranks, but a place of cultural enrichment. No longer do I look at a stone and think—dead person! That stone conveys a life and that life's love, anger, happiness, and place in family, community and society. I have found an interest to keep me happy for a long time.[11]

And so have we all, those of us responsible for the book you now hold in your hands. Some sixty years after the publication of Harriette Merrifield Forbes's landmark study, we may say that, like her and those who followed, we have searched for and listened to the voices of American culture in cemeteries across our land, and they have kept us happy—and busy—for a long time. And that is as it should be, for if stones indeed are so witty as to speak, should we not have sense enough to hear?

Notes

1.   Quoted in Harriette Merrifield Forbes, *Gravestones of Early New England and the Men Who Made Them, 1653–1800* (Boston: Houghton Mifflin Company, 1927), p. 7.

2.   See, for example, Simon J. Bronner, "'Visible Proofs': Material Culture Study in American Folkloristics," *American Quarterly* 35 (1983): pp. 316–39 (especially pp. 319–21); Thomas A. Adler, "Musical Instruments, Tools, and the Experience of Control," in *American Material Culture and Folklife: A Prologue and Dialogue,* ed. Simon J. Bronner (Ann Arbor: UMI Research Press, 1985), pp. 103–11; and Kenneth Ames, "Material Culture as Non-Verbal Communication: A Historical Case Study," in *American Material Culture: The Shape of Things around Us,* ed. Edith Mayo (Bowling Green, Ohio: Bowling Green State University Popular Press, 1984), pp. 25–47.

3.   "Culture, History, and Artifact," in *Material Culture Studies in America,* ed. Thomas J. Schlereth (Nashville: AASLH Press, 1982), p. 123. Beckow's remark brings to mind William Carlos Williams's assertion that "for the poet there are no ideas but in things." *The Autobiography of William Carlos Williams* (New York: Random House, 1951), p. 390.

4.   See, for example, Thomas J. Schlereth's apologia in "American Studies and American Things," *Pioneer America* 14 (1982), pp. 47–66.

5.   Simon J. Bronner, "The Idea of the Folk Artifact," in *American Material Culture and Folklife: A Prologue and Dialogue,* p. 24.

6.   See, for example, Terry G. Jordan, *Texas Graveyards: A Cultural Legacy* (Austin: University of Texas Press, 1982), p. 126; also several of the essays in this volume.

7.   Ibid., p. 7.

8.   See, for example, Richard V. Francaviglia, "The Cemetery as an Evolving Cultural Landscape," *Annals, Association of American Geographers* 61 (1971), pp. 501–9.

9.   On the need for multidisciplinary cooperative endeavor in the study and interpretation of material culture see Henry Glassie, *Pattern in the Material Folk Culture of the Eastern United States* (Philadelphia: University of Pennsylvania Press, 1968), pp. 238–39; and Bronner, "The Idea of the Folk Artifact," pp. 15–17. An entire collection more or less based upon this premise is Ian M. G. Quimby, ed., *Material Culture and the Study of American Life* (New York: W.W. Norton & Company, 1978).

10.   Complete bibliographic data on this and other works discussed in the paragraphs which follow may be found in the bibliography at the back of this book.

11.   Aaron Russell Ursey, Introduction to Folklore Field Collecting Project, Western Oregon State College, Monmouth, Oregon, June, 1986.

Icon and Epitaph

Icon and Epitaph

The monuments in our cemeteries speak to us in many ways—through their shape, their size, their composition (type of material), and even their positioning with regard to one another and the cemetery site as a whole. But of all their voices, it is the visual and verbal images they bear upon their faces which, be it symbolically or literally, seem to tell us the most of both the cultures and the individual lives which produced them. The four essays which comprise this section all deal with specific applications of this phenomenon, two of them focusing primarily upon the visual element, one upon the verbal, and one upon a combination of the two. Together, they consider American gravemarkers on a temporal scale ranging from the eighteenth to the twentieth centuries and encompassing the geographical breadth of the continent.

Ellen Snyder's analysis of the symbolic functions of Victorian children's gravemarkers concerns a period when the memorials erected for children first began to assume their own distinctive forms in America. (Prior to this time they generally tended to be diminutive versions of adult markers.) More importantly, it demonstrates the manner in which these forms mirrored the unique vision of childhood embodied within Victorian cultural mores. Edward Clark's study of the Bigham family of stonecarvers in the Carolina piedmont chronicles the growing emergence of a uniquely American self-awareness in the years following the Revolution by analyzing the metamorphosis of gravestone images from an older Scots-Irish clan iconography to the symbols of a new nation. My own essay on logger gravemarkers in the Pacific Northwest considers both visual and verbal statements in a contemporary context to demonstrate the manner in which gravemarkers often form an important expressive material component in the traditions of occupational folk groups. Concluding this section is an essay by J. Joseph Edgette examining the manner in which original verbal inscriptions—personalized epitaphs—frequently yield valuable insights into the cultural values and personality types of both the individuals they commemorate and those who remember them and mourn their loss.

1

Innocents in a Worldly World: Victorian Children's Gravemarkers

Ellen Marie Snyder

Victorian Americans lived in an era marked by rapid change. Technological advances, urbanization, expansive entrepreneurship, and a swelling population seemed to move society ahead at unheard-of rates. But as the rewards of civilization and the profits of business multiplied, concern rose over the consequences of economic prosperity and the environment that bred it. The thriving city marketplace was frequently depicted in sentimental Victorian literature as greedy, immoral, impersonal, and opportunistic.[1] In many ways, it seemed to embody the perils of the worldliness against which earlier puritan doctrine had railed.

At the same time this characterization of the outside world was solidifying, new adult attitudes towards children were emerging. This changing image of the child would come to stand in stark contrast to the image of the marketplace. By the late 1830s, the concept of childhood innocence was beginning to be highly valued.[2] Perceived as untamed blossoms, children were seen as pure, unblemished, and lacking in artifice. They were closely associated with the home, which stood in marked contrast to the world outside,[3] a world understood to be dominated by men. As innocent beings, small babes were untouched by outside forces; they were not part of "the world." And if they died, they were depicted in the cemetery in a way that would have been denied to them had they reached adulthood.

Children's markers—specifically, three-dimensional, sculptural depictions of children with domestic artifacts—are one of the most elaborate material manifestations of a standard urban, middle-class, Protestant, Victorian vocabulary. These markers had a unique role in the Victorian cemetery. Special poses and designs, created almost exclusively for children by adults well-versed in Victorian sentiment, conveyed visual messages about the sanctity of childhood and its separateness from the marketplace and the adult world of insincerity. These often elaborate forms were just one portion of a larger trade in Victorian children's markers, which were most often much simpler: unlike the plainer stones, they spot (rather than blanket) the cemetery landscape. But the sentiments they express share in a wider fascination with children and the potentially instructive occasion of their death that was characteristic of the era.[4]

These messages are best understood in the context of the adult world of the living. Generally held attitudes about gender roles and the home played a great part in the choices made in representing children who had died.

Victorian men, women, and children participated in an assigned social order derived from biological assumptions common to the evolutionary thought of the time. At one end of this spectrum were men. While the Victorian period saw the first real use of female labor in the factory system, and other women left homes to work in city occupations,[5] it was men who were perceived as the main players. They were the ones who "pushed the nation on its colossal course of empire."[6] The world of business into which they ventured forth and became associated with was seen at the same time as both exciting and refined and immoral and decadent.[7] As cities grew, and home and workplace became more separate, large numbers of men left the home to make their way in this world.[8] Ambitious men, out in the agressiveness and competitiveness of the marketplace, ran the risk of becoming tainted.[9] In his 1879 book, *The Coming Man is the Present Child,* Reverend W.F. Crafts captures this predicament through two stories spoken through the "omniscient" mouths of babes. The first chastises the errant fathers who are drawn away by the ever-pressing concerns of business: "There is a moral taught by the following conversation which needs to be learned by many fathers," writes Crafts. "Said a little four-year-old, 'Mother, father won't be in Heaven with us, will he?'—'Why not, my child?'—'Because he can't leave the shop.'"[10] In a related tale, Crafts reenforces the notion of the men of the outside business world as possibly being poisoned by its influences: "A GENTLEMAN who was unusually well pleased with a sermon remarked that he was carried right to the gates of heaven by it," recounts Crafts. "His precocious six-year-old son upon hearing him say this, exclaimed, 'Why didn't you dodge in father? It's the best chance you'll ever have of getting into heaven.'"[11]

This situation—heaven versus the shop—was a problem for Victorians who were worried that their concern with material prosperity was at odds with their Christian ideals. In the midst of this anxiety, and significantly at the same time that the United States was going through enormous changes as it became an urban industrialized society and left a rural agrarian past behind, the Victorian child came to stand for innocence. Unlike their seventeenth- and eighteenth-century predecessors, perceived as inherently depraved until the advent of a conversion experience, Victorian children were portrayed as uncorrupt, pure, artless, and close to nature from birth.[12] In a kind of literary cult of childhood that began around 1800 in England and developed throughout the nineteenth century in America, children's innocence and sincerity was juxtaposed against adult artifice.[13] By 1860, early liberal thinkers had been joined by most of the general population in an elevation of children into preconceived adult visions of desired goodness.[14] "In the common view," writes historian T. J. Jackson Lears, it was "especially children ... untainted by social artifice ... [who] embodied the moral innocence and emotional spontaneity which seemed increasingly absent from the public realm."[15] The child, genuine and sincere in a world marked by hypocrisy and the love of goods and business, became both relief and escape from "longstanding protestant anxieties about commercial prosperity."[16]

This role of the child as the antithesis to the marketplace was rooted in the unbreakable early association of children with the home. The Victorian era saw the home develop as a pure, sincere, safe sanctuary, ruled by women, where men who toiled in a competitive, unchristian economic sphere could be made civilized,[17] and where children were nurtured. There, society assigned women the special role of counteracting a deceitful world's hypocrisy.[18] "This is the true nature of the home," wrote John Ruskin in 1871. "It is the place of peace, the shelter. So far as the ... hostile society of the outer world is allowed by either husband or wife to cross the threshold it ceases to be a home. ... But so far as it is a sacred place, a vestal temple ... it is a home."[19] Christian morality was a means to this end: "There is no such school or Bible religion in the land as a happy, God-fearing home," wrote nineteenth-century minister Reverend Theodore Cuyler. "No church is effective for restraint from evil, and for growth in all Christian graces, as 'the church in the house.' There stands the domestic altar. There is felt the influence that moulds character from the cradle to the judgment seat; such a home on earth is the surest preparation for the home eternal in the heavens."[20] This was the cosmos of the child. Not the marketplace, not the world, but the home, with all its socially understood trappings. It was their own, and their only realm, since as tiny youngsters they were unable to part from it. This close connection bestowed upon children a great dose of purity.

With their assured sincerity and innocence, as well as their close connection to the Christian home, children assumed a special place in the Victorian social order which death only seemed to solidify. Dying as they did before they had to enter the grown-up marketplace insured their perpetual purity and spot in this order. "Their angel innocence shall remain unsullied by a breath from this sinful world," wrote the Reverend John H. Morison in 1842.[21] Dead children were safe children; ultimately and wholly pure and innocent. "Parents! spare your tears for those whom you have laid down to sleep in their narrow earth-beds, with the now withered rose-bud on their breasts," admonished Theodore Cuyler in *The Cedar Christian* (1867). "They are safe; Christ has them in his sinless school, where lessons of celestial wisdom are learned by eyes that never weep. Save your tears for your living children, if they are yet living in their sins, untouched by repentance. . . ."[22] Children who died had the surest guarantees of sinless afterlives, for their brief lives protected them from decay.

Such deep and unremitting feeling about the role of the child in Victorian society carried visibly into the cemetery, where it assumed a variety of material forms. Most common are plain markers which bear epitaphs and symbols associated with childhood, such as lambs, doves, flowers, and a number of other images. Three-dimensional sculptural representations of children with domestic artifacts—markers which actually assume the shape of a small person and a related prop with some dimension—are, as noted previously, decidedly much rarer than these markers. Cost is probably the largest factor in this discrepancy: more elaborate sculptures would have been far more expensive than plain markers. Examples such as the finely detailed sculpture of a reclining child which appeared in a trade catalog of the Philadelphia firm of Wood and Perot (fig. 1.1) would have been available (most likely through an undertaker) only to a more affluent middle-class audience. Hence, they tend to appear most frequently in large urban cemeteries patronized by the more well-to-do rather than in small churchyard cemeteries.

In the cemetery, sculptural portrayals of small children—with their vivid, often realistic appearance and size—reenforced the separateness of the childhood and adult states by establishing clear visual correlations between the child and the home, the purity of nature, and symbols of childhood. These portrayals stand in marked contrast to their adult counterparts, particularly men, for whom signs of the world of business or even the battlefield are reserved.

Of all the three-dimensional portraits of children, the most common is one of a sleeping child. The innocence of this simple act was a recurring Victorian theme. In *Agnes and the Little Key,* sleep becomes a tie between life and death. "Sights of her asleep, when her mother and I stood over her with lamp in hand, are as deeply stamped on my mind as views in the Alps," writes her father. "I could tell you every dimple which we detected as she lay on her back, a knee or an arm disengaged from her clothing."[23] Later, he recounts similar emotions on her death—a final sleep: "I fear that some

No.583

Wood & Perot. Phil
1861.

Figure 1.1.　Reclining Child Gravemarker, No. 583
From R. Wood and Co., *Portfolio of Original Designs of Ornamental Iron Work,* Philadelphia, 187?, p. 163.
(Courtesy Henry Francis du Pont Winterthur Museum Library: Collection of Printed Books and Periodicals)

of you will smile if I say she seemed to me the sweetest little thing that ever died; that, as she lay in her last sleep, no sight could be quite so beautiful and touching. . . ."[24] William Henry Rinehart's *Sleeping Children* (1859) (fig. 1.2) echoes this sentiment. An extremely popular parlor sculpture in its time, its imagery was easily translated into that of deceased children who found their place in the cemetery. In the small stone marker dedicated to Lydia and William Groot, brother and sister lay intertwined, sleeping, on a small bed (fig. 1.3). The reclining marble figure of Frank Percy Chadwick (fig. 1.4), who lays his head upon fluffy, raised pillows, equally expresses this vision of childhood sleeping as a most innocent, sweet function of their short lives, touching adults' hearts in its purity. And it also clearly makes a connection with the home, where they had once slept in life.

The use of the domestic setting in these examples made further connections with the home and children's place in it, placing them even more distant ideologically from the adult world. The bed imagery acted as a reference not only to the home and its many connotations but more specifically to the bedroom—not the bedroom of the adult, but that of the child. In houses where space had distinct uses and divisions, bedrooms were off-limit, nonpublic spaces intended for privacy. Bedrooms were purposefully separate in the Victorian home, generally upstairs, away from the eyes of visitors. Home decorating guides often did not even discuss these rooms through a sense of modesty.[25] But nurseries, which would have been home to children only, were not immodest, suspect, or tainted; on the contrary, they were perceived as kinds of moral incubators.[26] By the second half of the nineteenth century, a separate nursery for children, often away from the master bedroom, had evolved as part of the middle class home.[27] These controlled environments not only protected childhood innocence but proclaimed it, separating their inhabitants from the adult world. While adults's beds might have had some suspect connotations, children's beds were recurring, sexless, and safe symbols of the most innocent room in the home.

These visions of children safely tucked away in bed came to serve as visual metaphors for good children. In a poem titled "Saturday Night" by Ada Rowena Carahan, the children in bed are pictured as being at their most innocent—and in many ways at the closest to suggestions of their own demise. It is Saturday night, and a father muses upon their clothes laid out for Sunday school the following day. He then turns to their small forms, and says:

> The children are all washed; their shining faces
> Lie there together in the trundle-bed;
> They are our treasures; almost by those graces

Figure 1.2.   William Henry Rinehart, *Sleeping Children*, 1859
Marble, 15⅜″ × 26¾″ × 18¾″.
*(Courtesy National Museum of American Art, Smithsonian Institution, gift of
Mrs. Benjamin H. Warder; photograph Mike Fischer)*

Figure 1.3. Reclining Children Gravemarker of William P. (d. 1849)
and Lydia (d. 1846) Groot
Marble. White Plains Rural Cemetery, White Plains, New
York.
(Photograph Ellen Marie Snyder)

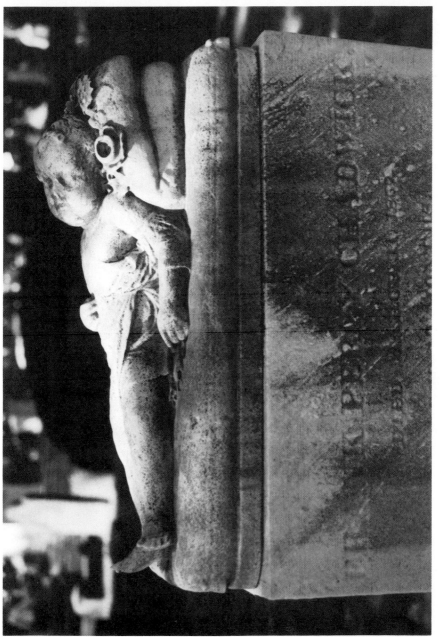

Figure 1.4. Reclining Figure Gravemarker of Frank Percy Chadwick (d. 1867) Marble. Mount Pleasant Cemetery, Newark, New Jersey. *(Photograph Ellen Marie Snyder)*

We count the happy years since we were wed.
Oh, what could fill for us their vacant places,
If they were laid away among the dead?[28]

When portrayed on gravemarkers, sleeping children are often further separated from adults through their asexual depiction. For one, they appear most frequently in only the barest form of dress. At a time when Victorian fashion indicated status—or when, far worse, it could be used as a disguise to conceal one's true, hypocritical identity[29]— this lack of clothing was a clear sign that these small babes had nothing to hide, no moral blemishes to cover up. In the embrace of brother and sister Lydia and William Groot (much as in the Rinehart sculpture), both children present a pose that is absent from adult markers, where it would have conveyed taboo associations. Their act of embracing is totally asexual, and this absence of sexuality reiterates the separate state of children from grownups and "the world." Visually, it relates the perception of childhood as the only stage of life that was still at home in the Garden of Eden.[30] Such meanings could be reenforced through additional symbols; the sleeping figures of Albert and Henry Noll (fig. 1.5) are a case in point. Each sleeping child is accompanied by a visual expression of purity: an angel, symbolic of Heaven, leans over the figure of Albert, while Henry lies down with a lamb, a familiar sign of innocence in the Victorian cemetery.

This pairing of a child with a lamb, a form that appears in fairly stock forms in many rural cemeteries, also expresses the particularly nineteenth-century vision of the child as close to nature. Nature, by the mid-nineteenth century, had become associated with peace and virtue in the face of an urbanizing nation.[31] The child—lying down with the lamb—expresses an affinity of which only he or she, in their young, unmarred state, was capable. Portraying the babe so closely allied with the natural world once again pointed to the disparity between the child and the overcivilized world created by adults[32] that was increasingly removed from nature.

Unfilled furniture also came to assume meaning as symbols for unfulfilled children's lives. As part of a Victorian visual genre of empty furniture which represented a deceased loved one, the sculpted rendering of a small bed (fig. 1.6) would have certainly jogged the memory of the mourner. In this marker, the sheets are pulled back, as if waiting for the child to whom it belongs. The broken flower bud on the footboard symbolizes the unfulfilled potential inherent in an early death;[33] and, as with the lamb in the Noll monument, it creates a symbolic link with the natural world with which children were identified. The simple word "Grace" on the headboard affirms the sinless state of the deceased child (though one cannot dismiss the possibility that it also may represent the child's name).

Figure 1.5.   Reclining Children with Angel and Lamb Gravemarkers of Albert Noll (d. 1859)
and Henry Noll (d. 1856)
Marble. Mount Auburn Cemetery, Cambridge, Massachusetts.
(Photograph Ellen Marie Snyder)

Figure 1.6. Bed Gravemarker, Inscribed "Grace" Marble, ca. 1849. White Plains Rural Cemetery, White Plains, New York. *(Photograph Ellen Marie Snyder)*

This "empty furniture" syndrome is recalled in Theodore Cuyler's popular consolation piece, *The Empty Crib: A Memorial of Little Georgie* (1869). Drawing on his own experience of having lost a son, Cuyler reiterates this bridge between empty and filled and evokes the kind of power such a symbol would have had for viewers in the cemetery. Musing on what he must have seen as an almost inevitable occurrence in an age of high infant mortality, the minister looks to the child-specific furniture in his home as a symbol that portends what is surely to come. "What sorrows this home hath in store for us, God only knoweth," says Cuyler. "Perhaps in yonder nursery a little crib may grow deeper until it deepens into a grave." When the prophecy was indeed fulfilled, Cuyler brought the domestic connection full swing as he mused upon the cemetery plot where his small son was buried. "Thousands and thousands of other little children are slumbering around him," he wrote of young Georgie, "for Green-Wood [Cemetery] is one vast nursery, in which cribs give place to little caskets and coffins, and no one is afraid to speak loud lest they wake up the silent sleepers."[34]

Such objects reenforced the child's connection with its former environment. But they also had the ability to evoke certain highly sentimental connotations. "The most trifling objects become endeared to us by tender associations," states *The Loved and the Lost,* a cemetery guidebook of the period. "Nothing is too little to yield us some sweet portion of condolence. Again and again we hang over a book, a toy, a simple article of dress or ornament of the dear departed. It is priceless to us now."[35] Such items are a part of the Adsit marker in Brooklyn's Green-Wood Cemetery—a small chair draped with the jacket of a deceased child whose empty shoes lie upon the seat (fig. 1.7). This tiny upholstered chair, clearly meant for a little one, becomes the symbol for the child now gone. The small shoes add further visual impact, recalling the sentiment of the message in the poem "My Darling's Shoes" which describes shoes as links to the other world. In the verses, a mother laments the loss of her children. They are revived as she looks at their shoes: "The little shoes are empty in the closet laid away," she cries. As she stands and holds the shoes, she sees her babes:

> And while I am thus standing, I almost seem
> to see
> Two little forms beside me, just as they used
> to be!
> I reach my arms out fondly, but they clasp the
> empty air!
> There is nothing of my darlings but the shoes
> they used to wear.

Figure 1.7. Child's Chair Gravemarker with Jacket and Shoe
Marble, ca. 1850–65. Adsit family plot, Green-Wood
Cemetery, Brooklyn, New York.
(Photograph Ellen Marie Snyder)

But she fears not, for it is almost better they are gone: "Be patient, heart! while waiting to see their shining way," she tells herself, "For the little feet in the golden street can never go astray."[36] By the nature of their small size and childhood connection, these objects have reminded the grieving mother that it is this very same smallness—this inability to ever achieve the full size of adulthood—which has kept her children pure and unsullied, separate and distant from the outside world.

While most common, beds and furniture were not the only objects reserved for children in these highly sculptural forms. Other trappings were also used to reinforce their distinct roles as separate entities from adults. Typically these were items which fell into the arena of playthings. Clutched in little Johnnie Siefert's hand as he lies upon his bed, for instance, is a rattle (fig. 1.8), a distinctly child-related prop. A more elaborate example is provided by the group of markers for the children of Clifton and Lizzie Bell in a rural cemetery in Denver, Colorado (fig. 1.9). Flanking a sleeping child (a daughter of the couple) are two other children of the Bells, Gracie (left) and Harley (right). Each playing child bears a toy: Gracie holds a doll, and Harley sits astride a rocking horse. Perhaps most significant about the two scenes is the choice of imagery on markers meant to stand as a lasting memorial to these children. The use of these toys in perpetuity reflects a growing nineteenth-century recognition of the naturalness of play and its importance to the proper upbringing of children.[37] This new Victorian ideology here translates into cemetery sculpture, becoming a lasting reminder of the separate worlds of adults and children.

In the cemetery the sleeping child, the vacant chair, and the tiny belongings became charged and potent symbols. Vastly different from representations of adult men with whom these children were most at odds, they signaled home, purity, goodness, and innocence. They were clear visual barometers of the changes in Victorian society, showing a separation between the world of children and that of adults. Their appearance of permanence in the cemetery must have been reassuring to Victorians who feared both physical and moral decay. The small forms, who slept in the cemetery as if they were still home, visually defied the progression of age. These children forever escaped what would have been an inevitable entrance into "the world," which was at best refined, at worst immoral, and in any case fraught with insincerity and the love of goods. The forms these gravemarkers took, and the props they utilized, placed them squarely in the realm of childhood—a realm totally removed from the adult world of men and the marketplace.

Ultimately, children in the cemetery remained forever young, more notable for their deaths than their short lives.[38] "They who have lost a child in infancy, have a child which shall not grow old," wrote John H. Morison

Figure 1.8.   Detail of Rattle Held by Reclining Figure. Gravemarker of Johnnie Siefert (d. 1888) Marble. White Plains Rural Cemetery, White Plains, New York. *(Photograph Ellen Marie Snyder)*

Figure 1.9. Gravemarkers for Children of Clifton and Lizzie Bell: (L-R) Gracie M. (d. 1881), unidentified daughter (d. 1881), Harley C. (d. 1887) Marble. Riverside Cemetery, Denver, Colorado. *(Photograph Ellen Marie Snyder)*

in his discourse. "Their other children advance with the advancing years. The seasons of life pass over them and they are changed.... But with the little one taken in childhood it is not so. No change is there. The same image comes always to their thoughts. Its countenance is not hardened into the rigid features of the man, but remains always the countenance of a child; Eternity has there fixed its seal."[39] Carved in stone or cast in metal, these sculptural portrayals of children and their belongings insured that they would remain ever part of the goodness of the home sphere, ever undisturbed and unchanging, and, most importantly, forever innocents in a worldly world.

Notes

1. Nancy F. Cott, ed. and intro., *Root of Bitterness: Documents of the Social History of American Women* (New York: E. P. Dutton and Co., Inc., 1972), p. 12.

2. "Children, Childhood, and Change in America, 1820–1920," in Mary Lynn Stevens Heininger, Karin Calvert, Barbara Finkelstein, Kathy Vandell, Ann Scott Macleod, and Harvey Green, *A Century of Childhood: 1820–1920* (Rochester, New York: The Margaret Woodbury Strong Museum, 1984), p. 10.

3. Nancy F. Cott, *The Bonds of Womanhood: "Woman's Sphere" in New England, 1780–1835* (New Haven, Conn.: Yale University Press, 1978), p. 58.

4. Ann Douglas, *The Feminization of American Culture* (New York: Avon Books, 1977), p. 240.

5. Cott, *Root of Bitterness,* pp. 12–13.

6. Perry Miller, *Errand into the Wilderness* (Cambridge, Mass.: Belknap Press of Harvard University Press, 1956), p. 208.

7. Simon J. Bronner, *Grasping Things: Folk Material Culture and Mass Society in America* (Lexington, Ky.: The University Press of Kentucky, 1986), p. 46.

8. David Schuyler, "Home as Castle: Architecture and the Ideology of Domesticity," *Susquehanna* 6 (July 1981), p. 32.

9. Karen Halttunen, *Confidence Men and Painted Women: A Study of Middle-Class Culture in America, 1830–1870* (New Haven, Conn.: Yale University Press, 1982), p. xiii.

10. Rev. W. F. Crafts, *The Coming Man is the Present Child: Or Childhood, the Text-Book of the Ages for Parents, Pastors and Teachers, and All Lovers of Childhood* (Indianapolis: Fred L. Horton & Co., 1879), p. 198.

11. Ibid., p. 210.

12. Norma Johnsen, "'Our Children Who Are in Heaven': Consolation Themes in a Nineteenth-Century Connecticut Journal," *The Connecticut Historical Society Bulletin* 51:2 (Spring 1986), p. 88.

13. T. J. Jackson Lears, *No Place of Grace: Antimodernism and the Transformation of American Culture, 1800–1920* (New York: Pantheon Books, 1981), p. 145.

14. Heininger et al., *A Century of Childhood,* p. 10.

15. Lears, *No Place of Grace,* p. 146.

16. Ibid.

17. Harvey Green, *The Light of the Home: An Intimate View of the Lives of Women in Victorian America* (New York: Pantheon Books, 1983), p. 181.

18. Halttunen, *Confidence Men and Painted Women,* p. 58.

19. John Ruskin, "Of Queen's Gardens," *Sesame and Lilies* (London, 1864; New York: Metropolitan Publishing Co., 1871), quoted in Gwendolyn Wright, *Moralism and the Model Home: Domestic Architecture and Cultural Conflict in Chicago, 1873–1913* (Chicago: The University of Chicago Press, 1980), p. 13.

20. Theodore L. Cuyler, *Christianity in the Home* (New York: The Baker & Taylor Co., n.d.), p. 9.

21. John H. Morison, *A Sermon . . . Preached before the First Congregational Society in New Bedford, Sunday Morning, November 27, 1842* (New Bedford, Mass.: Press of Benjamin Lindsey, 1842), p. 15.

22. Theodore L. Cuyler, *The Cedar Christian: And Other Practical Papers and Personal Sketches* (New York: Robert Carter and Brothers, 1867), p. 104.

23. Nehemiah D. D. Adams, *Agnes and the Little Key of Her Coffin, By Her Father* (Boston: J. E. Tilton & Co., 1857), pp. 9–10.

24. Ibid., p. 12.

25. Wright, *Moralism and the Model Home,* p. 39.

26. June Sprigg, "The Victorian Nursery in America," unpublished manuscript, 1975.

27. Karin Calvert, "Cradle to Crib: The Revolution in Nineteenth-Century Children's Furniture," in Heininger et al., *A Century of Childhood,* p. 53.

28. Ada Rowena Carahan, "Saturday Night" (n.p., n.d.; ca. 1860–76). The Brooklyn Historical Society Archives, Jacob Meyers Scrapbook, 1978.109.

29. Halttunen, *Confidence Men and Painted Women,* p. 29.

30. Calvert, "Cradle to Crib," in Heininger et al., *A Century of Childhood,* p. 37.

31. Heininger et al., *A Century of Childhood,* p. 12.

32. Ibid.

33. Deborah A. Smith, "'Safe in the Arms of Jesus': Consolation on Delaware Children's Gravestones," *Markers* 4 (1986), p. 90.

34. Theodore L. Cuyler, *The Empty Crib: A Memorial of Little Georgie. With Words of Consolation for Bereaved Parents* (New York: R. Carter and Brothers, 1869), pp. 12, 152.

35. N.A., *The Loved and the Lost* (New York, 1856), p. 10.

36. N.A., "My Darling's Shoes," from *The Portsmouth Journal,* ca. 1860–76. The Brooklyn Historical Society Archives, Jacob Meyers Scrapbook, 1978.109.

37. Calvert, "Cradle to Crib," in Heininger et al., *A Century of Childhood,* p. 36.

38. Douglas, *The Feminization of American Culture,* p. 240.

39. Morison, *A Sermon,* pp. 10–11.

2

The Bigham Carvers of the Carolina Piedmont: Stone Images of an Emerging Sense of American Identity

Edward W. Clark

In downtown Charlotte, North Carolina is located a small cemetery surrounded by tall buildings. The Old Settlers Cemetery, as it is called, contains several gravestones relocated from surrounding sites overtaken by construction—the city's slow pace has changed dramatically from the years when the textile industry dominated the region. Now this urban center is home to a rapidly expanding banking industry with its accompanying high-rise structures of steel and tinted glass. This small pocket of memorials contains gravestones that recall the preindustrial South of two centuries ago, when the newly created United States of America was young and in its first stages of self-awareness.

One stone in particular seems to encapsulate the turmoil of those times. Carved by a Scotch Irish stonecutter, the marker's inscription reads:

> In Memory of
> JOEL BARNHART
> who died Nov^r.
> 30th 1789 Aged 14
> Years.

During 1775, the year that Joel Barnhart was born, the British marched on Lexington and Concord and laid siege to Boston; the year of his death, George Washington was inaugurated as the first president of the United States. Thus, the adolescent's short life spanned the beginning and end of the Revolution, the drafting and ratification of the Constitution, and the installation of the Revolution's military leader as first president. The most striking feature of the memorial is the design of a musket that the stonecutter etched into the tympanum, an appropriate image for one whose short life had witnessed so much tumult.

Barnhart's marker was cut by one of the Bigham family of carvers who had settled at nearby Steele Creek where a community of Scotch Irish Presbyterians had established a church. The gravestones produced by several generations of the Bighams capture in stone a point in the American past when ethnic origins were being supplanted by an emerging sense of national identity. The gravemarkers they created from 1750 to 1780 reflect their having come from Northern Ireland; however, from the time of the Revolution until 1815, they incorporated distinctly American symbols of the young republic into their repertoire of designs.

The Bigham carvers of the Carolina Piedmont were descended from Bighams who had emigrated to Pennsylvania in the mid 1730s.[1] Their ancestor, a John Bingham, had dropped the *n* from the family's name to produce the current spelling. His great-great-great grandfather, Sir George Bingham, whose ancestors had lived in Dorset in England, served as Military Governor of Sligo on the western coast of Ireland in 1593 during the reign of Queen Elizabeth I. Some of Sir George's descendants remained in Ireland where they probably intermarried with the Ulster Scots, known in America as the Scotch Irish, who, in return for land, helped their English allies subdue the native Irish.

The Scotch Irish had served well on the various frontiers between the English and the native population in Ireland. When transplanted to the Pennsylvania frontier between the various Indian tribes and the English coastal settlements, their previous military experience also served them well. The Ulster Scot's Celtic heritage carried with it a reputation for hard drinking and hard fighting. Combining these traits with the kind of independent spirit fostered by their brand of Presbyterianism, they indeed made formidable adversaries.

It has not been established whether any of the Bighams were stonecarvers in Northern Ireland, nor is it known which of them specifically carved their gravestones found in several of the Presbyterian burial grounds near Gettysburg, Pennsylvania, where they arrived in 1749.[2] But the various renderings of coats of arms to be found on their stones attest to their understanding the importance of clan identity among the Ulster Scots.

Sometimes the Bighams carved a full coat of arms on their markers, while on other occasions they employed a certain element or elements taken from coats of arms and used singly or in a new configuration. They could carve a coat of arms like that found on the Robert McPherson stone (fig. 2.1), located in Evergreen Cemetery in Gettysburg, which contains the traditional elements of the crest, the mantling, and the shield. Here the crest

Figure 2.1.　Traditional Coat of Arms
Stone of Robert McPherson (d. 1749), Evergreen
Cemetery, Gettysburg, Pennsylvania.
(Drawing from photograph by Edward W. Clark)

area contains the figure of a cat; the mantling, as it does in a traditional coat of arms, flows out from the top of the shield and down its sides; and the shield contains a galley at its base, a gauntleted hand grasping a saber in the fess or mid-area, and a candle and holder in the chief or top third of the shield.

In the Belfast region of Northern Ireland coats of arms can also be found on gravestones contemporary to the McPherson stone. The George Woodside stone, located in the Templecorran cemetery in Ballycarry in County Antrim, uses, for example, the various elements of heraldry (fig. 2.2). In this case, a sheaf of wheat serves as the crest, a wreath (or torse, as it is sometimes called in heraldry) is placed atop the helmet upon which is carved a five-petaled Tudor Rose, and the mantling flows out from the helmet and ends in tassels. The motto is here placed above the crest rather than below the shield where it more conventionally occurs. The shield is divided bilaterally, with a tree flanked by two cross crosslets in the left division and three longbows with arrows in a line in the right division.[3]

Since the Bighams lived on the Appalachian Frontier far from those who regulated the use of coats of arms in Britain, they were able to experiment more readily with varied placements of elements and with the incorporation of new figures or designs than stonecarvers in Ulster. The John Brown stone, located near Gettysburg in the Great Conewago Presbyterian Cemetery, for example, leaves out some of the traditional heraldic elements (fig. 2.3). Although there is ample room for a crest, one is not carved. However, a wreath, upon which the crest always rests, is included. The helmet has been pared down to a simple form with three slanted parallel lines serving as the grille for a nonexistent visor. The Tudor Rose is rendered, but no motto is visible nor do any animals flank the shield as they would on a full coat of arms. Several objects are placed asymmetrically on the shield—a couped hand, a crescent moon, two pierced six-pointed stars, and a Scottish Thistle. Such seemingly random placement of objects on a coat of arms's shield would have been odd indeed in Northern Ireland if, in fact, it would have been permitted at all.

In the late 1750s and early 1760s many of the Scotch Irish moved from Pennsylvania to establish homesteads in the Carolina Piedmont. Once again, as they had in Northern Ireland and Pennsylvania, they settled in a frontier region, this time between the lowland plantation culture whose regional center was Charleston and various Southern Indian tribes, most notably the Catawba and the Cherokee. They named the three South Carolina upland counties of York, Lancaster, and Chester after counties in the Pennsylvania homeland they had left behind. The church at Waxhaw in Lancaster County, South Carolina served as the spiritual center for the Presbyterians of the region. Its pastor, Rev. William Richardson, was instrumental in coordinat-

Figure 2.2. Traditional Coat of Arms
Stone of George Woodside (d. 1730), Templecorran
Cemetery, Ballycarry, County Antrim, Northern Ireland.
Because of weathering much of the motto is not legible.
(Drawing from photograph by Edward W. Clark)

Figure 2.3. Modified Coat of Arms
Stone of John Brown (d. 1760), Great Conewago Presbyterian Cemetery, near
Gettysburg, Pennsylvania.
(Drawing from photograph by Edward W. Clark)

ing the missionary efforts of young men who had just recently studied at Princeton College in New Jersey to establish Presbyterian congregations throughout the area. One of the Bigham carvers cut a gravestone for Richardson that shows that perhaps the Bigham shop was acquainted with the Neo-Classical design, then in fashion New England, of the temple facade with a portrait disc positioned at the peak of the pediment.[4] On the Richardson stone the traditional coat of arms is replaced by a circle divided into three equal fields containing a lion, a unicorn, and a wolf (fig. 2.4). The mantling is kept, but the circle is surmounted by a crown.

Although the small cemetery at the Old Waxhaw Presbyterian Church contains several excellent examples of Bigham-carved stones, the best and most varied collection of their work can be found in the cemetery next to the Steele Creek Presbyterian Church, approximately forty miles from the Old Waxhaw Church. Although the structure no longer exists, the Bighams' workshop was located in the vicinity of the Steele Creek Presbyterian Church, which they attended and near which they lived. Evidence has been found in various wills and legal documents which establishes that at least six different carvers worked cutting gravestones in the Bigham workshop.[5] The oldest was Samuel Bigham, Sr., who arrived with his wife in the 1760s in Mecklenburg County, North Carolina. Samuel Bigham, Jr. might have been the most skilled craftsman of the shop; at least he was proud enough of his ability to follow his signature on legal documents with the initials "s.c." for stone cutter. Samuel Jr. may have been the son of Samuel Sr. although it is difficult to know for sure because there were at least four or five Samuel Bighams living in the area at that time.[6] Samuel Jr. had two brothers, William and Hugh, in the trade, who were joined by two apprentices, James Sloan and William McKinley. It has not yet been (and may never be) established which gravestones may be attributed to which carver, although one can see several distinctive hands or styles at work.[7]

Among the variety of traditional Scotch Irish designs the Bighams used, the Scottish Thistle, the Tree of Life, and the Dove of Promise seem to have been three of their favorites. We have already noted a rather crude rendering of the thistle on the John Brown stone. A more successful effort with this Scottish national symbol can be seen on the gravestone carved for the one-month-old infant John Elliott (fig. 2.5). Here two separate thistle blossoms are attached to the ends of two vines that are carved in relief below the dentil border of the tympanum. The Tree of Life, which occurs about as frequently as the Scottish Thistle, is often used in combination with another design. The Elizabeth McClellen stone (fig. 2.6) features a tympanum which displays a precisely carved swastika (or clubbed fylfot, to use the heraldic term) flanked by two miniature Trees of Life. Usually the Tree of Life design is rendered in a much larger size. Sometimes its trunk may

Figure 2.4.   Modified Coat of Arms
Stone of Rev. William Richardson (d. 1771), Old Waxhaw Presbyterian Church
Cemetery, Lancaster County, South Carolina.
(Drawing from photograph by Edward W. Clark)

Figure 2.5. Scottish Thistle Motif
Stone of John Elliott (d. 1781), Steele Creek Presbyterian Church Cemetery,
Charlotte, North Carolina.
(Photograph Edward W. Clark)

Figure 2.6.   Tree of Life and Swastika Motifs
Stone of Elizabeth McClellen (d. 1791), Steele Creek
Presbyterian Church Cemetery, Charlotte, North
Carolina.
(Photograph Edward W. Clark)

stretch over half the height of the stone, especially when carved on the back. Although carving on the back of gravestones does occur in Scotland and Northern Ireland, it is extremely rare in America. Perhaps the Bighams were acquainted with this practice in Ulster, or they might have imitated their German neighbors in Pennsylvania who did backcarving on their gravemarkers.

The Scotch Irish of the Carolina Piedmont often requested that the Bighams carve a Dove of Promise on their memorials, and it is perhaps the most frequently used in their canon of gravestone images. Usually the Dove of Promise occupies the center of the tympanum of a stone cut for a child or an adolescent, although it can be found on stones for adults as well. The Esther Zelefrow Feris stone (fig. 2.7) in the cemetery at the Ebenezer Presbyterian Church in Rock Hill, South Carolina, shows the Dove of Promise, with the traditional olive twig in its beak, on the shield of a coat of arms which one of the Bigham carvers perhaps tailor-made for this teenage girl's gravestone. Another Christian symbol, the fish, which the Bighams rarely used, is placed in the crest area.

The images of birds can be found with some regularity on traditional coats of arms. Other than the dove, the Bighams used two types of birds when cutting stones for people who wished to show their Scotch Irish background with a coat of arms drawn from traditional heraldry. The stone carved for Susanna Maxwell (fig. 2.8) features a shield containing a traditional gyron design created by passing a line through the shield's center-point and then rotating it to form eight sections. For the shield here a Bigham carver rendered four of the sections in relief; on a traditional coat of arms two different colors would be alternated to create a gyron. The curious head in the crest area at first seems to be an impish figure, but a closer inspection reveals that the pointed ears probably are those of a cat and what appears to be wings is part of the mantling. Flanking the shield are a pair of swans. The motto reads *SOLA VIRTUS INVICTA.* The Mary Carothers stone also uses a heraldic bird. In this case, hawks flank a shield containing a two-masted ship. The back of this stone shows a cleverly worked design of four bandlike sections running the width of the stone and separated by double-etched lines (figs. 2.9 and 2.10). Carved in the bands is a short but effective epitaph:

> Continued be
> As well as others
> The Memory of
> Mary Carothers

Figure 2.7. Dove of Promise Motif
Stone of Esther Zelefrow Feris (d. 1795), Ebenezer Presbyterian Church
Cemetery, Rock Hill, South Carolina.
(Drawing from photograph by Edward W. Clark)

Figure 2.8.   Coat of Arms with Swans
Stone of Susanna Maxwell (d. 1791), Steele Creek Presbyterian Church Cemetery,
Charlotte, North Carolina.
(Photograph Edward W. Clark)

Figure 2.9.   Hawks Flanking Shield with Ship
Stone of Mary Carothers (d. 1785), Steele Creek
Presbyterian Church Cemetery, Charlotte, North
Carolina.
(Photograph Edward W. Clark)

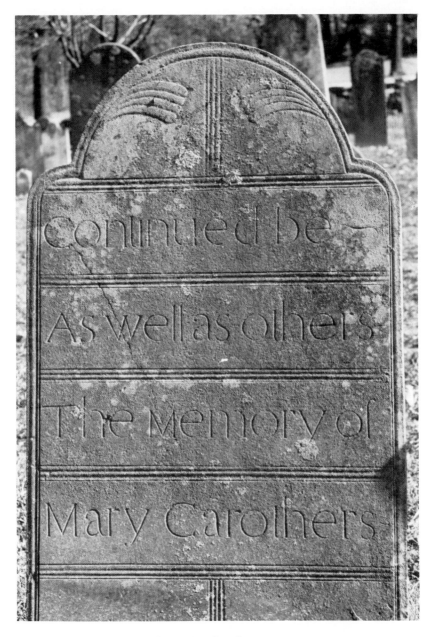

Figure 2.10.   Back of Mary Carothers Stone
Steele Creek Presbyterian Church Cemetery, Charlotte,
North Carolina.
(Photograph Edward W. Clark)

Both the Robert Campbell and Robert McCleary gravemarkers illustrate a continuing allegiance to a Scotch Irish heritage. The badly worn stone for Campbell uses one of the variants for the coat of arms for that famous clan (fig. 2.11). The gyrons in the first and fourth quarters of the shield are constant elements in the Campbell coat of arms while the other elements may vary according to the particular branch of the clan. Here we have a boar's head in the crest area, under the wreath four roundels, and ships in the second and third quarters of the shield. Lions rampant flank the shield, while the motto declares *VIXIA NUSTRA VOCO.*

The stone cut for Robert McCleary flanks the shield with lions like those for Robert Campbell. The four roundels are also positioned under the wreath like Campbell's. The shield has three swords in a pile pointing downward and carved in relief. The crest contains a couped arm with a clinched fist wielding a sword, but the carving for the hand and fingers is much better executed than the hands and fingers found on the John Brown and Robert McPherson stones. As we can see, the Bighams' craftsmanship in the carving and execution of their various designs improved considerably from the 1750s to the 1790s.

One of the best executions of a traditional coat of arms of any of the Bigham-carved stones is that found on the Hannah Greir marker (fig. 2.12). Here the entire coat of arms and the inscriptions are carved in relief. The English crown in the crest area, the columns flanking the shield, and the crenelated castle turrets in the shield make this one of the most noteworthy of all the Bigham markers. The dentil design along the border of the tympanum, the double-lined borders of the panels carved in high relief, and the miniature half-sun discs in the finials all add to this stone's unique artistic character.

While the Hannah Greir stone is an exceptional treatment of a traditional coat of arms, the stone carved for one of the Bighams' relatives, Andrew Bigham, is probably the most unusual of all the 800 or so gravemarkers they carved. On this stone the Bighams made use of a specifically American coat of arms—that of the seal of the Commonwealth of Pennsylvania. Although the eagle carved for the crest seems somewhat stiff, its awkwardness adds to the extraordinary nature of this remarkable gravestone (fig. 2.13). The spelling of independence with an *a* in the motto, in fact, suits its one-of-a-kind quality. The carver took pains to faithfully copy details from the seal. On the ship note the portholes, the forecastle, the ratlines on the masts, the unfurled sails on the yard arms, and even the design on the flag above the tiller. In the detail of the horse on the right side of the shield (fig. 2.14) one can see the horse's ears, eyes, nostrils, hooves, neck muscles, strands of hair in the tail, and the braidwork on the traces.

The fact that Andrew Bigham chose (or that his close relatives chose

Figure 2.11.   Variant of Campbell Coat of Arms
Stone of Robert Campbell (d. 1795). Steele Creek Presbyterian Church
Cemetery, Charlotte, North Carolina.
(Photograph Edward W. Clark)

Figure 2.12. Finely Executed Traditional Coat of Arms
Stone of Hannah Greir (d. 1788), Steele Creek
Presbyterian Church Cemetery, Charlotte, North
Carolina.
(Photograph Edward W. Clark)

Figure 2.13.   Seal of the Commonwealth of Pennsylvania
              Stone of Andrew Bigham (d. 1788), Steele Creek
              Presbyterian Church Cemetery, Charlotte, North
              Carolina.
              (Photograph Edward W. Clark)

Figure 2.14. Detail of Andrew Bigham Stone
Steele Creek Presbyterian Church Cemetery, Charlotte,
North Carolina.
(Photograph Edward W. Clark)

for him) to have a coat of arms that referred to Pennsylvania instead of Northern Ireland is important for at least two reasons. First, it shows that the old clan identity was fading, or at least was less attractive, to those who had lived most of their lives in America. Andrew's vital statistics, as recorded on his gravemarker, would place his birth at about the time when many Scotch Irish were emigrating from Northern Ireland to British North America. Those who made that arduous journey probably did not have much fondness for the English, who many Scotch Irish felt had treated them badly even though they had helped the English to conquer the Emerald Isle. Andrew Bigham could have been born in his distant ancestral home or in Pennsylvania. Regardless of where his birth did occur, he would have lived for at least thirty years in Pennsylvania before moving south. His memories were of growing up in Pennsylvania, not in Northern Ireland. Although the coat of arms on his gravestone owed its structure to the conventions of Scottish heraldry, its emotional content—the feelings associated with the image—belonged to an American place. By the time of his death, members of his generation thought of themselves more as Americans than as Scotch Irish. Secondly, the Andrew Bigham stone is important because it shows that the Bighams were willing to experiment, within certain structural limits, in using American symbols when constructing their coats of arms.

This trend toward American images can be seen even more concretely in two beautiful and complex gravestones the Bighams carved for members of the Steele Creek community. One commemorates a young married couple who died within six months of one another, William and Mary Barnet, and the other a relative of the carvers, Robert Bigham.

The coat of arms carved in relief on the Barnet memorial has what appears to be some type of eighteenth-century military headgear in the area where the traditional knight's helmet would be positioned (fig. 2.15). The shield contains traditional symbols of heraldry, but two of these symbols could very well have American associations in addition to their more conventional meanings. The first quarter of the shield contains a Dove of Promise, a symbol which the Bighams had used many times before. In the second quarter we find a couped, gauntleted hand which holds not a sword (as we might expect), but another cutting instrument—a scythe—which is placed beside it. Conventionally, when associated with death, the scythe symbolizes that the deceased's life has been cut short. Thus this iconographic device might refer in the Barnets' case to the ages of the young couple, twenty-seven and twenty-one. The third quarter holds a pair of crossed arrows, certainly a well-known image used for centuries in heraldry. But this could also suggest the bundle of crossed arrows in one of the talons of the American eagle, a symbol coming into use for the new republic about this time (1785). The spread-winged eagle of the fourth quarter seems

Figure 2.15.   Early Hints of American Symbols
Stone of William (d. 1785) and Mary (d. 1785) Barnet,
Steele Creek Presbyterian Church Cemetery, Charlotte,
North Carolina.
(Photograph Edward W. Clark)

closer to the conventional eagle seen in heraldry than it does to the American eagle; however, we shall see a variant form of the conventional heraldic eagle and an eagle in a new form on stones carved after 1800. This eagle can be considered a precursor, at least conceptually, for those that follow on later Bigham gravestones.

The Robert Bigham stone exhibits an exceptional carving skill and an ability to create a new coat of arms with clearly recognizable American symbolic content (fig. 2.16). Traditional crossed swords are placed in its crest area. A wreath is provided, and what appear to be palm branches extend outward from the top corners of the shield, perhaps a variant design of the mantling. But it is the shield itself which draws our closest attention. In each of the four quarters are placed three pierced five-pointed stars (or mullets, as they are called in heraldry). At the centerpoint is placed another star, making thirteen in all, obviously meant to represent the thirteen colonies. The motto—*ARMA LIBERTATIS*—leaves no doubt that Robert Bigham's allegiance was not to the English crown but to the newly created flag of the United States. Although he did not live to see the new republic actually gain its independence, the stars on his gravestone testify that Robert Bigham thought of himself as an American.

The stone carved for the infant John Price reveals that his parents wanted to make a direct statement about their national allegiance and that the Bigham carvers were willing to oblige them (fig. 2.17). This marker allows no room for ambiguity. Price's parents were Americans, and they wanted people to know that they would have liked for their son, had he survived, to have been one too. During the year of the Price child's death in 1794, George Washington was in the first year of his second term in office. The Constitution and the Bill of Rights had been ratified six years previously. If the parents of John Price, who were living in the backwoods of the Carolina Piedmont, could have the Seal of the United States of America carved onto their infant son's gravestone, then they explicitly declared to all their neighbors that they considered themselves neither British nor Scotch Irish but Americans.

In fact, after 1795 the Bighams carved very few fully developed traditional coats of arms on their gravemarkers. Instead they used images singly, in pairs, or groups of three, hardly ever placing them on a shield. One image they began to use at this time is instantly recognizable two centuries later. The eagle—as it occurs on the James Bigham stone of 1807—was a truly American eagle (fig. 2.18). Clutched in its left talon is a bundle of crossed arrows we recognize from heraldry, and in its right talon the olive branch that we have seen associated with the Dove of Promise—joining together the two embodiments of war and peace in our major national symbol. Born in 1777, even as the new nation was struggling toward its own birth, James

Figure 2.16.   Stars of a New Nation
Stone of Robert Bigham (d. 1777), Steele Creek
Presbyterian Church Cemetery, Charlotte, North
Carolina.
(Photograph Edward W. Clark)

Figure 2.17. Seal of the United States of America
Stone of John Price (d. 1794), Steele Creek Presbyterian
Church Cemetery, Charlotte, North Carolina.
(Photograph Edward W. Clark)

Figure 2.18.   The American Eagle
Stone of James Bigham (d. 1807), Steele Creek
Presbyterian Church Cemetery, Charlotte, North
Carolina.
(Photograph Edward W. Clark)

Bigham was of the first generation to grow into adulthood feeling themselves to be Americans. By the beginning of the nineteenth century the sense of being Scotch Irish perhaps only lived in the memory of those who had heard old men and women talk about Pennsylvania and the old country.

During the eighty-year period (1740–1820) in which the Bighams carved gravestones, one stone in particular seems to epitomize the history of the Scotch Irish Americans during those years: the marker carved for John Crockett. A contemporary of Andrew Bigham, he died in 1800 at the age of seventy and was buried at the Old Waxhaw Church Cemetery. On the back of his gravestone is carved a ship and an epitaph which tells of the circumstances of his birth:

> Born in a ship in the year 1730
> Born upon the sea near Pennsylvania shore;
> Lived in America til almost four score.
> Happy the man who has his sins forgiven,
> By our Redeemer who now lives in Heaven.

The ship and epitaph encapsulate the history of Crockett and his neighbors. In selecting them, he chose to remember his birth on a ship moored off the coast of Pennsylvania. He did not choose a coat of arms that would link him to a past in Northern Ireland and to a sense of clan identity, as did several of his neighbors buried around him. The Revolution that had ended in success seventeen years before he died made it possible, when he looked back over his life, to see his birth as an important beginning. A native son, he though of himself as an individual and as an American who owed his allegiance to other Americans rather than to an ethnic past that had begun to fade perhaps even before he was buried.

It was the men of Crockett's generation who had experienced so much during their lifetimes. Frontier warfare, whether it be with Indians or the English, was never far from their homes. Crockett almost certainly saw young Andrew Jackson, who was born nearby in 1756. As an adolescent, so the story goes, Jackson had acquired his lifelong hatred of the British when, at the Old Waxhaw Church, he saw the saber wounds inflicted on men like Crockett by the British cavalry under the command of Tarleton. The church had served as a hospital for the wounded and the dying after a Tarleton raid. Like Crockett, Jackson was Scotch Irish; his generation would also see great changes. Jackson, in particular, would permanently alter the way of American politics when elected to the White House three decades after Crockett's death.

The ship on the John Crockett stone serves as an emblem for the Scotch Irish in eighteenth-century America. It locates a place and a time that, in retrospect, marked a new beginning for the many Scotch Irish who emigrated to the American shore. The image of the ship symbolized a newfound land and a newly made country. On the front of the stone two Doves of Promise face one another, the olive twig sticking out from the beak of one dove and almost touching the twig of the other. In a way, the doves represent both the hope of peace in a new land and the promise of a spiritual harbor in heaven.

The Bighams carved particular designs on the gravestones cut for their Carolina neighbors as a visual means by which they could remember or imagine a distant past in a distant land. Newly created national symbols, like the American eagle or the seal of the United States, called to mind an immediate present—the turmoil of the Revolution, the birth of a new nation—and, by implication, a new future waiting to unfold for new generations. But, whatever image the Bighams used, those who gazed on their markers remembered Americans who had made that final journey to a place beyond earthly concerns where neither ethnic origin nor nationality mattered—the homeland of eternity.

Notes

1. The genealogical information on the Bighams comes from descendants of the Bighams living in the Charlotte area, Mrs. Roy S. Bigham, Jr. and her son David M. Bigham, and from Mrs. Edwin S. Brewster of Fullerton, California.

2. Directions from Dr. Daniel Patterson, Director of the Folk Life Division of the Department of English at the University of North Carolina at Chapel Hill, made it possible for me to locate some of the key burial grounds where Bigham-carved gravestones are found in the Gettysburg area. He was also instrumental in helping me locate their stones in the Charlotte, North Carolina area. Patterson has done all the digging through legal documents to determine who the particular Bighams were who worked in their shop in the Steele Creek community. He has been researching the Bighams at various intervals over the past ten years and hopes to publish a book-length study on these exceptional carvers in the near future.

    A Summer Research Fellowship provided by the South Carolina Committee for the Humanities made it possible for me to visit many of the sites where Bigham stones are located both in Pennsylvania and in North and South Carolina.

    I also attended a National Endowment for the Humanities Summer Seminar on tomb sculpture in Europe and America, directed by Dr. Ruth Butler of the Art Department of the University of Massachusetts, Boston in the summer of 1982, where my research project focused on eighteenth-century New England gravestones.

3. The main sources used for the information on heraldry in this essay are Hubert Allcock, *Heraldic Design: Its Origins, Ancient Forms, and Modern Usage* (New York: Tudor Publishing, 1962); Arthur Fox-Davies, *Heraldry Explained* (Rutland, Vermont: Charles E. Tuttle, 1906; rpt. 1971); Julian Franklin, *Heraldry* (New York: A.S. Barnes, 1965); and Francis J. Grant, ed., *The Manual of Heraldry: A Concise Description of the Several Terms Used, and Containing a Dictionary of Every Designation in the Science,* rev. ed. (Edinburgh: John Grant, 1924).

4. See Allan I. Ludwig, *Graven Images: New England Stonecarving and Its Symbols, 1650–1815* (Middletown, Conn.: Wesleyan University Press, 1966), especially chapter 2. Particularly good examples of temple facade designs and portrait discs can be seen at the Hillside Burying Ground, Concord, Massachusetts.

5. The source for this information is Dr. Daniel Patterson.

6. David M. Bigham of Charlotte, North Carolina, a descendant of the Bigham carvers, explained to me the problems he faced in trying to establish which Samuels belong to what branch of the family tree. The incomplete records may not make it possible to establish the exact relationship between Samuel, Sr. and Samuel, Jr.

7. Again, Dr. Patterson is my source for the names of the carvers and their apprentices.

3

Images of Logging on Contemporary Pacific Northwest Gravemarkers

Richard E. Meyer

It is a commonly held belief, even amongst many of those who have devoted considerable energy to the study of cemeteries and gravemarkers, that the contemporary American cemetery is a place devoid of any significant degree of interest. The general image is that of a bland, featureless conglomeration of flat markers set into a nondescript landscape somewhat resembling a poorly designed pitch and putt golf course. Certainly there is some justification for this conception: the contrasts between the evolving sumptuousness of cemeteries and memorials in nineteenth-century America and the dramatic decline of these qualities in the first half of the twentieth century are striking indeed, and it seems likely that not one but several factors played a significant role in this transformation. An emerging aesthetic based upon applied pragmatic ideals seems to have had a lot to do with it initially: as early as 1917, one commentator, touting his vision of the ideal new cemetery as "similar to that of a modern real estate development," would note with satisfaction that "there is a fortunate growing tendency away from gaudy and freakish display in all fields of art. This is happily noted in the use of monuments in the cemetery."[1] The notion of cemetery planning and management as a somewhat esoteric form of real estate development would indeed become exceedingly attractive to entrepreneurs in the middle decades of the century, and, with its attendant concepts of perpetual care, "preneed" planning, and, ultimately, combined services (i.e., mortuary, interment, monument), would have much to do with creating typical cemetery landscapes based upon the ideals of standardization, simplicity, and ease of maintenance. Added to all of this—and undoubtedly contributing to it as well—would be a growing disinclination of Americans to associate themselves personally with both the spiritual acceptance of death and the numerous practical necessities which traditionally accompany such acceptance, preferring instead to leave these matters to specialists responsible for the smooth and profitable operation of death-associated industries.[2]

Despite the essentially homogenizing effect of these trends, however, it is quite erroneous to assume that nothing exists within contemporary cemeteries to link them with the great traditions of funerary decoration. Indeed, while much undoubtedly remains to be desired in terms of restoring the cemetery setting to anything approximating the complex artistic and social functions it once served as a part of the American cultural landscape, certain encouraging developments are readily apparent to anyone who has taken the opportunity to spend some time recently in the newer sections of our cemeteries. For one thing, both decorative plantings and the use of upright markers are making a strong resurgence, owing in part to the development and use of tools such as the weed-eater, but equally or more so to a willingness on the part of a growing number of cemeteries to modify restrictive regulations in the face of increasing demands by patrons who wish to see their loved ones commemorated in a more personalized and aesthetically pleasing context. Even more striking is a trend which began to evidence itself in the decade of the 1960s and has continued to escalate in dramatic fashion with each passing year—a sudden reemergence of interest in gravemarkers which manifest a notable degree of verbal and visual imagery, in essence a renaissance of those primary elements, epitaph and icon, which have traditionally proven to be of greatest importance to those interested in sepulchral decoration.

If there is one notable difference, however, between this new imagery and that found on gravemarkers dating from the nineteenth century and earlier, it is in its dominantly retrospective emphasis, the manner in which, to a degree unprecedented in earlier eras, it conjures up vivid images of the deceased person's life.[3] Again, technological advancements in the industry seem to have achieved a high degree of coincidence with new interest in and attitudes toward commemoration of the dead. Perfection of sandblasting techniques, the advent of granite etching, and the use of sophisticated equipment such as lasers, computers, and other high-tech graphics devices have resulted in the ability to produce startlingly realistic and personalized images on stone at a cost far less than one might initially expect. At the same time, those wishing to commemorate their loved ones have embraced these new techniques as a way in which to celebrate the meaning, values, and memories of an individual life. As one monument dealer, defending these highly personalized images against certain detractors in the profession who find them undignified, recently put it: "They are sold not to art critics and philosophical debaters, but to persons trying to memorialize what they think should be remembered."[4] The percentage of contemporary gravemarkers bearing personalized imagery in any given cemetery may vary widely owing to a number of contributing factors, not the least significant of which might be the presence in the immediate geographic area of one or more monument dealers who actively promote this sort of memorialization. In any event, they still constitute a minority of the total stones being produced, though, as noted previously, their numbers have been growing dramatically on a year-by-year basis during the past several decades.

The retrospective imagery found upon contemporary gravemarkers may center upon virtually any aspect of a person's life deemed worthy of commemoration.[5] A fair proportion of it, in fact, emphasizes what might be termed recreational pursuits, and this is particularly so in the case of memorials for young people. Thus, one finds an astounding variety of cars, sporting scenes, musical instruments, and a host of other, sometimes highly esoteric, objects and activities visually displayed on newer markers. In many instances these are enhanced by epitaphs and other inscriptions which provide a verbal counterpoint to the pictorials. The other major area of personalized retrospective emphasis involves depiction of the deceased person's occupational status, and in this at least one finds a certain degree of precedent in the occasional use of occupational symbolism on gravemarkers from earlier eras.[6] Strolling amongst the newer stones in many cemeteries one is likely to encounter any number of visual images denoting occupation—tools and equipment of all sorts, from plumber's wrenches to welder's helmets, long-haul semis, heavy construction equipment, and fire-fighting paraphernalia, to name but several of the more frequently seen patterns. The largest proportion of these clearly fall into what are generally considered blue collar occupations, though one also finds identifying symbolism for engineers, doctors, judges, and college professors. Finally, in those instances where one or more occupations are strongly identified with a certain geographic region, it is highly likely that the careful observer will find this emphasis reflected in the stone testimonies of area graveyards.[7] Thus, the cemeteries of the Pacific Northwest, a region with strong historic and contemporary economic ties to commercial fishing, ranching, and the lumber and wood products industries, yield numerous and often fascinating examples of markers which commemorate the lives of those who practiced these trades.

Anyone is likely to be intrigued by artifacts such as these, but when viewed by a folklorist they take on an immediate and special significance, for they constitute a meaningful and yet little-studied aspect of what is generally referred to as occupational folklore.[8] Any identifiable folk group—whether it be defined by age, ethnicity, religion, recreational interest, geographic region, or, in this case, occupational status—shares certain things in common, and amongst them is a body of oral and material traditions which are highly instrumental in providing cohesiveness and self-identity to members of the group. Most distinct occupational groups, even some of the more recent to emerge, possess some degree of occupational folklore, and in the case of certain of them it is considerable. This seems to be most especially true amongst those whose history is fraught with elements of hardship and danger, and where the occupation itself is felt to have had a dominant impact upon the development of American society. Thus, among the most heavily documented traditional occupational folk groups in America one might number keelboaters, miners, railroaders, and cowboys.

Another group which fits these criteria is that of professional loggers. From the early days of American logging upon the eastern seaboard, through the years of dominant activity in the upper Great Lakes region, to its ultimate emphasis within the Pacific Northwest, the rigors and rituals of this profession have forged a strong bond amongst those who work the woods. [9] Not surprisingly, loggers as a folk group have developed an enormously rich and diversified set of oral and material traditions, including songs, oral poetry, specialized vocabulary, traditional clothing, and all sorts of woodcarving activity from whittling to chainsaw art.[10] There are also complex patterns of traditional humor, ranging from initiation rituals to contextually meaningful "in" jokes. For example, the back of a closed fist, from which extend upright the index and little fingers, is presented, together with the question, "What's this?" The answer: "An Oregon logger ordering four beers!" As this joke suggests, logging is—and always has been—an extremely hazardous occupation.[11] It is, indeed, this element of danger and imminent death which informs the inscription found on one of the earliest extant gravestones for a logger in the Pacific Northwest, that of Wm. F. Laymen (d. 1880), whose marker in the Brownsville, Oregon Pioneer Cemetery proclaims in an almost accusatory fashion that he was "killed by falling from a tree while working for J. L. Larkin."

Though the danger factor remains extraordinarily high in modern logging[12]—indeed a fairly high proportion of contemporary gravemarkers for loggers commemorate men who died in job-related accidents—a listing of the cause of death on the markers is, in fact, rather rare. Instead, the retrospective emphasis tends to focus upon other things, most particularly visual representations of objects and activities associated with the work itself and certain complementary verbal sentiments which serve to reinforce the pride, self-identity, and worldview associated with members of this occupational folk group.

At the simplest level of occupational emphasis, one encounters verbal inscriptions which serve as general identifiers, e.g., "The Logger," though

they may upon occasion more narrowly define the scope of activity—
"Donkey Puncher," "A Sawmill Man," "Old Time Faller."[13] Such identifiers
are not infrequently embellished by superlatives which, when combined
with the already esoteric nature of the language of this occupational group,
serves to identify the individual as a true "man among men." Thus, one finds
such appellations as "One Hell of an Offbear" and "A Real Timber Beast."

A similar function of identification is often achieved through the visual
depiction of one or more items of personal clothing or equipment instantly
recognizable to those in the know as being symbolically representative of
logging and loggers. As Barre Toelken points out, the distinctive clothing
worn by Northwest loggers in essence "constitutes a folk costume by means
of which loggers belong and recognize each other."[14] Amongst the separate
elements in this sartorial repertoire, the ones most frequently singled out
for symbolic depiction on logger gravestones are the hard hat, required by
law to be worn when working in the woods, and the distinctive caulked
boots referred to by loggers themselves as "corks" (figs. 3.1 and 3.2). In
instances where the full figure of a logger is depicted (e.g., figs. 3.3 and 3.4),
one is likely to see other typical items of clothing such as suspenders and
stagged (i.e., cut off above the ankles) pants. A number of personal tools of
the trade serve, either singly or in combination with other items of equipment or clothing, as additional visual identifiers. These may range from
tools and equipment recalling an earlier era of logging—axes, springboards,
"misery whips" (crosscut saws)—to that mainstay of contemporary logging,
the chainsaw. Upon occasion the tools as purely occupational symbols may
fit into a somewhat broader and more traditional symbolic context. Thus,
an unattended ax embedded in a fallen log (fig. 3.2) or a chainsaw left
sitting on a stump (fig. 3.5) may suggest several levels of association simultaneously: the occupation of the deceased, the notion of a life cut off before
its time (often represented in traditional gravestone symbolism through the
depiction of sheared off pillars, broken chain links, and severed tree or plant
limbs), and the somewhat more complex visual metaphor which implies
the absence of an essential binary element (as, for example, in the traditional mourning motif of the saddled, riderless horse).

A more complex form of visual identification is often achieved through
the depiction of a logger (presumably meant to represent the deceased
himself) engaged in some typical activity associated with the occupation.
He may be seen on his knees setting a choker, bucking fallen timber (i.e.,
cutting the tree into log lengths), or merely taking a break with his hat
tipped back and one foot resting upon a log. Fallers, those who actually cut
down the trees, are amply represented, whether standing atop an old time
springboard and vigorously applying one end of a "misery whip" to some
massive wonder of nature or wielding a modern chainsaw in a stand of

Figure 3.1. Logger's Hard Hat, Boots, Inscription
Elkton Cemetery, Elkton, Oregon.
(Photograph Richard E. Meyer)

Figure 3.2. Axe in Log, Logger's Boots, Inscription
Lone Oak Cemetery, Stayton, Oregon.
(Photograph Richard E. Meyer)

Figure 3.3. "Boom Cat" Logger with Pole
Murray Hill Cemetery, Clatskanie, Oregon.
(Photograph Richard E. Meyer)

Figure 3.4. Chainsaw-Carved Logger in Full Regalia
Forest Grove Cemetery, near Tenino, Washington.
(Photograph Richard E. Meyer)

Figure 3.5.   Chainsaw on Stump, Inscription
Lone Oak Cemetery, Stayton, Oregon.
(Photograph Richard E. Meyer)

second growth timber. While all of these activities bespeak an evident pride in their performance, it is even more apparent in those specialized woods functions involving the highest levels of skill and exposure to danger. One such specialization, for the most part obsolete in modern logging operations, was that of poler or "white water man." These athletic daredevils (whose function with regard to the massive log drives of the past was not dissimilar to that of the drovers on the great cattle roundups) were a breed which spawned the matter of legends and ballads. Louie Blanchard, an old time logger of the upper Great Lakes region, recalls that as a kid around the turn of the century "We saw lumberjacks ride logs through the rapids, holding their pike poles to keep their balance, and it looked like a job better than being President of the United States. Everybody looked up to these man who wore caulked boots and red mackinaws and walked on logs as they shot the rapids."[15] Today, one must attend a special logging show (the logging equivalent of a rodeo) to see these extraordinary skills demonstrated, but the visitor to Murray Hill Cemetery in Clatskanie, Oregon can also see them depicted on the gravemarker of Urho H. Korhonen (fig. 3.3), where they silently but proudly proclaim that this man was not only a logger but a "boom cat," one of those special types which the late logger-songwriter Buzz Martin dubbed "a vanishing breed of man."[16]

A large number of logger gravestones present visual depictions of various types of heavy equipment used in logging operations, serving in this fashion as well to give a clearer indication of the individual's particular specialization. Again, the emphasis may be at least partially nostalgic, linking the person with pride to some earlier era when logging was presumably even more demanding and meaningful an occupation than today. Thus, one finds images of various antique steam donkeys and other yarding devices, plus even earlier skidroad operations involving the use of oxen or horses. Far more numerous, however, are pictorials which demonstrate a wide variety of modern logging machinery, frequently shown in the course of performing some typical activity. One finds many examples of various types of logging tractors as well as both wheeled and crawler skidders (fig. 3.6), plus such specialized pieces of heavy equipment as feller-bunchers, yarding cranes, hydraulic loaders, and some items which could perhaps only be identified by an expert in the field.

Loggers, by most commonly accepted definitions, are generally considered to be those who work directly in the woods and who are engaged in one form or another in the actual harvesting and initial rough processing of timber. Taken as a whole, however, the modern wood products industry encompasses a number of separate, though obviously related, occupations. One such area—with, incidentally, its own set of long-standing folkloric traditions—involves the sawmill men who practice the skilled, and some-

Figure 3.6.   Logging Cat Engaged in Modern Skidding Operation
Gold Beach Cemetery, Gold Beach, Oregon.
(Photograph Richard E. Meyer)

times extremely hazardous, tasks of transforming raw timber into finished lumber,[17] and it comes, therefore, as no great surprise that individuals such as these also show an interest in visually emphasizing their specific occupational status on personalized gravemarkers (fig. 3.7).

The problem of transporting raw timber from the generally remote and sometimes virtually inaccessible areas where it is felled to the mills where it receives final processing has always posed significant challenges to the industry, resulting both in some ingenious solutions and a succession of workers with their own special sense of identity. Today, the modern descendants of the white-water men who worked the great spring log drives and the narrow gauge railroaders who manned the logging trains of the West are log truck drivers, a somewhat free-spirited set of individuals marked by an enormous amount of pride and self-assurance.[18] As might be expected, they are liberally represented in the gravestone imagery of a number of contemporary Pacific Northwest cemeteries (fig. 3.8). Central to all such imagery is a depiction of the truck and trailer combination itself, generally in its fully loaded configuration. The images may often become highly particularized, however, even to the extent that one may identify the specific make of truck (e.g., Kenworth, Peterbilt, or, in some cases, older types no longer on the market). The deceased's name and vital data may be engraved upon the stone truck's door (in a manner reminiscent of the way in which his name and other information might have been painted on the door of the truck he drove in life) or upon the load of logs being hauled. In one rather extraordinary design created by Oregon Memorials of Hillsboro, Oregon, a personalized marker for a log trucker depicts a fully loaded 16-wheeler, with the logs in front bearing the names of each of his children.[19] Like long-haul road truckers, log truck drivers frequently give personal names to their vehicles (e.g., "Bluebird," "Jennie Lee"), and in some instances these are also included in the pictorials. The same is true of individual CB "handles" (e.g., "Howler").

Pictorials are in some ways the most arresting form of personalization, but a fair amount of emphasis on contemporary logger's gravemarkers is also given to verbal inscriptions, frequently utilizing words or even whole phrases which have traditional status within the group. Thus, in addition to shorter identifiers such as those discussed earlier in this essay, one might encounter somewhat more complex notions such as those embodied in the utterance "May the Bull of the Woods Always Walk in Tall Timber" (fig. 3.1), wherein there is a blending of several traditional terms and sentiments, including the rather Elysian desire to "Always Walk in Tall Timber" and the title "Bull of the Woods," which can have several specific meanings but in each case denotes a man of high status within the community of loggers.[20] The phrase which seems the undisputed favorite amongst con-

Figure 3.7.   Modern Sawmill Worker
Dallas Cemetery, Dallas, Oregon.
(Photograph Richard E. Meyer)

Figure 3.8. Contemporary Log Truck
Calvary Cemetery, Tacoma, Washington.
(Photograph Richard E. Meyer)

temporary loggers, appearing in slightly variant form on a large number of markers throughout the Pacific Northwest, is the ubiquitous "Where There Walks a Logger, There Walks a Man" (fig. 3.2). Though it was popularized to a large extent in the 1960s by logger-songwriter Buzz Martin as the title song for his first album,[21] it seems to have enjoyed traditional status in the woods for some time prior to this,[22] embodying in succinct fashion one of the most fiercely held tenets of logger self-concept and worldview.[23] Upon occasion an inscription may yield other sorts of insights, as in the somewhat esoteric "Its All in a Day in the Bush with God" (fig. 3.5), where the term "Bush" (the word used by Canadian loggers as the equivalent of the American "Woods")[24] also seems to indicate the national origin of the deceased.

In some cases the verbal component reaches the proportions of a full-blown epitaph. The gravemarker of retired logger Paul Lennis Swank in the Canyonville, Oregon Cemetery lists a birth but no death date. In fact, Swank (taking no chances that his wishes as to epitaph not be honored after his death) wrote his own, and had the stone erected himself with the following quatrain inscribed upon it:

> Here under the dung of the cows and sheep,
> Lies an old highclimber fast asleep.
> His trees all topped and his lines all hung,
> They say the old rascal died full of rum.

This verse, which bears a strong affinity in its technical qualities to a great deal of contemporary logger poetry, is textually more complex than it might at first appear. To lie beneath the dung of cows and sheep is, in fact, a very real possibility in many unfenced rural Oregon cemeteries where domestic animals sometimes wander at will: the fact that the subject of the epitaph knows himself to be in such a situation is an ironic bit of self-deprecating humor given the disdain true loggers normally evince towards "flatlanders" (i.e., farmers) and all things associated with them. In the second line we learn that Swank is more than just a generic logger: he is a "highclimber," one of that daring and highly skilled elite cadre of old time loggers who would climb to dizzying heights and saw the tops off trees in order to prepare them for rigging. These tasks are alluded to in the next line, though with the solemn reflection that they have been completed for the last time, at least in this life. Whatever solemnity is produced by the third line, however, is washed aside by the poem's conclusion, which puts the final emphasis upon another semiheroic quality with which loggers sometimes stereotype themselves, their ability to consume prodigious amounts of alcohol. Thus, within the space of four brief lines we are given the measure both of an individual personality capable of mixing humor and serious reflection and of one who embodies in his belief system some of the most fundamental values and collective self-concepts which distinguish loggers as an occupational folk group.

The examples used in the discussion of logger gravemarkers up to this point have virtually all been of that type commonly supplied by professional monument dealers, which, in this case at least, has meant both flat and upright granite stones. There is, however, one other striking manner in which the graves of many Pacific Northwest loggers are marked—perhaps in the last analysis the most symbolically fitting of all—and this is through the homecrafted use of the very material with which they are occupationally identified. The cemeteries of rural Northwest communities traditionally associated with logging activities contain many examples of this ongoing phenomenon,[25] and they constitute their own unique and provocative form of symbolic statement. The very fact that they are almost always handmade, sometimes commissioned but more often fashioned by coworkers or loved ones, carries its own immediate significance. Furthermore, the options for originality and highly individualized personalization may, if anything, be even greater with the use of wood; and one encounters a seemingly endless number of possibilities in area cemeteries. Burial plots may be covered with bark dust or wood chips. The perimeter may be defined by the use of logs or finished wood products, such as railroad ties or 4×4s. Entire plot perimeter fences are frequently constructed, and in some instances one even finds a type of canopied shelter somewhat reminiscent of those encountered in traditional rural cemeteries of the upland South.

Wooden markers themselves present a similarly wide range of possibilities. Sometimes stumps are brought in, placed at the head of the grave, and carved to display vital data. In a few instances separate objects, such as hard hats or chainsaw blades, are mounted to the side or placed on top. Crosses may be formed from small logs (limbs actually) or milled lumber. Pieces of wood of every conceivable thickness, height, and shape serve as headpieces on graves. They may be unfinished, laminated, or painted; their essence may be that of simplicity or lavish adornment. One of the finest examples of this type of cemetery artifact, and one which also admirably fuses material form and verbal sentiment, is located in the Canyon City, Oregon Cemetery. Here, upon an enormous rough-hewn section of log marking the grave of logger Thomas Lamar Cameron (d. 1977) are carved the following words:

> Here in these timbered mountains
>   And green valleys
> He loved so much
> We inter our beloved dad.

Here can be seen the image
of his life
Which forever lives in the
Hearts of his
Family and friends.

Upon occasion, a particular style of wooden marker might come to dominate an entire cemetery, so that, for instance, in the Canyonville, Oregon Cemetery one finds more than a dozen examples of a type of handmade gravemarker which consists of a crosscut section of a log suspended over the head or center of the grave plot from a frame constructed of pipes (fig. 3.9).

Perhaps most elaborate of all in this hierarchy of wooden grave decorations for loggers are those examples of markers which bear evidence of great skill in woodcarving of one fashion or another. The family of William A. Peacock (d. 1978) chose to honor his memory by commissioning the carving of a massive block of redwood, replete with images of evergreens symbolizing his occupation (fig. 3.10),[26] and other examples of similar, though smaller, artifacts may be found in several rural Northwest cemeteries.

In certain notable instances, chainsaw carving, itself a form of folk art strongly associated with professional loggers, supplies a symbolic adornment to their graves. Chainsawed elk and bear have both been observed at gravesites, but what might well be the most spectacular instance of this phenomenon is found in Tenino, Washington's Forest Grove Cemetery. Here, upon the gravesite of George R. Sanders (d. 1980), stands a magnificently executed chainsawed logger, dressed and equipped as he might have been in life (fig. 3.4). Hard hat, suspenders, stagged pants, caulked logger boots: all are clearly identifiable on this three-foot-high redwood effigy, despite the weathering which has taken place in the years since it was erected. In his hands he holds a chainsaw—probably intended as a replica of the one he used on the job, for on the front one may barely trace out the weathered make and model number (Homelite XL 12). The blade, no longer attached to the statue, carried the inscription "One Hell of a Logger."[27] Local residents recall that the marker suddenly appeared in the cemetery one day several months after Sanders's funeral, apparently erected personally by his widow, who had commissioned its carving in Idaho.[28]

Long the economic mainstay of the Pacific Northwest, logging and the wood products industry in general fell upon devastatingly hard times in the first half of the decade of the 1980s. Though some recovery has been made, there is legitimate concern as to whether this industry and its dependent

Figure 3.9. Crosscut Section of Log Suspended from Pipe Frame
Canyonville Cemetery, Canyonville, Oregon.
(Photograph Richard E. Meyer)

Figure 3.10.   Elaborately Carved Wooden Marker
Summerville Cemetery, near Summerville, Oregon.
(Photograph Richard E. Meyer)

occupations will ever fully regain their former status. As the profession of logging changes rapidly through a combination of economic and technological influences, and as younger workers shaped by these conditions begin to replace those nurtured in earlier times and traditions, certain questions inevitably pose themselves to the folklorist. Which elements of past traditions will disappear over time? Which will continue? What sort of transformations will take place? And, perhaps most intriguing of all, what totally new forms will arise? The answers to these questions will undoubtedly come: the key, as always, is in knowing where to look. Still, if the lessons of past and present are any accurate indicator, it is perhaps worth suggesting anew that some of that looking be done in the cemetery.

Amongst many of those scholars who have contributed significantly to the contemporary study of material culture in America there seems to be agreement on one general principle—the notion that material objects are, in fact, "texts" which can be "read" by those attentive to the cultural messages they seek to convey.[29] Gravestone studies—at least the best of them—have always embraced this concept and placed it at the heart of their interpretive approach. "Artifacts," Henry Glassie has written, "are worth studying because they yield information about the ideas in the minds of people long dead."[30] In the case of contemporary gravemarkers, they can also tell us a great deal about the ideas in the minds of people more recently dead, as well as—and this factor cannot be emphasized too strongly—those who remain to both mourn their loss and cherish their memory. If the recurring image of the winged death's head is a key to our understanding of puritan cultural values, if the countless instances of the clasped hands motif on nineteenth-century gravestones tell us something of Victorian sensibilities, what may we conclude about contemporary American culture as a whole (not to speak of subgroups within that culture) by carefully studying the forms of retrospective imagery which, in our time, have come to assume so significant a role in the markers we choose to commemorate our dead?

Loggers, an occupational subculture which Barre Toelken aptly identifies as a "high context group,"[31] possess a rich and highly diversified body of esoteric lore within which we may see much which serves to articulate and reinforce both personal and collective value systems. In speaking of logger poetry, Robert E. Walls has noted that "While logger poems are very personal statements of one individual's relationship with his occupation, they represent, more importantly, a vital form of public expression for the group's worldview, acting rhetorically on whoever may be the audience by stating the worth and respectability of an often maligned profession."[32] As we have seen, logger gravemarkers in the Pacific Northwest fulfill essentially the same functions, providing, in the best American tradition of "speaking stones," the material equivalent of personal narratives and oral verse recitations.

In the Carman United Church Cemetery, Sardis, British Columbia, there stands a small granite marker in memory of Robin T. Rancier (d. 1980). Depicted on the stone is a chainsaw and the simple message "Gone Logging." That, for many loggers of today, would have pretty much the same meaning as a nineteenth-century marble headstone bearing the image of a finger pointing upwards and the words, "In Heaven."

Notes

Special thanks to the following, each of whom contributed materially to the development of this essay: Ken Graves, Phyllis Harrison, Finley and Jean Hayes, Linda Howerton, Jens Lund, Lotte Larsen, Doug Nicol, Sam Schrager, Walt Stempek, and Barre Toelken.

1. Herbert Blaney, "The Modern Park Cemetery," in *Passing: The Vision of Death in America,* ed. Charles O. Jackson (Westport, Conn.: Greenwood Press, 1977), pp. 219–20.

2. A great deal of attention has been focused upon this phenomenon in recent decades, perhaps best exemplified in the numerous writings of Elisabeth Kübler-Ross. Despite its age, the most comprehensive, albeit popularized, treatment remains Jessica Mitford's *The American Way of Death* (New York: Simon and Schuster, 1963).

3. Memorialists, those professionally engaged in the design, manufacture, and sales of contemporary gravemarkers, lump all aspects of this trend under the general rubric "personalization," and the importance it plays in their current thinking is demonstrated by the many and varied treatments of the subject found in their trade journals. See, for example, virtually any recent issue of *Stone in America,* the monthly publication of the American Monument Association.

4. Jacqueline Hanks, "Pictorials: Pro and Con," *Stone in America* 100:10 (October 1987), p. 30.

5. Trade journals aside, scholarly interest in the forms and symbolic meanings of these contemporary artifacts has been virtually nonexistent. For one notable exception see Carol Edison, "Motorcycles, Guitars, and Bucking Broncs: Twentieth-Century Gravestones in Southeastern Idaho," in *Idaho Folklife: Homesteads to Headstones,* ed. Louie W. Attebery (Salt Lake City: University of Utah Press, 1985), pp. 184–89.

6. For an excellent discussion of these devices on eighteenth-century Scottish markers see the section entitled "Emblems of Trade" in Betty Willsher and Doreen Hunter, *Stones: A Guide to Some Remarkable Eighteenth-Century Gravestones* (New York: Taplinger Publishing Company, 1978), pp. 62–120. For some representative nineteenth-century American examples see Leonard V. Huber, *Clasped Hands: Symbolism in New Orleans Cemeteries* (Lafayette, La.: The Center for Louisiana Studies, 1982), pp. 106–11; 133–41. Folklorist Warren E. Roberts has extensively researched the employment of occupational imagery on older tombstones in southern Indiana. See in particular the following: "Investigating the Tree-Stump Tombstone in Indiana," in *American Material Culture and Folklife: A Prologue and Dialogue,* ed. Simon J. Bronner (Ann Arbor: UMI Research Press, 1985), pp. 135–43; "The Sincerest Form of Flattery: Originals and Imitations in 'Rustic Monuments' of the Limestone Belt of Indiana," in *Viewpoints on Folklife: Looking*

at the Overlooked (Ann Arbor: UMI Research Press, 1988), pp. 145–61; "Tombstones in Scotland and Indiana," *Folk Life* 23 (1984–85), pp. 97–104; "Tools on Tombstones: Some Indiana Examples," *Pioneer America* 10:1 (June 1978), pp. 106–11 (repr. in *Viewpoints on Folklife*, pp. 133–44; "Traditional Tools as Symbols: Some Examples from Indiana Tombstones," *Pioneer America* 12 (February 1980), pp. 54–63.

7. Professor Barre Toelken of Utah State University, who was kind enough to read this essay in manuscript form, suggested to me that this is a point which merits further probing. If the identification of occupation with region provides an especially rich context in which cemeteries and their memorials can reflect shared values, it must be assumed that this is a consequential, and not merely a coincidental, phenomenon. The question than becomes—"Why?" What factors combine, in this instance, to allow the intensified, shared emotions inherent in both regional and occupational identification to find one of their most articulate levels in the form of gravemarkers? Consideration of these factors in any depth would carry me beyond the limitation of this essay, but I am grateful to Toelken for stressing their importance and hope that they will provide the impetus for further study.

8. Recent years have seen a number of significant analyses of occupational folklore, ranging from the highly specific to more generalized. For two extremely useful overviews see Robert McCarl, "Occupational Folklore," in *Folk Groups and Folklore Genres,* ed. Elliott Oring (Logan: Utah State University Press, 1986), pp. 71–89; and Roger Mitchell, "Occupational Folklore: The Outdoor Industries," in *Handbook of American Folklore,* ed. Richard M. Dorson (Bloomington: Indiana University Press, 1983), pp. 128–35.

9. There yet remains to be written a truly comprehensive history of logging and loggers in the United States. The most useful treatment to date is actually based upon Canadian materials: see Donald MacKay, *The Lumberjacks* (Toronto: McGraw-Hill Ryerson, 1978).

10. For a brief but extremely illuminating overview and contextual analysis of logger folklore see Barre Toelken, *The Dynamics of Folklore* (Boston: Houghton Mifflin, 1979), pp. 51–72. A variety of oral and material logging traditions are presented in "Loggers and Their Lore," a thirty-minute documentary videotape produced in 1987 by Jean Walkinshaw for KCTS-TV, Seattle. The ballad tradition within the logging profession has been well documented: see, for example, Edith Fowke, *Lumbering Songs from the Northern Woods* (Austin: University of Texas Press, 1970). Of several glossaries of logger terminology, the best remains Walter F. McCulloch, *Woods Words: A Comprehensive Dictionary of Loggers' Terms* (Portland: Oregon Historical Society, 1958). Examples of logger poetry may be found in virtually any issue of the monthly publication *Loggers' World,* many of which are reprinted in Finley Hays, ed., *Loggers' World: The First Ten Years* (Chehalis, Wash.: Loggers' World Publications, 1987), and several excellent examples by contemporary Northwest logger poets may be heard on "Northwest Logger Poetry," a 1987 audio tape produced by the Washington State Folklife Council. For an important analysis of the forms and functions of these oral texts see Robert E. Walls, "Logger Poetry and the Expression of Worldview," *Northwest Folklore* 5:2 (Spring 1987), pp. 15–45. The personal narratives of old time Northwest loggers are extensively examined in Samuel Alan Schrager, "'The Early Days': Narrative and Symbolism of Logger Life in the Inland Northwest" (Ph.D. dissertation, University of Pennsylvania, 1983).

11. For the relationship between traditional humor and the dangers of logging as an occupation, see Toelken, *The Dynamics of Folklore,* pp. 58–60.

12. For an in-depth journalistic treatment of this troubling phenomenon see "Logging: Oregon's Deadly Career," *Salem Statesman-Journal* (April 26, 1987), pp. 1G, 7G, 8G, 9G, 10G. An interesting historical analysis is found in Andrew Mason Prouty, *More Deadly than War!: Pacific Coast Logging, 1827–1981* (New York: Garland Publishing, 1985).

13. These and all other references in this essay to both verbal and visual images on Pacific Northwest gravemarkers are accurate representations of material documented through the author's fieldwork. With the exception, however, of these examples for which illustrations are provided and certain others discussed at greater length in the text, names, dates, and cemetery locations have been dispensed with in the interests of economy.

14. Toelken, *The Dynamics of Folklore,* p. 53.

15. Walker D. Wyman, *The Lumberjack Frontier: The Life of a Logger in the Early Days on the Chippeway, Retold from the Recollections of Louie Blanchard* (Lincoln: University of Nebraska Press, 1969), p. 48.

16. Buzz Martin, "A Vanishing Breed of Man," on *The Old Time Logger: A Vanishing Breed of Man.* Ripcord SLP 004. Martin's four LPs on the Ripcord label are filled with fascinating insights into the logging life and worldview, as evidenced by song titles such as "Strong Winds and Widow Makers," "Loggin' in the Bars," " Settin' Chokers in the Snow," "Since They Repossessed My Used Log Truck," "Timber up in Heaven," "Whistle Punk Pete," and the classic "Where There Walks a Logger, There Walks a Man."

17. For an account of working conditions and traditional practices in the early mills of the Pacific Northwest see the chapter entitled "Sawyers and Setters" in Paul Hosmer, *Now We're Loggin'* (Portland: Binfords and Mort, 1930), pp. 129–35.

18. A fascinating collection of oral histories relating to this occupational folk group is presented in Walt Wentz, *Bringing Out the Big Ones: Log Trucking in Oregon, 1912–1983* (Salem, Ore.: Oregon Forest Products Transportation Association,1983).

19. See Mike Major, "Adapting to the Trends: The Brownleewee Family Shows the Way in Oregon," *Stone in America* 97:5 (May 1984), p. 25.

20. See, for example, McCulloch, *Woods Words,* p. 21; Toelken, *The Dynamics of Folklore,* p. 54.

21. Ripcord SLP 001.

22. Finley Hays, editor/publisher of *Loggers' World* and as expert a voice as one could ever hope to find on Northwest logging history and lore, is of the definite opinion that the phrase had a certain degree of oral currency before Martin's use of it (telephone interview, December 31, 1987).

23. See Walls, "Logger Poetry and the Expression of Worldview," pp. 33–35.

24. McCulloch, *Woods Words,* p. 24.

25. One may also observe this association in cemetery artifacts other than gravemarkers. The cemetery signs, for instance, are invariably of wood, and in the case of Forest Grove Cemetery, near the logging community of Tenino, Washington, the sign consists of a huge log with the individual letters forming the name chainsawed out of the wood so as to stand in relief.

26. Interview with cemetery sexton, Summerville, Oregon Cemetery, August 7, 1986.

27. A photograph of the monument in its intact state may be seen in the *Tenino Independent* (May 26, 1982), p. 1.

28. Personal communication from Linda Howerton, Tenino, Washington, December 30, 1987.

29. See, for example, Simon J. Bronner, "Folk Objects," in *Folk Groups and Folklore Genres,* ed. Elliott Oring (Logan: Utah State University Press, 1986), p. 199.

30. *Folk Housing in Middle Virginia: A Structural Analysis of Historic Artifacts* (Knoxville: University of Tennessee Press, 1975), p. 17.

31. Toelken, *The Dynamics of Folklore,* p. 52. The "high context" notion, by the way, is applicable as well to a number of other folk groups, and in many instances one finds a significant manifestation of this identity on contemporary gravemarkers. In addition to other occupational groups such as cowboys, truckers, and railroad workers, a fairly large number of personalized and group-identifiable gravemarkers exist (often concentrated in cemeteries specifically chosen by the group) for members of "outlaw" motorcycle gangs.

32. Walls, "Logger Poetry and the Expression of Worldview," p. 15.

4

The Epitaph and Personality Revelation

J. Joseph Edgette

Scholars from many fields, and perhaps most particularly those engaged in folkloristic and other approaches to the study of material objects, have recognized for some time that memorials erected to honor the dead serve an important and often complex function within the society which creates them. Furthermore, it has become obvious that this function often signifies far more than the essentially utilitarian purpose of marking the location of the grave of the individual buried there. Upon these artifacts one finds inscribed words, and sometimes visual images, which convey a great deal of information about the departed person and, in some cases, serve as insights into their individual personalities. One verbal element in particular—the epitaph—is especially significant in revealing personality traits, and it shall be the purpose of this essay to explore briefly some pertinent examples of these intriguing voices from the American cemetery.

The epitaph has always been a source of interest to many, especially when found to be humorous, bizarre or unique. Definitions of what a true epitaph is vary widely, but for the purposes of establishing parameters of discussion within the current context a somewhat standardized dictionary definition seems most workable: "An inscription upon a tomb. Hence, occasionally, a brief composition characterizing a deceased person, and expressed as if intended to be inscribed on their tombstone."[1] Particular attention should be drawn here to the word "characterizing." Characterizing an individual usually involves the recognition of those specific, distinguishing traits that set them apart from others. Often this is a matter of personality. The intended inscription thus implies the notion that the epitaph be fitting and appropriate to the named individual. Epitaphs, by their nature, evoke images of the departed soul.

The epitaph has been in use since ancient times and flourished profusely in the United States from the seventeenth century until the end of the last century.[2] Today, we still find them in use, but in greatly diminished frequency when compared with the past. Reasons for the decline can be attributed to several factors: rising costs of gravestone carving (a per-letter charge is now common, making the cost of long inscriptions prohibitive for many); tighter restrictions as to what will and what will not be acceptable to cemetery administrations; and changes in society's views regarding the appropriate manner in which to commemorate our lost ones.

Epitaphs may be grouped into several appropriate categories based upon their structural denotation and/or their implied function. Verses taken from holy scripture, for example, are perhaps the most commonly found of all epitaphic statements. A favorite reads:

> I am the resurrection and the life;
> he that believeth in me, though he were dead,
> yet shall he live.
> —John 11:25.

In this instance, the particular source of the scriptural passage is also provided, though frequently this is not the case (owing perhaps to the assumption that the verses selected would be commonly recognized by all who read them). These verses taken from scripture tend to verify and document the influence of religion upon the departed person, or in any case within the family whose duty it becomes to erect the marker. Catholic burial places abound with examples using verses from their version of the Bible, whereas cemeteries associated with the various Protestant denominations feature markers which tend to make use of the somewhat more poetic King James version. Other holy books, such as the Koran, are also quoted under the appropriate circumstances.

Closely associated with the type of scriptural quotations noted above are the frequently used ejaculations or short, plea-like prayers. Most often the tone is one of asking for mercy or fair treatment for the soul of the departed. These ejaculations are extremely common in Catholic cemeteries, and include such typical examples as "Eternal rest grant unto them, O Lord" and "Our Lady of Perpetual Help, pray for us."

Following scriptural quotations and other forms of strictly religiously oriented statements, the next most popular type of epitaph, particularly on older stones, is that of poetic versification. The following poetic stanza, akin to many of those found on Victorian gravemarkers, illustrates iambic tetrameter. More importantly, perhaps, it also exemplifies the philosophic belief that, while earthly life is limited, an eternal life awaits in which all will be reunited:

The praise of those who sleep in earth,
The pleasant memory of their worth,
The hope to meet when life is past,
Shall heal the tortured mind at last.

Dozens of similar verses are quickly discovered by anyone who spends much time in our older cemeteries, and it is evident that an analysis of these versified epitaphs reveals any number of contemporary views and attitudes regarding the nature of the death experience, often in terms of those who survive the loss.

A large category of inscriptions somewhat below the level of full-blown epitaphs are those verbal utterances which convey the expression of grief over loss while simultaneously attempting to justify and accept the loss. Appropriate examples would include such ubiquitous statements as "Gone but not forgotten," "Only Sleeping," "At Rest," and the like. In the case of each of these, there is on the one hand an acceptance of the fact that the person has left this temporal plain, while at the same time it is implied that a reunion will be inevitable.

Epitaphs of the types so far considered all share a common feature: each in its own way denotes the passing of the loved one to a place of greater glory, a place of rest, a place of peace eternal. These kinds of familiar expressions, while worth considering for the cultural insights they provide, cannot compare in interest to those one-of-a-kind epitaphs which I would designate as belonging to the truly "original" category. These original epitaphs invariably reflect something about the nature of the deceased person's personality. Highly personalized and peculiar to one specific person, they are, so to speak, customized to fit one individual and one individual only.

Personality is an enigma which is both fascinating and at the same time frustrating in terms of our being able to fully understand its nature, its complexities, and its manifest behaviors. As a working definition, we may say that personality is the sum total of those inner human traits which, when revealed to others, will tend to enable or, conversely, disenable an effective, successful communicative experience with the potential of furthering a deeper interrelationship between the individuals.

How does personality relate to gravemarker epitaphs? As the deceased no longer exhibits behavior, it may be argued that personality cannot be said to exist. The point here, however, is that the essence of an individual personality is often revealed by an original epitaph, either selected by the person prior to his death or chosen following his death by those who knew him best. These epitaphs, then, unlike the standardized inscriptions noted earlier, become as varied and individual as the personalities they symbolize.

Upon his death in 1974, Julian C. Skaggs, a retired West Virginia coal miner, was cremated according to his own instructions. His family had his remains interred in the family burial plot and later had a stone placed upon the grave to mark its location. The casual stroller will read the inscribed data and will invariably laugh or at least smile when coming upon the epitaph. This "last word" is, indeed, worthy of the chuckle it brings and reflects a very strong sense of humor, one of Mr. Skaggs's most noticeable and remarked-upon personality traits. He loved people, and he loved to converse, cajole, and joke with them. It was said that Julian used to derive immense pleasure from watching the expression on a stranger's face when he would shake hands, step back, and leave the stranger holding his artificial hand (the result of a mining accident some years earlier). He liked, as he would put it, the idea of "giving a hand to a stranger." His epitaph (fig. 4.1) becomes a final indicator of his wit. Keeping in mind that Mr. Skaggs was in fact cremated, the use of the pun in this original epitaph—"I made an ash of myself"—is wonderfully appropriate. A quite literal reference to the disposition of his remains becomes at one and the same time a sure indicator of his personality. This *was* Julian, and no one who really knew the man was surprised by the epitaph. It was more or less the sort of thing they had come to expect from him. Julian Skaggs would undoubtedly be very pleased if he could see the smiles and hear the laughter his epitaph evokes today. Though he is no longer a member of living society, his personality is clearly conveyed and, in a sense, continues to manifest itself in the world he left behind.

In North Leominster, Massachusetts, the gravemarker of one Joseph Palmer, founder of Harvard Fruitlands (Utopian Society), displays an effigy of the fully bearded Palmer. The epitaph inscribed below the carved facial view of Palmer, who died in 1873, reads: "Persecuted for wearing the beard."[3] This man had the courage of his convictions. Despite public opinion in his community, where, prior to the Civil War, it was considered unorthodox and improper to wear a beard, he dared to be himself and to live as he wished, both signs of a strong willed individual. Like Julian Skaggs, Joseph Palmer is memorialized by a unique epitaph which speaks to us of the personality features he evinced in life.

Other strong-willed personalities, such as atheists and confirmed bachelors, have left their epitaphal marks upon the American cemetery as well. Of the former, perhaps none have elicited as much controversy as Joseph Coveney, who in 1874 had erected in the local cemetery of Buchanan, Michigan a massive Victorian monument bearing his name and covered with inscriptions such as "He died as he had lived, a disbeliever in the Bible and the Christian religion"; "The more Priests, the more Poverty"; "Nature is the true God. Science is the true Religion"; and "The more Religion, the

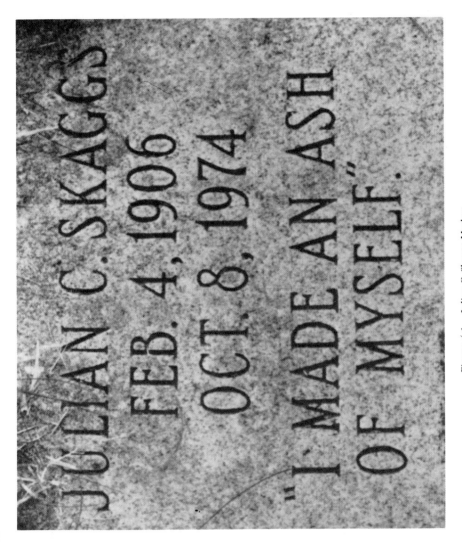

Figure 4.1. Julian C. Skaggs Marker
West Virginia.
(Photograph J. Joseph Edgette)

more Lying." Despite various attempts over the years to have the offending epitaphs removed, the monument still stands as originally erected, proclaiming to those who pass by the fiercely held convictions of Joseph Coveney.[4] One of the more extraordinary testimonials to the values of bachelorhood may be viewed in the cemetery of the small community of Myrtle Point, Oregon, where an impressive granite monument to William Hartley (d. 1913) bears the image of a gentleman dressed in Victorian attire standing upon a rock. Opposite him, on another rock, stands a woman with outstretched arms and beseeching gaze, while beneath the epitaph reads:[5]

> To an Independent good
> looking old Batchelor [*sic*]
> Who in his younger days
> Preferred living a
> Single life rather
> than get married and
> have a petticoat boss
> Ruling over him the
> Rest of his life and
> Perhaps through an
> Endless Eternity

In more recent times, Dr. Chalmers Cornelious of Bryn Mawr, a Philadelphia Main Line community, wished to have a marble, garden-type bench erected as his monument. Rather than having plain sides to the seat, however, he requested the carver to inscribe his own, specially selected words: "I shall sit thee down, tough seat." The H. C. Wood Monument Company of Lansdowne, Pennsylvania was commissioned to do the carving (fig. 4.2), which they did—to the letter. As was the case with the Julian Skaggs marker, Dr. Cornelious's bench illustrates some interesting wordplay. When reading the quotation and equating it with the man, a glimpse of his personality cannot help but come through. An educated individual, he conveys to those closest to him the sense of humor and cleverness so strongly known to be an integral part of his personality. Such epitaphs, however subtle, have the wonderful tendency to crystalize momentarily a minute but revealing particle from the personality of the deceased.

When attempting to interpret epitaphs correctly in terms of personality revelation, it is oftentimes extremely important to track down family members, personal friends of the deceased, or suitable documents which will help to confirm or modify the thesis overtly suggested by an examination of the marker *in situ*. This is illustrated in several of the preceding examples, but most particularly in those which follow.

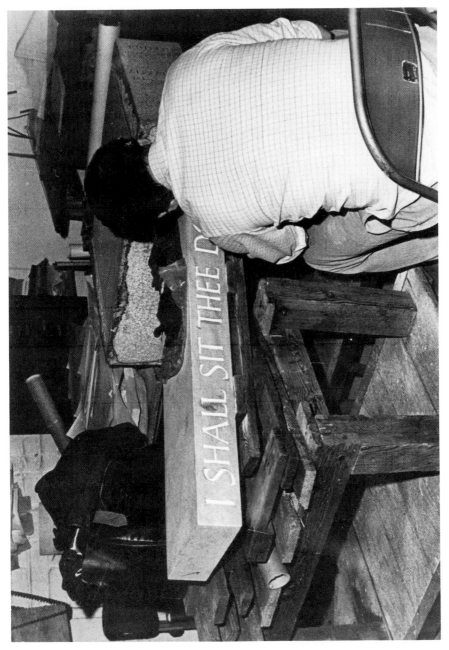

Figure 4.2. Cornelious Garden Bench Stone Bryn Mawr, Pennsylvania. (Photograph J. Joseph Edgette)

An attractive, socially poised woman, Elvira Grimaldi was equally comfortable in her roles both on and off the stage.

"Hail poetry thou heav'n born maid"
ELVIRA (Elvie) GRIMALDI
Oct. 18, 1926
Sept. 22, 1986

reads the monument recently erected to her memory. To those who knew her, the quotation at the top of the face of her marker serves as a most appropriate epitaph. Traditionally, epitaphs appear last on the marker, though this is by no means an inflexible rule. In this case, its initial placement is particularly significant, for, according to her husband, daughter, and closest friends, this epitaph is meant to be a strong statement regarding her personality. Elvie, as she preferred to be called, was outgoing and friendly. She had many friends and was a friend to them as well. Her voice was strong and melodious. As a result of her vocal talent, she became very actively involved with the theater, and her fondness for the stage grew more deeply with each year. Her last performance was *The Mikado,* which also served as the source for her epitaph. Because she loved Gilbert and Sullivan plays, and most especially *The Mikado,* her family selected this line, her favorite, and one which, in their view, encompassed all that was Elvie.[6]

Though one could argue the point that this epitaph might better reflect avocation or interest than personality, it is important to bear in mind that original epitaphs are often to a large degree private. They are intended primarily to convey a message to a select audience comprised of those who knew the deceased individual personally. Nonmembers of this audience, those of us who casually come upon these inscriptions, may often make incorrect assumptions or otherwise miss the point because we were not personally familiar with the personalities which inspired them. Elvie Grimaldi's stone most definitely reflects her essential personality: when friends and relatives view it, they vividly recall Elvie and her intense love for the stage. The stage was Elvie; Elvie was the stage. To them, her epitaph indicates far more than merely an interest she had in life: it is her own unique personality which continues to speak through these carefully chosen lines.

"Hooter," a young man whose complete legal name was William Scott Gibson, had recently married a divorcee with a young son. Hooter and his new wife were extremely happy, and her little boy loved his new "daddy" very much. While out riding one day on his motorcycle, Hooter and his wife were involved in a tragic accident which claimed his life.[7] Mrs. Gibson, who survived the wreck, had the following inscription placed upon her husband's headstone in suburban Philadelphia's Fernwood Cemetery:

WILLIAM SCOTT GIBSON
1944–1977
"HOOTER"
My buddy, My daddy
This is indeed a true bummer

Just how, one might ask, is personality reflected here? And, for that matter, whose is it? This marker, more than most, clearly implies the presence of several distinct personalities. It demonstrates, on the one hand, the affection and the degree of closeness shared by the survivors and the departed one, a closeness enhanced by the "buddy" and "daddy" labels. The "bummer" line is somewhat more subtle, but significant nonetheless in that it continues a pattern begun with the inclusion of Gibson's nickname, "Hooter" (undoubtedly an oblique reference to the old-time western film star "Hoot" Gibson). Language is, of course, one of the means by which we often gauge personality in contemporary society. The language used on this particular marker is indicative of a laid back, easygoing individual, and, in fact, has special relevance to the speech preferred by younger persons in the 1960s and 1970s. It mirrors, albeit indirectly, the basic personality of the deceased, and perhaps that of his wife as well. Because the survivors express their appraisal of the event in a form of language which would have been most typical of him in life, they are in fact preserving an essential trait of his which more than likely set him apart from others.

Porter H. Waite, an outgoing, personable, people-loving gentleman, had been a car salesman for many years in suburban Philadelphia's affluent Swarthmore area. His warm personality had a magnetic attractiveness about it. Upon his death, family members wanted an epitaph inscribed on his gravemarker which would reflect Porter's friendliness, his love of fun, and his fondness for people. The decision was made to simply combine three of his favorite expressions and to use these as his epitaph: "Hi everyone! Have fun. See you later" (fig. 4.3).

This specific epitaph is, in fact, the one which initially sparked my notion that personality revelation is possible through the analysis of certain original epitaphs. The thesis was confirmed during a lecture in 1984, where I had mentioned this idea in a public presentation on gravemarkers and their functions. In the audience was a middle-aged woman who was very excited about the Porter Waite marker, which I had used as an example. She stood up and proclaimed complete agreement with my hypothesis. She could verify my speculative comments because she was the sister-in-law of Mr. Waite. His personality, she affirmed, is clearly implied through the selected epitaph, and is especially treasured by those who knew him.

Unfortunately, not all personalities are pleasant ones. A curious marker,

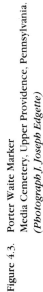

Figure 4.3.   Porter Waite Marker
Media Cemetery, Upper Providence, Pennsylvania.
(Photograph J. Joseph Edgette)

PORTER H. WAITE

DEC. 23, 1975

HI EVERYONE!

HAVE FUN, SEE YOU LATER

also in suburban Philadelphia's Fernwood Cemetery, is that of the Friend family (fig. 4.4).[8] Arranged in three columns, the inscribed data deals with the children and their parents in the left and right columns, respectively, with a long and especially revealing original epitaph in the center:

Marianne,
My sweetheart wife—
Glad love is mad love,
Deep as the sea!
Folks say it's madness
That you love me.
Long love is strong love.
Naught can subdue!
No one may measure
The way I love you.
Madness and gladness,
Love's always so!
The longer the stronger
The more love we know.
Only Gil,
Your Husband

Even the most casual observer will sense that this poetic epitaph stresses and reveals an obsession with love bordering on the psychotic. Marianne, as the marker notes, died in 1932, and she is interred next to husband Gilbert (d. 1933): "true lovers and sweethearts forever." It is not until one focuses upon the children's dates on the other side of the marker that an uneasy sense of peculiarity begins to arise. Helen, Robert, and Kenneth, born in 1927, 1925, and 1931, respectively, all died in 1933, the same year as did their father, and only one year after their mother. Would the bizarre undertone of the epitaph provide a clue to its author's personality? Sadly, the answer appears to be yes. Marianne Friend lost her battle with cancer in 1932. Gilbert, unable to cope with the loss of his "true lover" and "sweetheart wife," took the lives of his three children and then his own on a tragic day the following year. The macabre poem inscribed on the family marker was written by Gil Friend shortly after his wife's death. He then saw to it that the marker was carved and put in place before the fateful events which took place a year later. Despondency and instability, as reflected in the word "madness" repeated three times in the verse, become obvious in this self-composed, revelatory epitaph.

For a decidedly different emphasis, we might consider the Cellini husband-wife marker, situated high on a knoll in the Chester Rural Cemetery, Chester, Pennsylvania. Frank (1894–1982) also followed his wife, Grace (1905–1981), and, like Gil Friend, expressed his love through self-com-

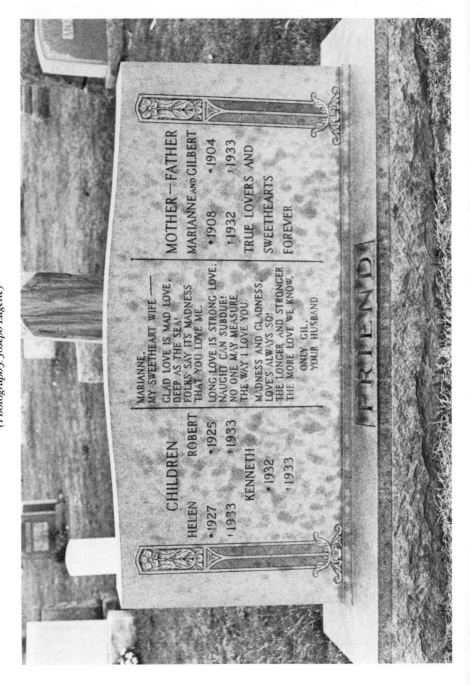

Figure 4.4. Friend Family Marker
Fernwood Cemetery, Upper Darby, Pennsylvania.
(Photograph J. Joseph Edgette)

posed words engraved in stone. The feeling conveyed here, however, is in no way similar:

Mary Grace Rosato
You were a courageous, friendly woman, your
husband artist, granite sculptor, erudite, sleeps
with you in eternity.
Frank

Frank Cellini, who also carved the stone in addition to composing its epitaph, is taking the opportunity here to both praise his wife and at the same time proclaim his own strengths. Thus, several facets of Frank's personality are revealed simultaneously: his role as an admiring loving husband is evident, but so, for that matter, is his pride in his own accomplishments. To all who knew Frank, such an epitaph was neither surprising nor inconsistent. To those who did not know him, on the other hand, the effect might be one of perceived pompousness, a feeling often described by students to whom I have shown a slide of this marker. All of which serves to reemphasize a point made earlier in regard to assessing personality revelation through epitaphs: it is essential that we make every effort to determine and acknowledge the "private" information held by relatives and close friends with regard to the individual whose epitaph we are considering.

At times, epitaphal inscriptions may go on to seemingly epic lengths. In the Media, Pennsylvania Cemetery, some five miles west of Chester, an elaborate tomb recently erected to the memory of Kathryn McMullen presents the following epitaph (fig. 4.5):

> TRIBUTE to a wonderful woman, Kathryn. She was kind and gracious to everyone and very intelligent. She acquired a world of knowledge in any field she entered. As the saying goes, "You only pass this way once." And we enjoyed every minute of it. Each time we returned home as we parked the car and walked to the front door, she would say, "I love our little house. This flicker of light or burning taper should remind us we are passing the same way." I was privileged and honored to have been associated with Kay for fifty years. For fifteen years we courted then were proudly married for thirty-five years of good health and happiness. She is dearly missed by me. She was my right hand.
>
> Kay's loving husband Curtis

Though lengthier than most, the epitaph fashioned for Kathryn McMullen again is geared toward a highlighting of a number of her chief personality traits. In this case, even though husband Curtis was the principal author of the epitaph, other family members contributed their thoughts and memories as well. Also, in a pattern seen in previous examples, Curtis, while striving to highlight Kathryn's personality, is revealing to a certain degree his own at the same time.

Figure 4.5. McMullen Tomb
Media Cemetery, Upper Providence, Pennsylvania.
(Photograph J. Joseph Edgette)

THE
McMULLEN

TRIBUTE TO A WONDERFUL WOMAN KATHRYN, SHE WAS
KIND AND GRACIOUS TO EVERYONE AND VERY INTELLIGENT.
SHE ACQUIRED A WORLD OF KNOWLEDGE IN ANY FIELD SHE
ENTERED. AS THE SAYING GOES, YOU ONLY PASS THIS WAY
ONCE, AND WE ENJOYED EVERY MINUTE OF IT. EACH TIME WE
RETURNED HOME AS WE PARKED THE CAR AND WALKED TO THE
FRONT DOOR SHE WOULD SAY, "I LOVE OUR LITTLE HOUSE."
THIS FLICKER OF LIGHT WAS TO REMIND US
WE ARE PASSING IN THIS SAME WAY. I WAS SO PRIVILEGED AND
HONORED TO HAVE BEEN ASSOCIATED. THEN WERE THEY MY RIGHT
YEARS, FOR FIFTEEN YEARS WE COULD OF GOOD HEALTH AND
MARRIED FOR THIRTY FIVE TEARS. SHE IS MY
HAPPINESS. SHE IS DEARLY MISSED BY ME. HER LOVING HUSBAND CURTIS.
HAND.

This essay has focused its attention upon the manner in which specialized personal inscriptions—epitaphs—serve to reveal significant personality traits of the individuals they commemorate, and in some cases those who remember them. It should not be forgotten, of course, that visual motifs are often used for similar purposes. Sometimes, in fact, the verbal and visual messages are deliberately paired so as to strikingly reinforce each other, and though it is beyond the scope of the present enquiry to pursue this particular phenomenon, it should be noted that the dedicated cemetery stroller will occasionally be struck by the appropriate and revelatory nature of markers with combined imagery such as the figure of a bowler with the epitaph "Scoring in Heaven," or that of a semi truck with the inscription "Last Load Delivered."[9]

As endorsed by the American Monument Association, the epitaphic inscription is a permanent document of sentiment; and the expression of such sentiment is the essence of commemoration.[10] Further, epitaphs, regardless of source, often provide us with statements directly associated with the essential personality traits of the departed souls to whom they refer. In those few serious studies of epitaphs conducted to date, attention has been primarily given to inscriptions whose sources are scriptural or traditionally poetic. From time to time there have also appeared various small pamphlets or booklets listing examples (largely spurious) of "humorous" epitaphs. This essay, it is hoped, has pointed the way towards another, potentially more profitable manner in which to consider the essential functions of the epitaph. For, even in death, it seems, the personality of the loved one can be immortalized when incorporated though epitaph into the other, more essentially utilitarian purposes of the gravemarker.

Notes

1.   *Oxford English Dictionary* (1971). Vol I: A-O, p. 884.

2.   Edwin Valentine Mitchell, *It's an Old New England Custom* (New York: Bonanza Books, 1946), p. 132.

3.   Edmund V. Gillon, Jr., *Victorian Cemetery Art* (New York: Dover Publications, 1972), p. 91.

4.   See "Monumental Gall," *American Heritage* 26 (1975), pp. 100–102.

5.   Information on the Hartley monument was supplied to me by Richard E. Meyer.

6.   The informant supplying information about Elvie Grimaldi was her daughter, Maria Walker.

7.   This information was related to me by Harvard C. Wood, III, the stonecutter who carved this gravemarker.

8. Background information on this marker was obtained from the records of the H.C. Wood Monument Company, Lansdowne, Pennsylvania.

9. For several examples of this phenomenon on contemporary gravemarkers, see the essay by Richard E. Meyer in the present volume.

10. American Monument Association, *Memorial Symbolism, Epitaphs and Design Types* (Boston: American Monument Association, Inc., 1947), p. 30.

Origins and Influences

Origins and Influences

There is, to be sure, an element of dynamic evolution in American cemeteries. They reflect changing cultural realities, and they take on distinctive flavors relating to regionalism, ethnicity, religious influence, and a whole host of other factors. They also allow for considerable personal innovation, as can be attested to by anyone who has spent much time exploring their infinite variety. At the same time, however, they represent one of the most conservative features in our cultural landscape, preserving in their sites and artifacts forms, and sometimes practices, which extend back centuries to other lands and cultures which shaped our own. Some of the most rewarding past investigations of American cemeteries and gravemarkers have involved consideration of the various origins and influences which were predominant in creating these cultural landscapes as they exist today, and the two essays which comprise this section continue that tradition. Gregory Jeane, a cultural geographer, has been interested for some time in defining the specialized characteristics which go to make up a distinctive element of the American cultural landscape known as the Upland South folk cemetery complex. In his present essay, he searches for the roots of these characteristics, an enquiry which ultimately leads him to challenge a number of prevailing theories. Art historian Peggy McDowell, in her treatment of tomb design in New Orleans's distinctive early cemeteries, examines the enormous influence exerted by the arrival in nineteenth-century New Orleans of French-trained architect J. N. B. de Pouilly, an influence still highly visible today when touring these most European-seeming of American cemeteries.

5

The Upland South Folk Cemetery Complex: Some Suggestions of Origin

D. Gregory Jeane

Few landscape features are as enduring as a burial ground. Although they disappear from the landscape through both neglect and intentional destruction, cemeteries, once sited, usually remain relatively resistant to change. There is a fascination with these holy grounds, containing as they do the mortal remains of our ancestors, and reminding us constantly not only of our individual frailty but of life's ultimate mystery. This perhaps explains why there is a general reluctance to cavalierly alter the geography of a burial ground. In any case, because of this reluctance, cemeteries are a good place to accumulate information that can provide insight into a community's social and economic structure, its religious tenets, and its ethnic composition. In addition, the occurrence of relatively unchanged burial grounds can provide a window into the recent past and, thus, one avenue for reconstructing historical landscapes. An important historical vestige of the cultural landscape of the rural South is the Upland South folk cemetery.

The Upland South is generally taken to be the area of significant log construction as determined by Fred Kniffen and Henry Glassie in their folk house studies.[1] The academic debate over the extent of the Upland South centers on the use of the terms Upland and Lowland South, each identified by specific cultural criteria. Glassie has relegated the Upland South to the interior of the southeastern United States, suggesting that topography has at least as much to do with determining the boundaries as does culture. Milton Newton, one of Kniffen's most ardent students, has challenged the restricted boundaries approach. For Newton, culture is the major definitive component; and he bases the areal extent of the Upland South on the presence of distinctive culture trait assemblages or associations not found in other parts of the eastern United States. The result of his research is a substantially larger areal extent for the Upland South. Field investigation of rural Southern cemeteries tends to confirm Newton's areal definition of the Upland South.[2]

The Upland South folk cemetery is a distinctive type of burial ground widely dispersed across the rural South (fig. 5.1). The folk cemetery is a complex of cultural traits significant for its association of traits rather than for any single identifying element. It is characterized by hilltop location, scraped ground, mounded graves, east-west grave orientation, creative decorations expressing the art of "making do," preferred species of vegetation, the use of graveshelters, and cults of piety.[3] "Making do" is expressive of folk resourcefulness in accomplishing some task with materials or skills at hand. Grave decorations and construction of gravemarkers are particularly expressive of the art. A cult of piety is an organized event intended to show reverence for the memory of deceased family members. Graveyard workday, homecoming, and monument dedications are a few of the pietistic activities that were historically important examples of this phenomenon.

Some of the traits defining the Upland South folk cemetery can be observed in various other parts of the world, and certainly even in some other parts of the United States. It is, however, the traits as a complex which give definition to the folk model and which establish it as a unique cemetery type. The regional distribution of the type coincides with the Upland South culture area and thereby is to be found across a broad swath of the southeastern United States. It is the cemetery as a distinctive regional type, rather than a stylistic form of a national generic type, that identifies it as a critical element of the Southern material cultural landscape and a significant spatial artifact useful in reconstructing the historical geography of the region.

The Upland South folk cemetery is expressive of the dynamic character of culture: because culture continuously changes, the folk cemetery can be thought of as an evolutionary landscape phenomenon. Several phases have evolved, each with its peculiar assemblage of identifying traits but with substantial adherence to the integrity of the traditional form established at the time of initial occupancy. Since the type was introduced to the American cultural landscape in the late eighteenth or early nineteenth century, three phases of evolution can be recognized—pioneer, transitional, and modern (fig. 5.2). Each phase clearly reflects the dynamic aspect of the culture. The sacred landscape of the South contains examples of all three phases, making it difficult both to generalize about the rate of evolution and to track regional changes. The diversity and permutations of basic types, while complex, provides a fascinating insight into both the evolution of attitudes toward death and the material expression of those attitudes.

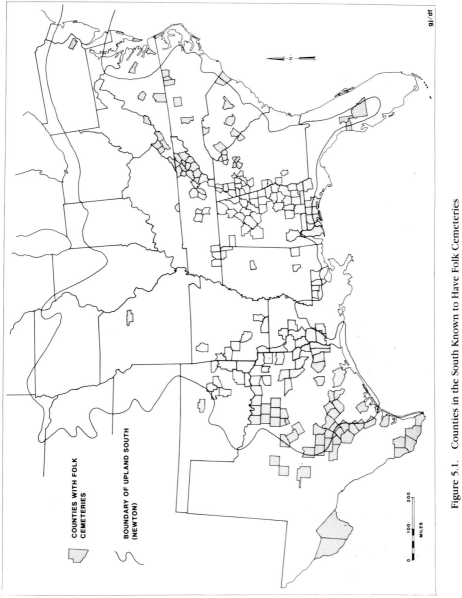

Figure 5.1. Counties in the South Known to Have Folk Cemeteries
(*Distribution map by D. Gregory Jeane. Upland South boundary based upon
the work of Milton B. Newton, Jr.*)

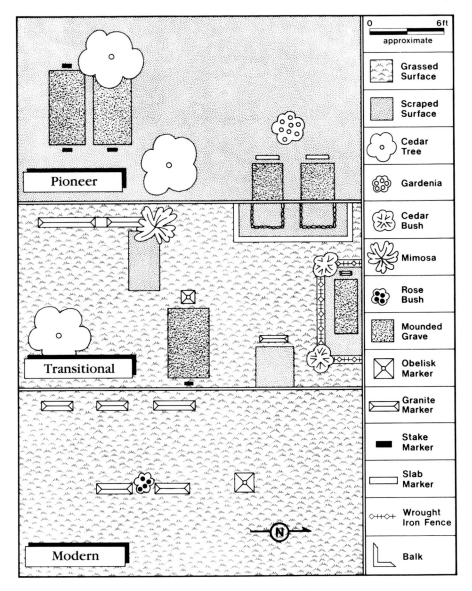

Figure 5.2. Evolutionary Phases of the Folk Cemetery
(Diagram by D. Gregory Jeane)

The folk cemetery's clearest historic image is to be found in "remote" rural burying grounds, where, for a broad array of reasons, the practices associated with proper cemetery upkeep have withstood the pressures to modernize the cemetery in accordance with mainstream American culture. The chance discovery of one of these pioneer phase graveyards gives one the impression of being caught in a time warp.

The pioneer model of the southern folk cemetery is identified by the existence of all or nearly all of the definitive traits outlined above—hilltop location, scraped ground, mounded graves, east-west grave orientation, preferred species of vegetation, creative decoration, graveshelters, and evidence or practice of cults of piety (fig. 5.3). This model is a landscape feature associated with initial settlement for most of the Upland South of the late eighteenth or early nineteenth century. While the earliest occurrence of the folk cemetery cannot be determined, it appears to have been well-established across much of the South by the 1830s.

As early settlers began to push westward from the Atlantic coast, the initial barrier of the Appalachians turned them southward along the Piedmont, rapidly diffusing their culture over a broad area. The diffusion of the Upland South culture rests upon Scotch Irish advancement of the frontier, well under way by the end of the eighteenth century and aggressively spreading in the nineteenth. Because the general flow of settlement was from east to west, even with the southward sweep around the lower Appalachians, older examples of the model are found in the eastern portion of the South. Examples are correspondingly more recent the father west one travels. Upland South cemeteries in the eastern Georgia Piedmont, for example, were established as early as 1810–1820. Preliminary investigation in western North Carolina and Virginia, the recognized hearth area for Upland South culture, indicates that the type may have been in the Appalachian mountain area in the last quarter of the eighteenth century. Similar folk cemeteries in eastern Alabama, on the other hand, date from the 1830s to the 1840s, while in western Louisiana they originate several decades later.

The Upland South settlement pattern is a dispersed one, distinctive from the clustering pattern which evolved in the coastal lowlands of the Atlantic and the Gulf. An essential requirement of the new frontier communities was to designate space for formal burial of their dead, an act that often preceded construction of a church. While one might presume a correlation between churches and cemeteries, field investigation indicates a wide variance between site selection for the two, making the association of church and cemetery a generally unsound basis for predicting cemetery sites. The Upland South cemetery is not a churchyard in the tradition of English or of Lowland South burial grounds. The British churchyard is consecrated ground adjacent to the church and enclosed by a fence or stone wall. Other

Figure 5.3. A Folk Cemetery on the Georgia Piedmont, ca. 1935
Note the scraped ground, mounded graves, lack of manufactured stones, and
preferred species of vegetation (oak and gardenia).
(Courtesy Library of Congress)

European countries have a similar tradition, particularly the rural parts of Catholic nations such as France and the Germanic countries. The British tradition was diffused with the early settlers to America, and the Lowland South burial grounds, dominated by the Anglican church, were virtual carbon copies of their English counterparts.

By contrast, land for cemeteries in the Upland South was often set aside or deeded long before congregations established houses of worship. It is thus as common to find the cemetery a discrete landscape feature as it is to find it adjacent to a church. In actuality, the cemetery was one of a broad assortment of dispersed central functions which served the needs of the Upland South community, other examples being schools, mills, general stores, and churches.[4]

The dispersed settlement of the Upland South accounts in large part for the prolific number of cemeteries which pepper the region today. The individual folk graveyard in the pioneer phase was small, often less than an acre. In the same way that folk cemeteries were not churchyards, neither were they necessarily family burying grounds of the type associated with many Southern plantations. More widely distributed than plantation burial grounds, the Upland South cemetery mirrors the extended family ties characteristic of the rural South, ties based on kinship patterns which evolved through intermarriage of frontier families.

The most distinctive trait of the pioneer folk cemetery model, and that most striking to outsiders, is the absence of grass. A barren patch of ground punctuated with neatly mounded graves aligned on an east-west axis presents a stark visual image. In conjunction with a hilltop location, it creates an impression not quickly forgotten. Grass is entirely removed from the cemetery once or twice a year. Repeated scrapings of the surface means eventual loss of all topsoil, exposure of clay beds or parent material, and can result in a hardened surface similar to concrete. Although hardy weeds will take root in the meanest of soils, actively maintained folk cemeteries would be relatively easy to keep clean, and a clean cemetery came to symbolize reverence for ancestors and the "proper" way for the community to express its devotion.

Grave mounds accentuate the vertical dimension of the pioneer folk graveyard. Unlike the common pattern found in urban cemeteries (or, for that matter, in later phases of the rural folk cemetery), gravemarkers are uncommon. Mounds served several purposes. One, of course, was grave location. Since markers were wooden, or of local stone, decay or displacement could result over time in the gravesite being lost. A more practical value in mounding was compensation for settling of the grave. A sunken grave, particularly one that caved in and exposed the burial, was simply unacceptable. Mounds are often not more than eighteen to twenty inches high. Historically, their size did not vary significantly, and one is struck by their uniformity in cemeteries where the practice is still active.

Where gravemarkers *are* found, they reflect one aspect of the creative practice of "making do." If available, a piece of field stone might be placed at each end of the grave, with the larger stone generally at the head. In rare instances a name or date will be crudely inscribed. Some graves have only a cedar or pine stake at the head of the grave or perhaps a wooden shake at either end of the grave mound. Occasionally, the wooden markers will be shaped: circles and diamond shapes are preferred, with the circle frequently at the head of the mound. My own fieldwork has yielded several excellent examples of "making do" in western Louisiana and eastern Texas cemeteries, where small, slightly curved, clay turpentine cups were stacked to form a marker. In other cemeteries these same kinds of cups were used to outline the perimeter of an individual grave or a family plot within the folk graveyard. What is decidedly missing is the frequent use of commercially produced gravestones of granite or marble. In areas where the settlement was post-Civil War, manufactured stones are more prevalent because of increased availability, better economic conditions for many, and an increasing sense that the manufactured stone represented the proper gravemarker, an idea that appears to have diffused from the urban settlements.

The use of distinctive forms of grave decoration is another revealing trait, particularly interesting in its reflection of personal tastes. While decorations of any kind were probably not abundant in the early cemeteries, they did reflect the pioneer trait of practicality while still demonstrating sincerity. Both adults' and children's graves were decorated, but those of children more frequently and with a greater variety of items. Items peculiar to an adult's grave would include eyeglasses, eyecups, mugs, shaving articles, or other personal items. A child's grave might have marbles, toys, or dolls. It is not uncommon to discover toys placed on adults' graves as well.

Common to all graves was the practice of decorating with shells. The most frequently used were conch, freshwater mollusks, and saltwater bivalves. Shells were arranged variously to include single placement along the axis of the grave mound, lining the axis of the mound from head to foot, surrounding the grave or several graves, and completely covering the grave mound.

Adding to the starkness of the pioneer folk cemetery landscape is the use of selected species of vegetation. The dominant species is eastern red cedar (*Juniperus virginiana*), a tree so commonly associated with burial grounds that is known across the South as the "cemetery tree." Various species of pine might also be used, primarily because of its evergreen character (symbolic of immortality), or, on occasion, oak. It is not always possible to distinguish between trees specifically planted and those allowed to remain on a site that was cleaned. What is strikingly observable, however, is the distinct preference for the cedar and other evergreen species. Ornamental shrubs and flowering plants do not appear to have been widely used.[5]

The horizon may also be broken by the presence of a graveshelter, a small, rectangular, gable-ended structure placed over the grave. These shelters have been observed across the South in white cemeteries, but also among Indian groups.[6] No graveshelters have been observed in black graveyards. Gravehouses usually cover a single grave, perhaps two. Only rarely were they constructed to cover large numbers of graves. They were of simple construction—four corner posts, often surrounded by picket fencing, supporting a shallow, gable-ended roof.

Cults of piety are especially characteristic of the pioneer folk cemetery. The most significant of these cults was graveyard workday, an annual event, usually in the late summer or early fall, when all members of the community gathered to pay homage to the memory of deceased loved ones.[7] It was often an all day affair, sometimes spanning two days in communities with large graveyards, and it served a number of functions for the social group. First and foremost, it was intended to maintain the cemetery according to the established values of the community. All grass was scraped from the graveyard, graves were mounded, gravemarkers placed or replaced if necessary or desired, and decorations placed on the graves. Graveshelters would be built or repaired as need dictated, and all tree limbs and vegetative trash removed. Originally men did the strenuous labor of scraping and hoeing grass, removing tree limbs, and mounding graves. Children had menial clean-up tasks but were commonly free to play. Women would rake or sweep the cemetery, the final touch in cleaning the graveyard.

Other social needs were met as well by the practice of graveyard workday. It served as a de facto family reunion, an opportunity to reaffirm extended family bonds, particularly for families which had moved out of the community. There was a traditional, communal noon meal, and there might even be a sermon and singing. Young folks often courted, and some recall that the menfolk might conduct a bit of horse trading or even discreet drinking and gambling.

The first cemeteries in the Upland South, therefore, contained an association of cultural traits assembled across centuries of use, traits whose origins and rationale for use had often long since been lost to the settlers carving out a niche on the American frontier. Nonetheless, out of these traditions, both those consciously and subconsciously observed, was forged a concept of what constituted a proper cemetery landscape for the group at that time and place. The high mobility of American settlers, however, subjected traditional frontier values to a constant array of influences from other groups of people, some just moving through the region, others set-tling down for a period of time. The incorporation of new ideas and values into the pioneer community gradually produced a different landscape ex-pression of the folk cemetery, a new accepted set of practices for the arrangement and care of the cemetery. Thus the folk cemetery entered a period of transition, a phase still evolving in some areas of the Upland South today.

The transition phase spans a lengthy period. Because of cultural dyna-mism, changes in the traditional folk cemetery began practically with its establishment. The transition phase may date from the mid-nineteenth cen-tury, certainly from the latter half, and is still widely distributed across the region.[8] It is characterized by visible demarcation of family plots, a mixture of scraped plots and grassed interspaces, new species of preferred vegeta-tion, a decline in creative decorations, and the virtual disappearance of organized cults of piety (fig. 5.4).

Significant changes occurred in folk practices during this phase. While large portions of established cemeteries continued to have scraped ground, grassed areas within the site arose from expansion of the cemetery. The result was a mixed pattern: new ground was left grassed, and individual burials or plots continued to be scraped clean. Grave mounds, however, began to disappear entirely. To compensate for the mound's value as a grave locator, two substitutions were introduced: the number of gravemarkers significantly increased, and graves of immediate family members were in-corporated into family plots. How the plots were outlined reflects the highly individualistic character of Upland Southerners and their tendency to "make do." Some families used concrete; others used wooden rails; still others used inverted turpentine cups. Whatever material was readily avail-able was used to define the perimeter of the plot, apparently without any particular medium establishing a norm.

New and different species of vegetation were introduced. Though the traditional cedar remained, magnolia, crape myrtle, mimosa, and aborvitae were popular. Flowering shrubs such as roses, azaleas, forsythia, cape jas-mine, and spirea were added. Vegetation was still selective and visually attractive, and all species were self-sustaining once established.

Decorations changed as well during the transition phase. Use of per-sonal objects on adults' graves virtually disappeared, while shells continued to be used. As a very recent addition to the transition phase, artificial flowers have displaced fresh bouquets. Since the mid 1950s the artificial flower is ubiquitous in all southern folk cemeteries. Children's graves con-tinued to exhibit a wide variety of decorative items, still largely personal, but increasingly supplemented with a wide assortment of store-bought toys and bric-a-brac. With the use of commercially produced gravestones came

Figure 5.4.   A Folk Cemetery in the Transition Phase
Note in particular the contrast of grassed and scraped areas and the dominance
of the family plot.
(Photograph D. Gregory Jeane)

also the use of portraits as a means of decoration. While not abundant, the practice was widespread enough to be considered common rather than unusual.

The graveshelter also began to disappear. Constructed of wood, these structures were not always substantial and gradually rotted. Families tended not to rebuild them once they had deteriorated beyond reasonable repair. A peak in elaborateness of decoration appears to have occurred in the latter quarter of the nineteenth century, with a rapid decline in popularity after 1900. Changes in taste with respect to cemetery architecture resulted in some communities eventually forbidding the erection of graveshelters, citing them as unsightly.

The variety of cults of piety actually increased for a time during the lengthy transition phase, but had begun to disappear by World War II. Graveyard workday continued to be the most significant annual event associated with the cemetery, but gradually this too dwindled, becoming increasingly difficult to organize as a community event.[9] The continued demise of cemetery cleaning led to individual families taking responsibility for a community function. Ultimately workdays were supplanted with modern maintenance techniques based on the hiring of a groundskeeper, provided one could be found. Where these measures failed, the cemetery eventually devolved into a weed patch, the ultimate Upland South symbol of disrespect for the dead.

Other traditional cults of piety included the observance of Decoration Day and Memorial Day, and monument unveilings. Decoration Day is often confused with Memorial Day, yet it was often different in many parts of the Upland South. Decoration Day might be associated with Confederate Memorial Day, but was generally a time set aside to decorate graves prior to the annual revival or as a community tradition evidencing respect for ancestors. If a cemetery were associated with a church, and an annual revival were traditional, there would be a time established just prior to the revival when the cemetery would be cleaned and decorated. This special preparation might or might not coincide with the annual graveyard workday. Memorial Day eventually became an important time to honor war dead across the United States, including the South, and the practice has not entirely disappeared.

Monument unveilings in the South were associated primarily with fraternal, or semifraternal, orders. The most significant organization in the Upland South associated with unveilings was the Woodmen of the World Life Assurance Society (W.O.W.). This semifraternal insurance organization had numerous "camps" scattered across the South, and practically every man belonged. Part of the membership creed supported the concept of a right to the dignity of a marked grave. A policyholder could, therefore, arrange to have a monument engraved with the Woodmen of the World logo erected on his grave, the cost covered by a modest rider on the holder's insurance policy.

Woodmen of the World monuments were dedicated and unveiled in formal ceremonies conducted by the local camp, usually on Memorial Day or at a convenient date set by the camp. The unveilings were formal events attended at times by a parade of the camp members to the cemetery and always with a moving eulogy for the deceased member. On Memorial Day flowers would be placed as well on the graves of other camp members.[10] Later changes in the by-laws of the W.O.W. admitted women to the order and they too could have a marker with the W.O.W. logo. By the time women were allowed, however, unveilings had begun to decline precipitously, and no evidence of unveilings for women has been found. By World War II, cults of piety of all kinds (with the exception of some Memorial Day observances) had virtually ceased to exist.

Although the South remained largely a rural environment until after World War II, new ideas about cemetery care were being brought into the region from an early date. Rapid urbanization outside the region affected urban centers in the South, which in turn influenced the rural areas adjacent to them. The Victorian cult of death had a significant effect upon urban American cemeteries, particularly expressed in the compartmentalization of the cemetery into family grave plots, in new designs for the arrangement of graves, and in the profusion of elaborate gravemarkers. The evolution of the Upland South folk cemetery may have begun slowly, but the process of cultural transformation gradually picked up speed. By the end of World War II the modern phase of the folk cemetery was evident on the Southern landscape.

The South experienced a spectacular cultural metamorphosis following World War II, a process still in progress. Everything about traditional rural life seems to have been affected. Three phenomena were particularly influential in hastening change in the rural South: the advent of the automobile and the blacktop road, the restructuring of local employment, and urbanization. Traditional Southern burial customs did not escape the wave of progress any less than in other regions of the country; the pace of progress was simply somewhat more leisurely. Urban cemetery organizations were pushing, had been pushing for several decades, for modernization of the Southern cemetery. The pressure to be fashionable resulted in marked changes, especially in the Southern urban cemetery but in rural graveyards as well. The modernized Upland South cemetery has two landscape expressions—a rural version of the urban memorial garden and the true perpetual care mortuary complex.

The rural version of the urban memorial garden continues to contain vestiges of the transition phase. All graves have grass on them. Some plots still have fencing or coping surrounding them, though brick may be used instead of concrete blocks or wood. More graves have standardized, commercially produced gravestones. Traditional gravemarker symbolism has been replaced by symbols of a new age—couples walking hand in hand into the future, the Good Shepherd, double wedding bands—and epitaphs have largely disappeared except for a cryptic line or short Biblical quote. Plastic flowers are ubiquitous and seasonally predictable (e.g., poinsettias at Christmas and white lilies at Easter). The cemetery is periodically mowed by members of the church or by a hired caretaker.

Similar in some, though not all ways, is the perpetual care form of the folk cemetery, which is characterized by the disappearance of coping or balks surrounding family plots, the carpeting of all burial space with grass, the replacement of creative and personal decorations with the ubiquitous artificial flower, and maintenance responsibilities, originally centered in acts of piety by family members, relegated to various forms of "perpetual care" programs. Upland South communities closest to expanding urban areas have changed the most.

It is still possible, however, to observe a rural church and folk cemetery, or just a folk cemetery, surrounded by suburban sprawl. The contrast is usually startling and is an immediate barometer indicating the range of difference between traditional and contemporary values (and the attendant pressures from the contact). Although, because of their sacrosanct nature and the high cost involved, the church and cemetery are seldom actually moved, it is usually a matter of time before the values of the newer and more dominant urban community supplant those of the weaker rural one. The church is gradually "modernized" and, eventually, so is the cemetery.

The unique character of the southern folk cemetery described above automatically generates speculation about the origin of the traits that give the complex its distinctive character. Limited research has been conducted into the origin of some of the folk cemetery's more dramatic traits, but nothing to date has been totally satisfying.[11] The Upland South folk cemetery is a complex of cultural traits associated with white Anglo-Saxon communities. Blacks living in the same communities share some of the same cemetery traits, but there is little convincing evidence that they were a significant source of diffusion to the white community. Both Jordan and Vlach attribute important diagnostic traits in the folk cemetery to African origin. Vlach implies, for example, that the peculiar decorative traits of Southern blacks, which include the use of shells, mounding, broken pottery, and an assortment of personal artifacts, are not to be found in nonblack communities.[12] Yet it can be clearly demonstrated that Upland South folk cemeteries, dispersed over a far greater geographic area, also contain many of the same objects and practices. Jordan is more emphatic still, contending that some African cemetery traits, notably scraping of the ground, diffused from blacks into the white culture.[13] Jordan also attributes the origin of graveshelters to Amerindian influence.

Neither of these approaches satisfactorily accounts for the broad distribution of the Upland South cemetery, nor for the occurrence of shared traits. An African origin for certain definitive folk traits, apparently diffused to the South via the slave trade and thence throughout the region, does not account for the significant presence of the folk graveyard in Southern regions minimally affected by slavery or black culture in general. Neither does an African or Amerindian origin give adequate recognition to the dominance of European culture in creating the accepted norm for proper disposal and remembrance of the dead, to say nothing of establishing social norms for virtually all other aspects of Southern culture until the mid-twentieth century.

The general reluctance to disturb cemeteries implies a conservative attitude on the part of most culture groups when it comes to adopting new customs for the "proper" burial and care of the dead. It would appear more logical that the pioneers arriving on the Southern frontier already had a system acceptable to the group for choosing and properly maintaining the group's sacred ground. The survival of the pioneer trait complex into the twentieth century would suggest something about its antiquity as well as its resistance to wholesale alteration. Suggesting that the region's dominant culture would eschew most aspects of black culture for two centuries, but openly and wholly accept African burial traditions over time-honored European ones does not make sense. Thus, it is to Europe that one must look for the basic cemetery traditions that diffused with the settlers who fanned out across the Southern frontier.

A number of the traits characteristic of the southern folk cemetery have, in fact, been linked to a European origin, either from the northwestern or Mediterranean areas.[14] The origin of traits worked out by Jordan represents a significant contribution to the understanding of the folk graveyard landscape, and there is no need to duplicate his efforts here. Briefly, his research indicates a European origin for such traits as the mounding of graves, the use of shells, the preference for flowers as a mortuary offering or gift, the use of gravestones, lamps or lights associated with the grave, and the preferential use of cedars or evergreens.[15]

What is striking about the shared cemetery traits of the two racial groups in the South is the rationale for practicing them. This is where the critical difference between the two lies. It is generally accepted that blacks have a richer tradition of spirit worship than whites.[16] Jordan's research into and explanation for the use of shells as a decorative item in Anglo cemeteries, for example, does not contradict that of either Vlach or Thompson for the use of shells in black cemeteries. When it comes to other personal artifacts, however, there is a major difference. Blacks, for example, placed personal artifacts on graves to appease wandering spirits, or to keep them *from* wandering. One aspect of this black practice is the ritual breaking of grave goods. Whites characteristically did not break personal items placed on graves.[17] Thus, the decorative practices of the two cultures may indeed share some common traits, but the rationale for practice represents two very different traditions. What may be just as significant as attempts to interpret or define the cultural context of these acts is the realization that, for the Europeans at least, perpetuation of the tradition became more important than the rationale behind the practice.[18] From a general interest point of view, the European tradition may be less colorful than its African counterpart. Because of man's fascination with death and all its rituals, there is a tendency to focus on the unusual. This is evident in recent years for material pertaining to black culture, emphasizing some aspects as unique while ignoring similar customs in white culture. All cultural traits are important and scholars must be careful not to read more into either group's practices than is merited.

Significantly overlooked by Jordan in the European burial tradition is the widespread practice of scraping, more common on the continent than in the British Isles, but found there as well (fig. 5.5). In addition, there appears to be ample evidence that the Europeans, especially the inhabitants of the British Isles, were more than casually aware of the house-form tomb, which may be a more likely precursor of the graveshelter in folk graveyards than Amerindian spirit houses. There is as well the strong visual similarity of the English lychgate to the Southern graveshelter, not only in form but in function, and this may be even more important in the evolution of the gravehouse as a cemetery trait in the rural South.

The practice of scraping grass from the cemetery has always been one of the most striking traits of the southern folk cemetery. Its broad distribution across the Upland South indicates it was probably brought over as part of the cultural heritage of our European ancestors. The role of vegetation as a cemetery element has been a topic exhaustively debated in the history of burial.[19] Although the use of vegetative material, and even the presence of trees in burial grounds, has its origin in antiquity, the authorities responsible for the design and location of cemeteries in Europe from the Renaissance forward expended much effort toward educating the public on the positive and negative aspects of vegetation. Of interest here is the popular notion, officially expressed in the sixteenth century, that all vegetation should be excluded from burial grounds for reasons of health.[20] My own fieldwork in Europe indicates that the practice of scraping vegetation from

Figure 5.5.   The Cemetery of Huise, Belgium; April, 1985
Note in particular the removal of all grass; also the predominance of east-west
grave alignment and the European preference for individually demarcated graves.
(Photograph D. Gregory Jeane)

cemeteries is widespread. Given its antiquity, European immigrants to the New World would certainly have been aware of the trait. It is not unrealistic to assume that the trait was more widespread in the past than at present and that it may have been common in some areas of Europe several hundreds of years ago even though rare today. The European tradition suggests that our Southern frontier settlers may have been accustomed to the practice of scraping cemeteries when they arrived in America. The fact that people of other cultures, notably Africans, practiced cemetery scraping is not denied, but it seems unrealistic to suggest that the idea was indigenous to Africa and that a direct cultural transfer took place when Europeans and Africans were thrust together as a consequence of the slave trade.

The lack of extensive vegetation in Mediterranean cemeteries may to some extent be as much a function of the environment as any other factor. Summer drought in the Mediterranean creates an environmental stress condition unique to the region's climate type. Grass is not common in the cemeteries of Italy or Greece, for example. Trees such as cypress and pine are plentiful, and the ancient symbolism of the cypress and immortality is common knowledge (fig. 5.6). What one can observe, however, is that even where water is relatively abundant, such as in northern Italy, the cemeteries still have little or no grass. It may be, in fact, that the sixteenth-century Catholic directive prohibiting vegetation may have a stronger influence than previously considered. The cemeteries may have flowers and live plants on the grave, but space between graves is clean (either bare earth, gravel or even concrete).

In Austria and Germany, one can observe scraped cemeteries as well. Again, individual graves may contain numerous flowers and other live plants, but all ground between the graves is clean. In addition to the scraped ground one finds the occurrence of grave mounds or, in some cases, the use of a coping around the individual grave. Similar traits have been observed in Poland as well.

The practice of scraping is especially well developed as a cemetery trait in France and Belgium. In both of these areas, where drought is not a problem, the cemetery is dramatically bare. Mounding of graves is not especially prominent except for recent burials, but can be occasionally observed on older graves. The prevalence of scraping cemeteries clean in areas dominated by the Catholic church at least hints at the impact of church doctrine on the preservation of traditional beliefs.

The two dominant cultural groups on the Upland South frontier were the Germans and the Scotch Irish. The scraped cemetery tradition, as we have seen, is known in Germany and in Germanic countries in general. What about the British Isles? My own field investigation of cemeteries in England and Scotland indicates that the tradition of cleaning individual

Figure 5.6. Isola San Michele, Venice, Italy; July, 1984
Note the predominance of cypress as the preferred
species of vegetation; also the scraping of all grass from
the cemetery.
(Photograph D. Gregory Jeane)

graves does exist there, though it is less clear that entire cemeteries were scraped. Scraped and mounded graves occur in eastern England, in Essex and Cambridge counties, in the Yorkshire counties, and also in Wiltshire in the south of England. In Scotland, the practice of scraping is slightly different than in England. Although I also noted individual graves without grass, the existence of outlined family plots appears to be more widespread. The entire plot is cleaned and the cemetery in some respects resembles the transition phase of the Upland South folk graveyard (fig. 5.7). In Scotland I have found no instances of mounded graves.

The gravehouse is another feature which would seem to have a European origin. There is little evidence to suggest that its origin can in any way be attributed to Amerindian influence.[21] Two elements of the European burial landscape may have influenced the development of the gravehouse. One of these traditions is the widespread occurrence of the house-tomb. In Italy, and other Catholic countries, the use of a house structure over crypts is quite common. Although the graves are above ground, the tomb is surmounted by a rectangular, gable-ended structure. It is not particularly significant in Germany, although it is common in Catholic Germanic countries. Austria in particular has numerous examples, as do parts of Switzerland.

The house-tomb in the British Isles is of a different type. Although the tradition of subterranean burial is dominant there, the chest-type grave is no less significant. The use of a rectangular chest with gable ends is of considerable antiquity[22] (fig. 5.8). Invariably, house-tombs in the British Isles are built of stone. Frontier settlers in the rural South had little stone to work with, certainly not much of the workable quality found in Scotland or England. Nonetheless, some of the very earliest graves found in cemeteries on the Georgia Piedmont are small stone houses similar to their larger British counterparts. House-tombs which I examined in Dundee, Scotland, for example, average five feet in length, nearly three feet in width and three to four feet in height (fig. 5.9). The largest similar tombs that I have observed in the Upland South are smaller, rarely over two feet wide and under two feet in height. Because there is frequently no gravestone, uniformity of the tomb size does not reveal whether the form was used for adults or children, or both. In any case, the striking similarity leaves little room for doubt that the concept of the grave as a house was diffused from northwestern Europe.

Another British cemetery trait that may also be significant in the concept of the gravehouse is the lychgate. Although these gateway houses to English burial grounds vary considerably in size and dimension, they share certain universal traits. Nearly all lychgates are rectangular, open-sided, gable-ended structures that resemble a house (figs. 5.10 and 5.11). In some

Figure 5.7.   Churchyard in Dollar, Scotland; August, 1983
Note the scraped plots; also use of the shell as a decorative item. In the
background is a yew, sacred tree of British cemeteries.
(Photograph D. Gregory Jeane)

Figure 5.8.   House-Tomb, Dundee, Scotland; August, 1983
Note the use of stone and the distinctive gable-end.
(Photograph D. Gregory Jeane)

Figure 5.9.   House-Tomb, Dundee, Scotland; August, 1983
A later and more elaborate variant of the house-tomb shown in figure 5.8. Note
details in roof and gable-end.
(Photograph D. Gregory Jeane)

Figure 5.10.   Lychgate, All Saints' Church, Steep, Hampshire, England;
August, 1983
This fine structure is backed by an avenue of yew trees
leading to the church porch. Note the gate's rectangular
shape. Though not apparent here, the sides are open.
(Photograph D. Gregory Jeane)

Figure 5.11. Lychgate, Gringley-on-the-Hill, North Yorkshire, England; August, 1980
A fine example of the traditional English lychgate, showing its rectangular, open-sided, and gable-ended form.
(Photograph D. Gregory Jeane)

English churchyards, and in graveyards not associated with churches, the lychgate is large enough to accommodate a funeral party and contains built-in benches and space for the coffin to be placed in the center.[23] The use of the lychgate as a protected place for a party to wait until the priest arrives to conduct the funeral ceremony has important symbolic connotations; and, interestingly, the most frequent reason given for building a graveshelter in the Upland South is to protect the grave from the weather.

Yet another churchyard related structure that may have significance for the evolution of the Upland South gravehouse trait is the church porch. These appendages to the side entrance of the English church are rectangular, gable-ended structures. Similar to open-sided lychgates, the porches provide protection from the elements for people waiting to enter or leave the church. The immigrants who flocked to America from the British Isles would have been intimately familiar with the form and function of both the lychgate and the church porch. The translation of these forms to a shelter to protect the grave would not have been difficult.

Although much European fieldwork remains to be done, the initial results are encouraging and seem to clearly suggest that Europe is a significant source area for the diffusion of cemetery traits characteristic of the Upland South folk graveyard.

In summary, it should be emphasized that the folk cemetery has evolved considerably since its introduction to the South in the late eighteenth and early nineteenth centuries. The pioneer phase characterized by all or most of the definitive traits outlined earlier quickly evolved into a transition phase. While many of the traits of the pioneer phase were retained, changes occurred in several areas: individually scraped graves predominated, rather than entirely bare cemeteries; new species of vegetation were introduced; and attitudes about respect for the dead changed rapidly, as evidenced in changing patterns of cults of piety. The modern phase began shortly before World War II but swiftly diffused following the 1940s. Important in this phase has been the loss of the tradition of scraping, the profusion of manufactured gravestones, and the virtual elimination of cults of piety.

A tremendous amount of research still needs to be done before any definitive analysis can be proffered for American cemetery landscapes in their totality. The material available for scholarly review is difficult to obtain and even that often tends to focus on the unusual or bizarre. And yet the fact remains that land designated for burial represents one of the most enduring and revealing cultural modifications which man has brought to his environment. The cultural traditions that have evolved concerning proper location, internal arrangement, and care of the dead offer critical insights into the lives of our ancestors and can be used to reconstruct historic landscapes.

This essay has focused upon one type of cemetery landscape, and it represents the best evidence to date for the classification of a distinct American cemetery type. The intent here has been to place the Upland South folk cemetery within a local, regional, and national context (in the manner recommended by Wilbur Zelinsky as critical to building the base from which methodical analyses of cemetery landscapes can be conducted), and to offer suggestions for the origin of some of its definitive traits.[24] A primary goal has been to suggest, strongly, that the origins of burial traditions in the Anglo-Saxon-dominated rural South are best sought in the source areas of the original immigrants. Although African culture traits have been recently incorporated into the American cultural fabric, particularly since the 1960s, the conservative nature of the region's population argues more favorably for Europe as a source area for the region's religious values and traditions than for any part of the world. The widespread occurrence of similar folk burial traditions across Europe supports the validity of the theory.

Notes

1. Fred Kniffen has been credited with popularizing the term Upland South among cultural geographers, primarily through his research on folk housing. Kniffen and Henry Glassie fleshed out this region in their article, "Building in Wood in the Eastern United States: A Time-Place Perspective," *Geographical Review* 56 (March 1966), pp. 40–66. Glassie later abandoned the more expansive regional boundaries for a much more restricted area in the heart of the southeastern United States. See also Fred Kniffen, "Folk Housing: Key to Diffusion," *Annals, Association of American Geographers* 55 (December 1965), pp. 549–77; and Milton B. Newton, Jr., "Cultural Preadaptation and the Upland South," *Geoscience and Man* 5 (June 1974), pp. 143–54.

2. See Henry Glassie, *Pattern in the Material Folk Culture of the Eastern United States* (Philadelphia: University of Pennsylvania Press, 1968), p. 39. For the opposing approach see Newton, "Cultural Preadaptation," p. 149.

3. Milton Newton is, as far as I know, the originator of the term "cults of piety."

4. See Newton, "Cultural Preadaptation," p. 151. See also Milton B. Newton, Jr., "Settlement Patterns as Artifacts of Social Change," in *The Human Mirror: Material and Spatial Images of Man,* ed. Miles Richardson (Baton Rouge: Louisiana State University Press, 1974), pp. 339–61; and Newton, "Route Geography and the Routes of St. Helena Parish, Louisiana," *Annals, Association of American Geographers* 60 (March 1970), pp. 134–52.

5. Terry Jordan has stated that the rose is common in Texas graveyards, noting that it was a preferred plant. However, many Upland South folk cemeteries in east Texas do not have roses, nor is it particularly common as a cemetery plant across much of the rural South. See Jordan, "'The Roses So Red and the Lilies So Fair': Southern Folk Cemeteries in Texas," *Southwestern Historical Quarterly* 83:3 (January 1980), pp. 227–58.

6. See Donald B. Ball, "Observations on the Form and Function of Middle Tennessee Gravehouses," *Journal of the Tennessee Anthropological Association* 2:1 (Spring 1977), pp. 29–62. (Hereafter cited as "Tennessee Gravehouses.") Ball has fairly conclusively indicated that the American Indian tradition of building gravehouses is late and almost surely a tradition accepted from the Europeans (see specifically pp. 30–32).

7. William Humphrey has poignantly described the observance of cemetery workday in a fictitious northeast Texas community around the turn of the twentieth century in the opening chapter of his novel *The Ordways* (New York: Bantam Books, 1966). The accuracy of his description would imply some personal familiarity with the traditional practice of graveyard workday and contains an interesting description of the familial (read communal) values that perpetuate the tradition.

8. The dating of the cemetery phases poses special problems. It is still possible to observe all of the folk graveyard's evolutionary phases today. The pioneer phase came in with initial occupancy and has different dates of origin depending on the part of the South to which you are referring. By the 1830s it was widespread across the South as the typical cemetery in white communities. Modifications began shortly after initial occupancy, and so transition means something different in terms of dates for the same reason. One can think of the transition phase as peaking in the last quarter of the nineteenth and first quarter of the twentieth centuries. It is easier to assess the initiation of the modern phase, beginning shortly before World War II, because there are people who can distinctly and accurately remember when significant changes began to become commonplace.

9. A review of newspaper notices of graveyard workday published in one south Alabama area, Covington County, is illustrative of the decline of this once important community event. Advertisements in local newspapers were a common form of announcing when a particular cemetery would have its graveyard workday. Particularly abundant in the period 1890–1915, the notices in this particular area began to drop off as World War I approached. Following the war it was not unusual to see notices reprinted with alternate dates for previously established cleanings and with a plea for all interested parties to attend. After 1930 the notices become scarce and by World War II were rarely printed. That communities were aware of changes taking place can also be deciphered from editorials even as early as the turn of the century lamenting the deplorable condition of city and rural cemeteries alike.

10. A newspaper notice in the 1920s is illustrative: "The members of Magnolia Camp No. 381, met at the WOW Hall at Opp Sunday at 8:30 AM. After instructions were given by the Master of Ceremonies, the group went to Hickory Grove where five graves were decorated. At 11:00 they went to Opp Cemetery where six graves were decorated. They met again at 2:00 when they went to Valley Grove where two graves were decorated. From this place they went to Mt. Gilead where one grave was decorated." (*Opp Weekly News,* June 16, 1927, p. 6)

11. Terry Jordan's articles on Texas folk cemeteries and churches have addressed the origin of traits. See specifically his previously cited article "The Roses So Red." See also his "Forest Folk, Prairie Folk: Rural Religious Cultures in North Texas," *Southwestern Historical Quarterly* 80 (October 1976), pp. 135–62. His book *Texas Graveyards: A Cultural Legacy* (Austin: University of Texas Press, 1982) is considered the major geographical work on folk cemeteries. Another important work dealing with origins of folk cemetery practices and traits is John Vlach's "Graveyards and Afro-American Art," in *Long*

Journey Home: Folklife in the South (Chapel Hill, N.C.: Southern Exposure, 1977), pp. 161–65.

12. Vlach, "Graveyards and Afro-American Art," p. 161.

13. Jordan, "The Roses So Red," p. 232.

14. See Jordan, "The Roses So Red," p. 233. Unless otherwise indicated, I have drawn heavily on his analysis for an overview of some trait origins.

15. See also Frederick Burgess, *English Churchyard Memorials* (London: SPCK, 1979), p. 69. Burgess believes that the custom of mounding may be tied to the prehistoric use of tumuli and barrows dating from the Neolithic.

16. A classic source is Lyle Saxon's *Gumbo Ya-Ya* (Boston: Houghton Mifflin Company, 1945), pp. 316–65. Another important folklore resource is the voluminous *Frank C. Brown Collection of North Carolina Folklore* (Durham: Duke University Press, 1952). Volume I, on beliefs and customs, is particularly important for its revealing bits about death lore and ritual among blacks. An important new work dealing with the topic of African cultural influence is Robert Farris Thompson's *Flash of the Spirit: African and Afro-American Art and Philosophy* (New York: Vintage Books, 1984), pp. 132–42. Thompson's explanation of the decorative use of shells by blacks gives no acknowledgment to the widespread distribution of this trait among culture groups around the world, but more specifically makes no point that it is at least as common in white cemeteries throughout the South, is known in Europe as well, and is older in Anglo cemeteries in the South than in black cemeteries.

17. The breaking of objects as a funerary rite has an ancient origin. See L.V. Grinsell, "The Breaking of Objects as a Funerary Rite," *Folklore* 72 (September 1961), pp. 475–91 and "The Breaking of Objects as a Funerary Rite: Supplementary Notes," *Folklore* 84 (Summer 1973), pp. 111–14. Yet there does not appear to be any significant continuation of this practice in western European culture beyond the Bronze Age, occurring only sporadically in widely dispersed locations of Europe.

18. Grinsell quotes from Sir James Frazier: "Customs often live for ages after the circumstances and modes of thought which gave rise to them have disappeared, and in their new environment new motives are invented to explain them. . . . Sometimes people give no explanation of their customs, sometimes (much oftener than not) a wrong one." See Grinsell, "The Breaking of Objects," (1961), p. 476.

19. See Richard A. Etlin, *The Architecture of Death: The Transformation of the Cemetery in Eighteenth-Century Paris,* (Cambridge: The MIT Press, 1984).

20. Ibid., p. 90. See also his footnotes on "The Naked Cemetery," p. 380. Etlin indicates the proscription of all vegetation from cemeteries to be a long-held European tradition.

21. See Ball, "Tennessee Gravehouses," p. 32.

22. Burgess, *English Churchyard Memorials,* pp. 85–99. See also James Walton, "Hogback Tombstones and the Anglo-Danish House," *Antiquity* 28 (June 1954), pp. 68–77. Michel Ragon's *The Space of Death: A Study of Funerary Architecture, Decoration, and Urbanism* (Charlottesville: University Press of Virginia, 1983), contains an extensive section on the tradition of houses of the dead.

23. Mark Child, *Discovering Churchyards* (Aylesbury, England: Shire Publications, Ltd., 1982), pp. 19–22. See also Pamela Burgess, *Churchyards* (London: SPCK, 1980), p. 8.

24. Wilbur Zelinsky, "Unearthly Delights: Cemetery Names and the Map of the Changing American Afterworld," in *Geographies of the Mind: Essays in Historical Geosophy in Honor of John Kirtland Wright,* ed. David Lowenthal and Martyn J. Bowden (New York: Oxford University Press, 1976), pp. 171–95.

6

J. N. B. de Pouilly and French Sources of Revival Style Design in New Orleans Cemetery Architecture

Peggy McDowell

To many modern visitors who travel to New Orleans and tour the city's early cemeteries, the rich variety of above-ground tomb types and materials creates an opulent impression of a veritable city of the dead. The visual sensation is often enhanced by somewhat romantic associations of the early cemeteries with the varied cultural traditions of the past. The names of extended families, often dating from the early nineteenth century and the several colorful periods of New Orleans history, are frequently inscribed on plaques of family tombs. When these tombs, with their imposing arrays of names, confront the visitor, the effect is very different from that of modern twentieth-century lawn cemeteries in which the graves and markers are unostentatiously incorporated into the landscape, or of the traditional churchyard cemetery with its redundant headstones.

The effect created by these sites is also different from that of the picturesque rural or metropolitan cemeteries that were planned in nineteenth-century America. The earliest major cemeteries, St. Louis Cemetery I, established in 1789, the Girod Street or Protestant Cemetery, begun in 1822, and St. Louis Cemetery II, begun in 1823, predate the establishment of such significant metropolitan or rural cemeteries in America as: Mount Auburn, Cambridge; Green-Wood, Brooklyn; and Laurel Hill, Philadelphia, all of which began in the decade of 1830–40. Instead of meandering roads and paths winding through green landscapes filled with trees, lawns, and flowers, with horticulture as part of the designed effect, the typical cemeteries in early New Orleans had gridlike crowded paths and avenues lined with tombs and monuments placed in close proximity one to another. Land was used judiciously in building tombs as well as homes in New Orleans. In cemeteries such as Laurel Hill, Mount Auburn, or Green-Wood, grave-markers of varying sorts dominate, whereas above-ground tombs and mausoleums are interspersed sporadically along the avenues or paths. In New Orleans cemeteries, on the other hand, above-ground tombs are the predominant burial structures. Architecture dominates the landscape. Along with tombs that were surrounded by grassy lawns, shrubs, and trees, mausoleums in nineteenth-century metropolitan cemeteries in the eastern United States were occasionally built into hillsides with only the front of the structures visible. In this way the tombs became literally integrated into the landscape. This effect obviously was not adaptable to the flat terrain of New Orleans. A study of the monuments in these early New Orleans cemeteries reveals practical economical influences and cultural tastes. The tastes of the French dominated, and if indeed monuments may be said to speak, the voices heard here reveal a strong French accent. Jacques Nicolas Bussière de Pouilly, a French-born architect, was a stimulating influence on the evolution of New Orleans cemetery monuments from functional-but-simple to functional-but-sophisticated designs.

The French founded New Orleans on a crescent of land bordered by marshy swamps, the Mississippi River, and Lake Pontchartrain. The exceptional conditions of the environment, a frequently humid, inadequately drained site below sea level, especially influence the structural character of the earliest cemeteries. Burial in the ground was practiced in the first settler's cemetery, which was eventually abandoned and demolished. Inhumation also occasionally occurred in the two St. Louis cemeteries; however, because of the extensive numbers of deaths during the devastating epidemics of 1832 and 1833, underground burial in St. Louis I and II was forbidden. When burials did occur in the local cemeteries, water sometimes filled the graves before the coffins could be lowered into place. A contemporary account notes:

> In most of the cemeteries, interment in the ground is wholly interdicted, elevated vaults and tombs only being used. The necessity of this method of entombment, for all who can afford the expense, is easily explained by referring to the topography of the city. A grave in any of the cemeteries, is lower than the adjacent swamps, and from ten to fifteen feet lower than the level of the river, so that it fills speedily with water, requiring it to be bailed out before it is fit to receive the coffin, while, during heavy rains it is subject to complete inundation. The great Bayou cemetery is, sometimes, so completely inundated, that inhumation becomes impossible, until after the subsidence of the water, the dead bodies accumulating in the mean while. I have watched the bailing out of the grave, the floating of the coffin, and have heard the friends of the deceased deplore this mode of interment.[1]

However influential the peculiar conditions of the location might have been, it was cultural attitudes that inevitably contributed the most to the evolution of the character of the New Orleans cemeteries and their monuments. Even after the drainage problems had been relieved in the nineteenth century and the soil was more conducive to below-ground burials, the majority of citizens in this cosmopolitan city continued to prefer above-ground tombs. Pride and persistence of heritage and tradition helped encourage this practice, which has continued into the late twentieth century.

Before becoming a part of the United States in 1803, the New Orleans territory had been under the political domination of France and, for a shorter time, Spain. The nineteenth-century population of New Orleans was an amalgamation of American, Spanish, and French cultures, among others. The two European cultures that dominated New Orleans society, the Spanish and the French, brought with them attitudes, tastes, and customs that were modified by or assimilated into the New World. After control of Louisiana had passed from the French to the Americans, French families continued to immigrate. They were often troubled by political problems in early nineteenth-century France or were attracted by the possibilities of starting a new life in the Louisiana territory where French was frequently spoken. This elite society was a dominating force in Louisiana history and often competed politically and economically with the English-speaking population.

In 1833, Jacques Nicolas Bussière de Pouilly, a French-trained architect born at Chatel-Censoir in 1804, immigrated to New Orleans.[2] Accompanying the architect were his wife and baby daughter. De Pouilly had married in Paris in 1825; his bride, Mlle Drigny, was the daughter of an architect. De Pouilly's decision to make New Orleans his new home must have been motivated by the promise of financial success in the expanding and developing city. He was later joined by his younger brother as an associate in his architecture firm. For the next forty-two years, until his death in 1875, de Pouilly made his mark on the developing city. Although his designs are numerous, including churches, private dwellings, and businesses, his tombs and funerary monuments perhaps best reveal his creative versatility.

De Pouilly was a major influence in introducing and encouraging revival style design in the local commemorative arts. He brought with him a thorough understanding of the revival styles and contemporary trends in French architecture. The main sources of his funerary designs were from his academic studies of antique monuments and from current Parisian monuments and tombs such as those in Père Lachaise. Père Lachaise Cemetery, also called the *Cimetière de l'Est,* had been established in 1804 as the first of three metropolitan cemeteries serving Paris.[3] At the turn of the century, churchyard burial had been limited in Paris and in some instances had been forbidden entirely. The environment within the precincts of the new metropolitan cemeteries offered men of all backgrounds, funds permitting, the opportunity to create for themselves the ideal burial place. It also provided monument designers with opportunities of creating tombs and markers to satisfy the tastes of a wide variety of clients. Architects and clients found the Revival styles especially appealing, versatile, and applicable to cemetery designs in form and symbolism. As the metropolitan cemetery movement spread to other cities and countries, the popularity of Revival style designs followed. Eventually an international vocabulary of Revival style forms could be discerned in cemetery art. Classical, Gothic, Egyptian, and eventually Eastern or Oriental Revival designs became popular in American cemetery arts as rural or metropolitan cemeteries were developed. Much of de Pouilly's work for New Orleans clients reveals parallel trends in nineteenth-century American commemorative arts, especially in the more extensively developed cemeteries such as Green-Wood Cemetery, Brooklyn, or Laurel Hill Cemetery, Philadelphia. De Pouilly's designs are similar in that he, like other nineteenth-century architects and designers, used Classical, Gothic, and Egyptian Revival styles and types. The repertory of Revival style designs, forms, and types offered numerous options; De Pouilly's choices were primarily influenced by his French heritage.

St. Louis Cemeteries I and II contain the majority of de Pouilly's tombs and mausoleums. When he arrived, these cemeteries contained comparatively few artistically significant monument designs. The earliest monuments typical to these sites were more practical than elegant. Architectural features, when present, were simple and decorative elements minimal. The view of St. Louis Cemetery I (fig. 6.1) features several of the early normative types. Most of the tombs were plastered brick, rectangular in shape, and contained one or more vaults. The treatment of the tops varied. Some were flat or stepped-top with one or two layered courses of bricks; others had a simple pitched roof and occasionally a barrel-vaulted top. Sometimes the builder added an elevated facade topped by a triangular or arched-shape pediment to the basic rectangular form. The designs were probably the work of the cemetery sextons or of brick masons who specialized in cemetery work. It would be difficult to consider them products of architects. These simple early styles were economical and functional, and because of their practical nature they continued to be used throughout the nineteenth century. In some instances, builders translated these basic styles into more permanent material (such as granite), but with little change to their original character. During the 1830s and 1840s, a variety of new designs enlarged this repertory of types. One major source for these designs was J. N. B. de Pouilly, who had arrived in Louisiana at a fortunate time. Marble and granites from the eastern United States were becoming more readily available

Figure 6.1.   St. Louis Cemetery I
(Photograph Peggy McDowell)

as quarry firms established outlets in New Orleans. More fashionable clients wanted more fashionable or individualized tombs, a trend that in part can be attributed to the rise of an elite middle class and an expanding economy.

The study of de Pouilly's funerary designs is facilitated by a sketchbook, now in the Historic New Orleans Collection, in which the architect recorded a plethora of architectural renderings. Inside the front cover, the date February, 1834, is noted and an index follows that includes entries for houses, edifices, churches, and tombs. There are about sixty pages devoted to tombs, sometimes with several sketches or architectural details on the same page. Notations often include scale, the material, and the client's name. Several designs for the same client are sometimes included, with "project adopted," the builder, and the date for the final choice. There is no chronology to the sketchbook format and no evolution of style can be discerned.

A study of the drawings in this source gives the researcher invaluable insight into the options that de Pouilly offered his clients, the original designs with details, and the final choice, occasionally modified (especially in terms of decorations). Most clients in New Orleans apparently were rather conservative, and the decorations were often minimal. The sketched monuments include Classical Revival styles, Gothic Revival, Egyptian Revival designs, and occasionally, imaginative combinations of these styles. The most frequently rendered and constructed were Classical Revival designs. Egyptian Revival monuments were next in number in the sketchbook, with Medieval Revival styles last. The priorities given the different styles probably reflect the preferences of the local clients as well as de Pouilly's personal tastes.

Types of commemorative designs include family and society tombs with multiple vaults within one or more of the exterior walls; family and society mausoleums in which the vaults are located within a room or chamber accessible to visitors (described in de Pouilly's sketches as a "chapelle" tomb); and an occasional marker of a grave site. A society tomb, it should be clarified, is a monument with multiple vaults used by members of an organization such as a fraternal or benevolent society or a society especially organized to assure members of a burial vault within the crowded cemetery. The wall vaults that surround the cemetery grounds were the only other option, except in-ground burial, for those who did not want or could not afford an individual tomb or did not own a family vault. As was the tradition in New Orleans, the vaults in all these tombs were usually used numerous times—another practical way of saving expense and land. After a respectable length of time, the remains of the deceased were pushed to the back of the vault or removed and placed in a small receptacle within the tomb. Wooden coffin remains were usually burned.

As noted above, there were two basic variations of society tombs that were popular in the New Orleans cemeteries and which can be illustrated by de Pouilly designs. The Iberia Society tomb (fig. 6.2), designed by de Pouilly, dated 1843–45, and located in St. Louis Cemetery II, represents the most prevalent type. (The design was originally planned for the Cazadores Voluntes in the sketchbook notation.) This type of society tomb employs multiple rows of burial chambers across the outside walls. Numerous New Orleans tombs for mural burials present this economical vertical and horizontal stacking of vaults. The New Lusitanos Society tomb (fig. 6.3), dedicated October, 1859 and demolished with Girod Street Cemetery in 1957, demonstrates the other basic mausoleum type of society tomb—that in which the structure encloses the vaults. In this case, there is a central hall with vaults on either side. De Pouilly gives these society tombs a classical character by using antique inspired acroteria on the top corners of the Ibera Society design and the centralized portico with marble doric columns on the plastered brick New Lusitanos Society mausoleum.

Classical Revival types offered many possibilities in shapes and styles. De Pouilly's designs inspired by ancient Greek and Roman prototypes were primarily the sarcophagus, the temple, and, occasionally, the column. The sarcophagus type was usually based on an antique design that employed a pedimented, architectonic top (originally a lid in antiquity), with acroteria on the four corners. The type is marvelously flexible—it can be used inside other monuments or as an independent structure; it can be small for one-vault burials or can be enlarged in height and width for multiple vaults. Optional decorations, depending on the taste of the client, also provided variety. This type was sufficiently well known in nineteenth-century American commemorative arts that even John Haviland's *Practical Builder's Assistant,* 1830, illustrates in plate 54 a basic classical sarcophagus with pediment and acroteria.

De Pouilly's inspirations for use of the sarcophagus were French in origin. He probably had studied the illustrations in J. N. L. Durand's *Recueil et parallèle des édifices,* 1800, in which several pages were devoted to Roman altars and sarcophagi. Durand was commonly studied by students in the Parisian "écoles," and de Pouilly, according to family information, studied at the Ecole des Beaux Arts, or probably in the more specialized Ecole Polytechnique. De Pouilly was also familiar with similar monuments in Père Lachaise, and the architect reportedly owned a book of illustrations from this cemetery.

The Louis Foucher family tomb, in St. Louis Cemetery II, is typical of his basic interpretation of the sarcophagus design (fig. 6.4). It is dated 1836 in his sketchbook and was built by P. H. Monsseaux, who translated most of de Pouilly's designs into stone. Inverted torches ornament the corners.

Figure 6.2.   Iberia Society Tomb, St. Louis Cemetery II
(Photograph Peggy McDowell)

Figure 6.3. New Lusitanos Society Tomb, Girod Street Cemetery
As seen in 1957, before destruction of cemetery.
(Photograph Guy F. Bernard)

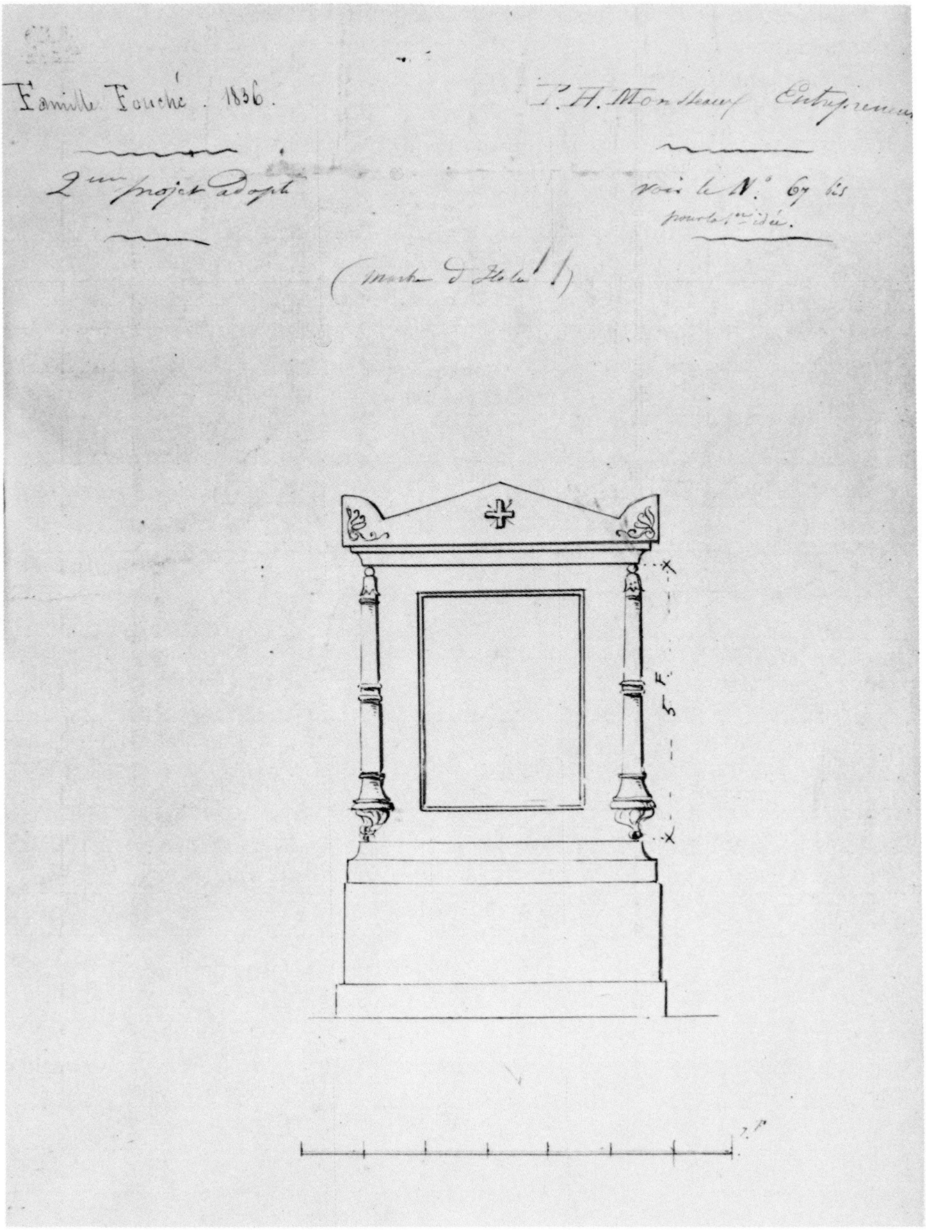

Figure 6.4.   Foucher Family Tomb, St. Louis Cemetery II
(Photograph Peggy McDowell)

An illustration of a double sarcophagus identified as the Jean Alex. Gervais Hennecart tomb in de Pouilly's Père Lachaise book shows a similar type with comparable use of such torches (fig. 6.5). The Foucher design is essentially a single version of this type. Interestingly, the McCall and Jones families' tomb (fig. 6.6), constructed in St. Louis Cemetery I, literally duplicates the Père Lachaise illustration and is attributed to de Pouilly; however, if it is a de Pouilly design, it demonstrates more eclecticism than is characteristic of his work. The monument, which is signed Monsseaux, 1857, may have been borrowed by de Pouilly's favorite builder from the book of Père Lachaise illustrations, or it may not have been officially signed or claimed by the architect because it was too eclectic a copy of another's design. It does not appear in his sketchbook, nor does the architect's name appear on the tomb as designer, a common feature of de Pouilly's constructed monuments. One may assume, however, that it was built under the Frenchman's influence. There are several versions of this type of monument in the New Orleans cemeteries. Variations include the rustication (i.e., clearly delineated separation) of stone joints and courses and the addition of sculptural details including an urn atop the structure, a traditional funerary accoutrement incorporated into several of de Pouilly's designs.

Along with the sarcophagus, the temple of Greek and Roman antiquity often served as an inspiration for tombs and mausoleums. De Pouilly explored numerous options of this type. The design he most often rendered was prostyle (a plan with columns that support a front portico) in which two doric columns supported a shallow porch. Like the society tombs designed by de Pouilly, his Neo-Classical temple tombs reveal two basic types drawn from his repertory of plans. One version features a wall of vaults sheltered beneath the portico. This version can be demonstrated by de Pouilly's designs for the Lacost family tomb, the Plauche family tomb, and the Miltenberger family tomb, all in St. Louis Cemetery II. The Miltenberger family tomb (fig. 6.7) uniquely employs a less conventional roof based on the same type. Another design variation seen in the Peniston and Duplantier families' mausoleum (also fig. 6.7) employs a shallow front chamber. De Pouilly labels this a "chapelle" tomb. In this version, doors, usually of wrought or cast iron or bronze, could close the vestibule and limit access to the mural vaults inside. This type of mausoleum was popular in nineteenth-century Parisian cemeteries. An illustration from Père Lachaise of the Rebut and Feyerick families' mausoleum (fig. 6.8) reveals similar design elements. De Pouilly, like his fellow architects in France, drew from the same sources of inspiration and their products were understandably similar. There is, however, one structural difference: many of the mausoleums in Père Lachaise had a lower crypt in which the bodies were interred, and a sarcophagus or altar ornamented the upper chamber. This

Figure 6.5. Hannecart Tomb

From illustration in *Le Père La Chaise*, n.d., Quaglia, Paris.

(Courtesy Leonard Huber Collection)

Figure 6.6.   McCall and Jones Families Tomb, St. Louis Cemetery I
(Photograph Peggy McDowell)

Figure 6.7. Miltenberger Family Tomb (left) and Peniston and Duplantier Families Mausoleum (right), St. Louis Cemetery II *(Photograph Peggy McDowell)*

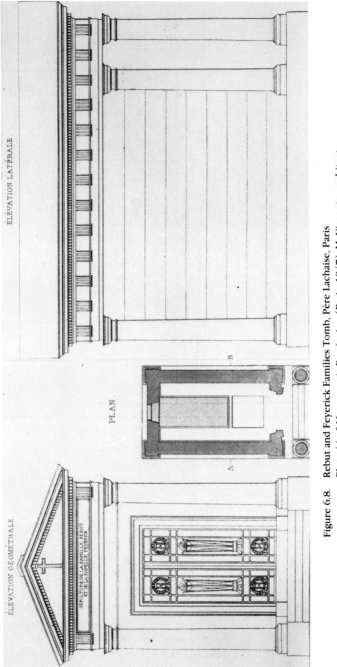

Figure 6.8. Rebut and Feyerick Families Tomb, Père Lachaise, Paris
Plate 44 of *Monuments Funéraires* (Paris, 1847). M. Visconte, architect.
(Courtesy Archive and Rare Book Collection, University of New Orleans)

configuration could not be duplicated as well in New Orleans; even basements are rare in the homes of the city. In the local mausoleums, instead of a roomy interior, wall vaults usually dominate, and no underground crypts were used for burials.

De Pouilly assuredly had a preference for the Classical Revival styles, and he used the Classical Revival vocabulary with facility in a variety of his designs. A major example of its application on an extensive scale was found in the design by de Pouilly and his brother of the impressive St. Louis Exchange Hotel (now destroyed). The domed Neo-Classical hotel and the passageway (alley) to it were inspired by the Rue de Rivoli in Paris and were a center for New Orleans, especially Creole, culture.[4] The local population exhibited a preference for the Classical Revival forms, and the years from 1835 to 1850 have been identified as a peak period for the use of the Greek Revival in New Orleans architecture.[5] It is, therefore, understandable that the interest by architect and client in the Classical Revival style extended to funerary designs.

De Pouilly rendered a variety of examples of Egyptian-inspired monuments; only two constructed Egyptian Revival mausoleums, however, those for the Grailhe family and the Kohn family, can be identified from his sketchbook designs. The Grailhe tomb, dated 1850, is located in St. Louis Cemetery II. There are two different versions of Egyptian style mausoleums sketched by de Pouilly for this family. The constructed tomb uses freely adapted interpretations of Egyptian motifs (fig. 6.9). The door is framed by banded roll moldings and is topped by a cavetto lintel. Ornamented pilasters flank the door and support the entablature. The cavetto cornice that tops the tomb is decorated on the center front by the winged disc, which is repeated again on the metal door and gate. The cornice sides are decorated by papyrus plant motifs. The original sketch included some minor decorations that were not translated into the final stone version. The original drawing for the Kohn family tomb is, however, much more ornate than the constructed mausoleum, which is located in Cypress Grove Cemetery, New Orleans. Stripped of all its decorations, it is more austere than the Grailhe tomb and loses much of the original character of the de Pouilly sketch. It seems from his few sketches that de Pouilly was somewhat interested in Egyptian designs even though the majority of his Louisiana clients were not.

De Pouilly was not the only local source of Egyptian Revival monuments. Although not as significant in architectural features, there are a few examples of Egyptian Revival designs that appear in New Orleans cemeteries in the first half of the nineteenth century. A modest brick pyramid topped by a ball was constructed in St. Louis Cemetery I before 1834. In 1840, the Egyptian pylon entrance gates to Cypress Grove Cemetery were

Figure 6.9.   Grailhe Family Tomb, St. Louis Cemetery II
(Photograph Peggy McDowell)

designed by Frederick Wilkinson, a transplanted New York engineer. James Gallier, an Irish-born and trained architect who moved to New Orleans in 1834 after working for a short time in New York, sketched a battered-wall Egyptian style tomb topped with an obelisk in 1841. The sketch is in the Historic New Orleans Collection. A tomb similar to the Gallier design was actually erected in Cypress Grove Cemetery for Henry Hohn (d. 1854). Unlike his French-trained counterpart, however, Gallier was not particularly active in cemetery design. In the first half of the nineteenth century, a rather conventional design with battered-wall and cavetto cornice was occasionally constructed in brick or stone. This simple interpretation of Egyptian elements was probably a stock design used by various local builders, and several examples can be found in St. Louis Cemetery II.

The general use of Egyptian decorations and the inspiration to create tombs in the Egyptian Revival style can be attributed to several influences. In France, the most significant influence came from the contact between France and Egypt in the early nineteenth century as a result of the Napoleonic expeditions. From this contact, by orders of his majesty the emperor Napoleon, there appeared a series of volumes that provided Europeans with detailed information on ancient and contemporary Egypt (fig. 6.10). Published between 1809 and 1828, twenty-one volumes included numerous large folio-size drawings of Egyptian temples, reliefs, ornaments, tombs, and maps. Collectively, they bore the title *Description de l'Egypte,* and were based on observations and research done in Egypt during the expedition of the French Army.

The Egyptian Revival had symbolic qualities that especially appealed to designers of monuments. Ancient Egypt suggested sturdy, permanent architecture and an impressive tradition of funerary arts and rituals, features that helped make the style applicable to nineteenth-century funerary designs. Perhaps it was for these reasons that de Pouilly, like many other nineteenth-century designers of tombs, found the Egyptian Revival especially useful for commemorative art. The Egyptian styles offered sufficient options to satisfy the needs and the tastes of clients. In addition to temple designs, Egyptian influences are also apparent in several other forms popular in nineteenth-century commemorative arts. Two other frequently repeated types were the obelisk and the pyramid, neither of which, however, seems to have had much appeal to de Pouilly (although he did sketch a pyramid on one of his unrealized society tomb designs).

The final revival style that de Pouilly applied to his funerary designs was the Gothic. The association of Gothic architecture with the Church and Christianity was certainly part of its appeal. To be buried in the Church was a religious ideal, and for hundreds of years the European elite of church, state, and society were indeed literally buried within the church structure.

Figure 6.10. Frontispiece, *Description de l'Egypte,* Vol. 1
*(Courtesy Archive and Rare Book Collection,
University of New Orleans)*

Figure 6.11.   Caballero Family Tomb, St. Louis Cemetery II
(Photograph Peggy McDowell)

In nineteenth-century American and European funerary designs, the Gothic Revival approached the popularity of the Classical Revival. Curiously, de Pouilly and his New Orleans clients did not find the Medieval Revival styles very appealing. Mausoleum designs inspired by the middle ages did not become especially popular in New Orleans commemorative arts until the second half of the nineteenth century. However, the de Pouilly designed Caballero family tomb in St. Louis Cemetery II, 1860, is an ornate example of Gothic style (fig. 6.11). As indicated in his sketchbook drawings, the family chose a Gothic over a Classical Revival design. In both design and decoration, the Caballero mausoleum stands out as unique alongside its neighbors. Comparable tombs can be seen in Père Lachaise and other con-temporary Parisian cemeteries, and the use of relief tracery inspired by the Gothic Revival styles was especially apparent in nineteenth-century French monuments. Relief work decorates all sides of the Caballero tomb, and the enclosing cast iron fence emulates ornate Gothic tracery. Fence patterns were usually coordinated with de Pouilly's tomb designs. The fences around most of his Classical Revival designs are simple, geometrical patterns much like those found in Père Lachaise, and the Egyptian Revival Grailhe tomb included Egyptian motifs on the fence gate.

It is hoped that these few examples serve to illustrate the dominant Revival repertory used by de Pouilly in New Orleans. Some eclectic combi-nations of styles also appear in his sketchbook, and there are numerous other tombs constructed from his designs.[6] His work in funerary arts was extensive and revealed the tastes and interests of his New Orleans clients. This interest in funerary and commemorative arts reflects a widespread trend in nineteenth-century Western cultures, a trend in which de Pouilly played a part by helping to introduce the Revival styles into New Orleans commemorative designs. It was an auspicious introduction for all con-cerned. Fortunately for New Orleans, this gifted architect brought with him a sensitive interest in funerary design based on his French heritage and a talent that allowed him to excel creatively in this field. Inspired by his creative leadership, the Classical, Gothic, and Egyptian Revival monuments that stand in the early New Orleans cemeteries speak in the international language of the Revival design forms: their accent, however, remains most decidedly French.

Notes

1.   Bennet Dowler, *Researches upon the Necropolis of New Orleans* (New Orleans: Bills and Clark, 1850), p. 7. The "great Bayou" cemetery referred to by Dr. Dowler is not identified. It may have been a cemetery established near Bayou St. John during the yellow fever epidemics of the early 1830s. This cemetery was probably used for underground burials during this emergency period. Its exact location, however, is not known. Further informa-

tion about the quality of the early cemeteries can be found in Albert E. Fossier, *New Orleans: The Glamour Period, 1800–1840,* published 1957, in which a chapter is devoted to the "City of Wet Graves," pp. 419–20.

2. Not much is published on this architect. Edith Long did the first major research on de Pouilly and interviewed his surviving relatives to supplement available documentation. Her research is partially published as a chapter in L. Huber et al., *New Orleans Architecture: The Cemeteries* (Gretna, La.: Pelican Publishing Company, 1974). Additional research on de Pouilly can be found in a brief pamphlet about a house designed by de Pouilly entitled *Madame Olivier's Mansion,* written by Edith Long in 1965.

3. Among the several publications that include the history of Père Lachaise is Frederick Brown's *Père Lachaise: Elysium as Real Estate* (New York: The Viking Press, 1973).

4. The relationship between the St. Louis Exchange Hotel and the facades of the buildings along Exchange Place and the Rue de Rivoli in Paris was noted by Samuel Wilson in Part II of *Plan and Program for the Preservation of the Vieux Carré,* a study conducted by the Bureau of Governmental Research for the City of New Orleans, 1968, p. 17.

5. See Samuel Wilson, Jr., and Bernard Lemann, *New Orleans Architecture: The Lower Garden District* (Gretna, La.: Pelican Publishing Company, 1971), p. xiv.

6. A list of the constructed tombs and other illustrations of de Pouilly's funerary designs can be found in Huber et al., *New Orleans Architecture: The Cemeteries,* pp. 72–104.

Ethnicity and Regionalism

Ethnicity and Regionalism

American cemetery and gravemarker study affords fascinating opportunities to observe different aspects of ethnicity through the material records of death left by various groups. These may range from distinctive types of markers, such as the metal cruciforms favored by certain German and Russian groups or the strong penchant for the inclusion of photographs of the deceased prevalent amongst those of Asian, Mediterranean and Eastern European heritage, to highly particularized landscape features such as the *Feng Shui* (geomancy) pattern observable in certain of the traditional Chinese cemeteries of Hawaii and the Pacific Northwest. Sometimes it is simply a matter of observing the prevalence of certain surnames on the gravemarkers in a given area. From these records we may learn much of the values which infused the traditional cultures of those who erected them, cultures in the process of evolving to become a part of a newer American culture. Another factor which often accounts for the distinctiveness of particular American cemeteries and gravemarkers is that of regionalism, a factor which may on a number of occasions actually correlate with ethnicity (as is the case with several of the essays in this section). A whole host of other considerations have also had their part in shaping the distinctive regional characteristics of American cemeteries—climate, topography, economic and occupational ties, events of major historic impact, to name but a few—and evidences of all of these may be read by those who take the time to look for them.

In a sense, all four essays in this section deal with ethnicity, and, for that matter, with regionalism as well. Ann and Dickran Tashjian's examination of our earliest extant Afro-American burying ground provides valuable insights into the lives of black Americans during the colonial period, demonstrating the manner in which material records can enrich our cultural understanding of historic groups for whom so little remains in written form. Folklorist Keith Cunningham takes us from colonial New England to the starkness of the desert Southwest, where he analyzes the manner in which the worldviews of three distinctive ethnic groups are reflected in the physical sites they choose and the customs they observe when death occurs in the community. Carrying on the notion of community and traditional practice, Lynn Gosnell and Suzanne Gott report on their findings based upon a long-term study of contemporary family-oriented grave decorating rituals in a large urban Mexican-American cemetery, noting, amongst other things, the manner in which certain traditions tracing back to old Mexico and further have been transmuted to cultural forms familiar in contemporary lifestyles. The section's final essay, by cultural geographer Thomas J. Hannon, demonstrates the manner in which intensive demographic analysis of a subregion's cemeteries, in this case, those of Western Pennsylvania, can lead to a broader understanding of the cultural and historical forces which shaped the area and helped provide its distinctive character.

7

The Afro-American Section of Newport, Rhode Island's Common Burying Ground

Ann and Dickran Tashjian

The Common Burying Ground of Newport, Rhode Island, has now been a place of general and particular fascination for centuries. Since 1650 the life of the city has moved along Thames Street and up Farewell to celebrate communal sorrow at the graveyard. This is not a garden cemetery, a place for casual strolling and picnics. Hidden and askew in tall grass, old bushes, and ivies (both benign and poisonous), the stones are packed into a space seemingly smaller than its ten acres bounded by Farewell and Warner Streets (fig. 7.1). According to one source, there are 8,072 graves marking the merchants, ministers, and their families who once populated the wealthiest and busiest seaport in eighteenth-century North America.[1]

Here, too, can be found inscribed on slate the names of servants who would otherwise be all but forgotten: Newport Redwood, Primus Gibbs, Neptune Sisson, Portsmouth Cheeseborough, Margaret Cranston, and Duchess Quamino, whose epitaph describes her as being "of distinguished excellence: / Intelligent, industrious / Affectionate, honest / and of / Exemplary Piety." (No wonder, then, that she was reputed to be the most celebrated cake baker in all of Rhode Island.)[2] These servants lie buried in a relatively small section on the most northern edge of the graveyard—an area reserved primarily for the burials of both the free and slave black inhabitants of Newport.[3]

This black section continued to be used, though sparsely, up through the mid-twentieth century. Newport's black families, well-established by the eighteenth century, may have continued to bury their dead there even after relatives had moved quite far away. The graves of persons described as French, Belgian, Cape Verdean, and from Worcester, Massachusetts, and San Francisco, California, are also to be found there. The area came to be

Figure 7.1. View of the Afro-American Section in the Common Burying Ground, Newport, Rhode Island

(Photograph Ann Tashjian)

reserved for those who, like blacks, were considered by the dominant white population not to be full members of the local community. From the beginning, then, this plot of land denoted the ambiguous if not marginal social status of those buried within its borders. Its demarcation by Dyre Avenue, the main street within the graveyard, subtly established a break in the terrain while maintaining an illusion of spatial continuity. Blacks in death thus mirrored their former social life in Newport, where they had been situated in the larger community but were not wholly of it.

The existence of a sizable black population in eighteenth-century Newport can be taken as a measure of this seaport's prosperity, which was based upon a trans-Atlantic trade in rum, slaves, and molasses that sailed the triangular route from Newport to the west coast of Africa and the Caribbean.[4] Africans who survived the horrors of the middle passage and landed in Rhode Island experienced a fortune different from those shipped down to Charleston, North Carolina, and other points south. Slaves were kept in Rhode Island to work the large South County plantations that raised dairy herds and grains for a growing brewery industry. In Newport many blacks served as household domestics and engaged in work that ranged from child rearing to manual labor and handicraft.

The life of servitude in an alien culture and society remained hard, despite the elegiac claims that the deceased servant was "faithful and well beloved of his Master." In rural Narragansett, for example, the Reverend James MacSparran, Presbyterian rector of St. Paul's Church, worked side by side in the fields with his slaves during haytime. Bodily labor, however, did not overshadow a concern for their souls. In his diary MacSparran often recorded his obligation to catechize "negro's & white children."[5]

Religious education and spiritual commitment, however, remained problematic. In 1743 the Reverend MacSparran confessed in his diary that he was "perplexed" by the sexual conduct of thirty-year-old Maroca (whom he had baptized at age thirteen). Despite her Christian status, he claimed, she "seems not concerned about her soul nor minds her promise of chastity, which she has often made me." Two years later MacSparran felt compelled to lash Maroca for receiving presents from Mingo, another slave. "I think it was my Duty to correct her," he reassured himself, but the whipping troubled Mrs. MacSparran, as revealed by his concluding remark: "and w'ever Passion passed between my wife and me on ye occasion, Good Ld forgive it." Whatever the nature of their tension, she would be nonetheless eager ("my poor passionate dear") to lash another slave after her husband's allotted strokes. Inclined to run away, the "headstrong and disobedient" Hannibal was exiled to another household on Conanicut Island and then casually sold a few months later.[6]

Failing to understand "the gift of chastity," as MacSparran put it, these slaves were caught in the crosscurrents of radically different cultures.[7] The hard life began at that cultural intersection, transcending the field work of rural Narragansett and infiltrating urban and urbane Newport, finally ending at the margin above Dyre Avenue in the Common Burying Ground.

In the summer of 1971 Ann Tashjian came upon this section of the Newport graveyard and realized that it was probably the only remaining burial site of blacks in colonial New England. The black graveyards of Boston and Providence are scattered if not virtually destroyed. An antiquarian source indicates that blacks in rural sections of Rhode Island were buried without headstones: "The earth in the lower and eastern portion of the old Narragansett churchyard still undulates with the nameless graves of the slaves, whose masters slumber in the upper part. . . ."[8] In an effort to forestall complete oblivion, she decided to photograph and transcribe all of the eighteenth-century gravestones still standing in the black section north of Dyre Avenue in the Common Burying Ground.[9]

In the autumn of 1986, after the project had been held in abeyance for many years, we discovered that even more stones had vanished or were broken beyond repair. The Guy . . . [a] Negro stone had been in ruins since at least 1971, but the Mintus Brenton stone (fig. 7.2), one of the finer carvings by John Stevens III, was more recently vandalized, and the Jesto Sisson stone (fig. 7.3) has simply disappeared.

This collection of photographs and transcriptions, however incomplete because of the depredations of time, may well be the only record of an eighteenth-century black burial ground in New England. Approximately half of the gravestones still standing and identified by name on a map of the graveyard drawn in 1903 (deposited at the Newport Historical Society) have been photographed. The collection, then, consists of 225 photographs of gravestones, all of which are accompanied by texts transcribed as faithfully as possible, plus some twenty texts transcribed from gravestones that are not photographed. These record the names of men, women, and children buried in the black section of the Newport cemetery during the eighteenth century. They are alphabetized by their given names rather than their surnames, which are usually those of their owners or are occasionally missing.

Town lore recorded in antiquarian histories has identified this section as reserved for blacks through ancient custom. There are also other sources to determine that the deceased were blacks and slaves. Even though only eleven epitaphs specify the deceased as "Negro," their given names are a source of identification that is corroborated by external evidence (diaries and journals, for example), which cite similar names for "Negroes."

The stones, as one might expect, record some of the usual stereotypes: Mimbo, Sanbo, and Chocolatt; but there are also place names: Newport,

Figure 7.2.　The Mintus Brenton Stone, 1774
Slate, 24½″ × 18½″.
(Photograph Ann Tashjian)

Figure 7.3. The Jesto Sisson Stone, 1774
Slate, 17½″ × 13¼″.
(Photograph Ann Tashjian)

Portsmouth, and Cambridge; Biblical names such as Sarah, Hannah, and Adam are outnumbered by names of classical origin: Cynthia, Phillis, Cato, Caesar, and Jupiter. Such names reflect Neo-Classical tastes on the part of owners, and suggest (as in the South) aspirations for a classical civilization which in its supposed "Golden Age" justified slavery. There was also the common ironic inversion of "Prince" brought low as a slave or servant, along with genuinely exotic names such as Cuffe, Cujo, Quarko, and Quash, some or all of which may have had African origins.[10] These names, like the graveyard segregation itself, were ways for whites to maintain difference, to keep a distance between supposed superior and inferior beings. At the same time, these names preserved a sense of an African past for slaves cut off from their homeland.

The social status of these blacks is more difficult to ascertain, although a clue can be gained from the names once again. On many of these stones for blacks a given name is often only implicitly associated with a surname, which is that of the family for whom the deceased was a servant. A typical example runs: "In Memory of / Newport a Faith / full Ser.t to Mr. / Jonathan Easton. . . ." From an owner's perspective, the casual omission of a surname benignly suggested that black "servants" were part of the family, whereas it actually set them apart from the dominant society even as it made them dependent upon a white family structure for identity.[11]

There are forty-five gravestones which indicate the servitude of forty-seven people. Variations within that broad category indicate a Negro servant or identify a master if not an owner. Cato Almy (who died in 1763), for example, was identified as having two successive masters. The term servant probably meant slave—as suggested by an epitaph for "Pompey (a beloved servant of Josias Lyndon) / died Sept. 11, 1765—aged 28 mos and 9 days" (fig. 7.4). Obviously, baby Pompey, scarcely two years old, was born into his servitude.

Although only Duchess Quamino was described as a "free black" on her gravestone, there was a sizable free black population in Newport prior to manumission in 1784. Many Quakers who owned slaves early in the eighteenth century had second thoughts about slavery, freed their slaves, and urged others to do so as well. Consequently, one cannot say with certainty that those blacks designated as servants were in all instances necessarily slaves. At the same time, however, of the forty-four identified as servants, only six were so described after 1784. Since it is unlikely that there was a radical shift in jobs after manumission, the omission of the title "servant" on a gravestone after 1784 may indicate a change in the legal rather than the occupational status of the deceased. In its reference to blacks on their gravestones, "servant" may well have been a euphemism for "slave," serving to assuage the conscience of surviving white families.

Figure 7.4. The Pompey Lyndon Stone, 1765
Slate, 20″ × 12¼″.
(Photograph Ann Tashjian)

Given the unique existence of this black burial site, what can be learned from the gravestones, individually and collectively? The anthropologist James Deetz has noted that "there is no better place in all of New England to stand face to face with the past than in the old burying grounds.... From the designs of these stones, and the way they vary in time and space, we may learn much."[12] Is, one might ask, his enthusiastic claim challenged by these artifacts? There is no evidence of African survivals, as in the instance of burial artifacts on the Georgia Sea Islands, where blacks had a measure of independence from white acculturation. Thus only the terrain demarcated within the graveyard sets these stones apart from those for the dominant society. And within the corpus of New England stonecarving these markers are hardly unique. The art of early New England stonecarving is not conspicuous in this section. Clearly, the absence of finely carved gravestones was less an index of talent and skill than economics and social status. Nevertheless, the presence of a strong craft tradition in the Old Burying Ground of Newport had an important impact on the cultural configuration of black gravestones.

Just as Yankee artisans suppressed an African craft tradition, so too did the religious values of New England Puritanism prevail in the graveyard. The carved images along with the verbal statements of piety expressed the religious expectations of the dominant community. While church rolls give a better indication of the names and numbers of blacks who attended the different churches of Newport, some gravestones state specific church affiliation for the deceased. Thus, four markers indicate that the deceased was a member of one of the various Baptist sects in the town. Cato Brindly was described as a "worthy member" of the Baptist Church under the "pastoral care" of the Reverend Gardner Thurston, as was Toney Taylor. Flora Flagg, a "worthy member of the Sabbatarin Baptist Church," "fell asleep in Christ": surviving "friends" were admonished to "wipe off your tears, / Here I must rest till Christ appears." Whereas the prominent church status of a deceased white person was often noted on the epitaph, blacks did not achieve such status with their limited participation in Newport's churches. Moreover, the cost of added lettering for an elaborate epitaph would have militated against such statements in the epitaph.

There is no way of knowing what individual blacks actually believed, even with the documentation that they were increasingly admitted to the various churches of Newport in the eighteenth century.[13] The inculcation of religious belief provided a subtle means of social control far more insidious than the codes governing the civil life of blacks in Newport. At the same time, Christian indoctrination was thought to "civilize" blacks, thereby eventually motivating some ministers to advocate the abolition of slavery. Did blacks give themselves completely over to Christianity? Some undoubtedly did, and to their advantage in the acculturation process. Others may have modulated a synthesis of disparate belief systems.

Although these gravestones did not frequently verbalize a Christian ideology, the carved imagery fell well within the parameters of traditional New England iconography, which expressed the survivors' hopes of life everlasting for the deceased. Because most of the surviving gravestones cluster around the mid-to-late eighteenth century, only three markers in this collection display the earliest images of winged skulls (which symbolized death and resurrection, a metamorphosis from this world to the next). Thus, a winged skull was carved on a stone for "Ann a Negro child / Belonging to Mr. Robert Oliver & / Daugr to his Negro / Mimbo aged 2 yr / Died June 1743" (fig. 7.5). The 1723 marker for Moll Barker (fig. 7.6) displays another early image derived from the seventeenth century, that of an hourglass, crudely incised, but with the strong lettering characteristic of John Stevens, first in the line of a prominent family of stonecarvers in Newport.

In the eighteenth century, stonecarvers gradually shifted their use of images from winged skulls to angels and cherubs, which are predominant among these gravestones for Newport's blacks. The prototype can be seen on the 1732 gravestone for Frankey and Judey, "two Negro sarvants to Mr. Edward Baner" (fig. 7.7). Among the carved cherubs can be found some minor variations: a different set of the wings here (the Lucia Johnson stone, 1783), an illusion of levitation there (the Jesto Sisson stone, 1773, fig. 7.3), or an elegant tip of the wing, as displayed on the Margaret Rivera stone, 1771 (fig. 7.8).

Most of the markers bearing cherubs, however, have a formulaic quality about them. These are obviously not the most expensive gravestones in the cemetery. At the same time, it should be acknowledged that these stones do not radically diverge in quality from so many carved for the dominant white population throughout Rhode Island and the rest of New England. (The slate used in this graveyard for both whites and blacks also tends to be inferior to that used elsewhere in New England.)

Variation in imagery otherwise occurs rather subtly in the designs cut upon the pilasters. But even this is not peculiar to these black gravestones but common to all gravestones with formulaic imagery. Pilaster variation provides some embellishment even for the most prosaic carvings. The Primas DeBlois stone (1775), for example, shows bold tulips on the pilasters (fig. 7.9), while the Sarah Burdin stone (1728) has some lyrical foliage that spills into the epitaph area from the pilasters (fig. 7.10).

The wealth and prosperity of Newport provided the economic base that sustained the enterprises of many of the finest Colonial craftspersons in cabinetry and architecture. This was no less true of gravestone carving. In the Common Burying Ground appears the work of the three generations

Figure 7.5   The Ann Oliver Stone, 1743
Slate, n.m.
(Photograph Ann Tashjian)

Figure 7.6.   The Moll Barker Stone, 1723
Slate, 14″ × 13″.
(Photograph Ann Tashjian)

Figure 7.7.   The Frankey and Judey Baner Stone, 1732
Slate, 23″ × 18″.
(Photograph Ann Tashjian)

Figure 7.8.   The Margaret Rivera Stone, 1771 (?)
Slate, 19½″ × 17¼″.
(Photograph Ann Tashjian)

Figure 7.9. The Primas Deblois Stone, 1775
Slate, 23″ × 15″.
(Photograph Ann Tashjian)

Figure 7.10.   The Sarah Burdin Stone, 1728
Slate, n.m.
(Photograph Ann Tashjian)

of John Stevenses as well as that of John Bull, a contemporary of young Stevens III, and their helpers, slaves, and/or servants.[14] Bull carved many of the cherubs for these deceased slaves with a characteristic clarity and flat elegance of line and proportion, as evidenced on the Cambridge Bull stone (1769) (fig. 7.11), the stylistic culmination of which would have been the marker for Elizabeth Sisson (1774), an upper-class white woman (fig. 7.12).

John Stevens III signed no fewer than thirteen gravestones for blacks in our collection, as exemplified by the Solomon Nuba Tikey stone (1785) and the slightly more elaborate Neptune Sisson stone of 1794. Stevens III also carved gravestones for Dinah Wigneron (1772) (fig. 7.13), Pompey Brenton (1772) (fig. 7.14), and Mintus Brenton (1774) (fig. 7.2). These angelic figures convey spiritual portraits with the particularity of tightly curled hair for Pompey Brenton and Mintus Brenton. Stevens's signature evidenced his growing self-consciousness as an artist emerging from a colonial craft tradition. These elaborate gravestones were a sign that these slaves were held in high regard by their masters, whose expenditure also displayed their own social prominence in the community. The Brenton family, for example, were major landowners in the colony and included a governor among their numbers.

Stevens III has also been credited with carving the gravestone for Phillis Lyndon Stevens (fig. 7.15), who was the "faithful servant" of Josias Lyndon, former governor of Rhode Island.[15] She died March 9, 1773 in giving birth to Prince, who died thirteen days later. This poignant image of mother-and-child is iconographically related to young Stevens's famous gravestone for Mercy Buliod, who died in 1771 (fig. 7.16). The logic of developing skill in the craft would suggest that young Stevens carved the stiff and even awkward image of Phillis Lyndon Stevens before the Mercy Buliod stone. Yet, even though families were known to commission gravestones long after a relative had died, this sequence seems unlikely because the Mercy Buliod stone conforms stylistically with other work by Stevens III in 1771. Thus, the Phillis Lyndon Stevens stone remains anomalous.[16]

With this inconsistency it is reasonable to suggest that the Phillis Lyndon Stevens stone may have been carved by someone other than John Stevens III. This carver probably worked with the Stevens family because the stone bears lettering from their shop if not from the hand of Stevens III himself. There is the possibility that the Phillis Lyndon Stevens stone was cut by Pompe Stevens. She is identified in the epitaph as the wife of Zingo Stevens, whose name appears as the "colored servant of John Stevens" on the baptismal rolls of the Second Congregational Church in 1770. Pompe's surname and practice of signing the gravestone strongly suggests that he

Figure 7.11. The Cambridge Bull Stone, 1769
Slate, 23½″ × 15½″.
(Photograph Ann Tashjian)

Figure 7.12.   The Elizabeth Sisson Stone, 1774
Slate, 35¼″ × 31½″.
(Photograph Ann Tashjian)

Figure 7.13.   The Dinah Wigneron Stone, 1772
Slate, 23″ × 16½″.
(Photograph Ann Tashjian)

Figure 7.14.   The Pompey Brenton Stone, 1772
Slate, 21¼″ × 18¾″.
(Photograph Ann Tashjian)

Figure 7.15.   The Phillis (Lyndon) Stevens Stone, 1773
Slate, 27″ × 22¼″.
(Photograph Ann Tashjian)

Figure 7.16.   The Mercy Buliod Stone, 1771
Slate, 29″ × 22″.
(Photograph Ann Tashjian)

worked in the John Stevens shop. Even so, without other evidence, this provenance must remain speculative.

Pompe Stevens is the only black eighteenth-century stonecarver whom we can identify by virtue of his own statement on a marker for his brother, Cuffe Gibbs (fig. 7.17):

> This Stone was
> cut by Pompe
> Stevens in Memo
> ry of his Brother
> Cuffe Gibbs, who
> died D[ec.] 27.th 1768
> [Aged . . .] Years

Pompe Stevens also signed a marker for baby Pompey Lyndon ("Cut . by, P:S"), who died in the Josias Lyndon household in 1765 (fig. 7.4).[17]

Although it is remarkable that Pompe Stevens signed his work, his signature has survived on only two gravestones, and those were for close kin and hence of particular emotional significance; otherwise, the two stones are unremarkable in their display of formulaic cherubs among many other formulaic cherubs in the black section and elsewhere. Thus it is extremely difficult to document the carving of Pompe Stevens. One possibility is to examine kinship patterns recorded on the markers. He might have carved gravestones for kin related by blood or white family ownership. Pompe Stevens may have been the brother of Zingo Stevens. There was in all likelihood a fourth brother, Primus Gibbs, who died in 1775 (fig. 7.18). Pompe, Zingo, and Primus had their own families. With Silva Gould, Pompe Stevens had a son Prince, who died in 1759 (fig. 7.19). After the death of Phillis, Zingo married Elizabeth, who died in childbirth in 1779, and then Violet, whose stone shows her death in 1803. There are no gravestones in the Common Burying Ground for Pompe Stevens himself or Zingo Stevens, whose three wives stand shoulder-to-shoulder as though in chorus. Primus Gibbs had a daughter, Susey Howard, who died in 1770. And there is a Jem Howard, twin of Quam, and son of Phillis, who died in 1771. Thus, in addition to Stevens and Gibbs, blacks of the Howard, Gould, and Lyndon families are implicated in an extensive kinship pattern by marriage and birth.

With these names serving as a nucleus, one might also examine markers dating from 1760 to 1775 for clues to reveal traces of Pompe Stevens's carving within a period that might reasonably span his engagement in the craft. The task is hardly compelling, however, because these gravestones are not visually distinguished, and we can assume that Pompe Stevens did indeed carve or had a hand in carving many stones simply by working in

Figure 7.17.   The Cuffe Gibbs Stone, 1768
Slate, 17½" × 17¼".
(Photograph Ann Tashjian)

Figure 7.18.   The Primus Gibbs Stone, 1775
Slate, 24¼″ × 17¾″.
(Photograph Ann Tashjian)

Figure 7.19. The Prince Stevens Stone, 1759
Slate, 13" × 12½".
(Photograph Ann Tashjian)

the Stevens family shop. (It is, of course, always possible that he was primarily a common laborer in the shop and tried his hand at carving only those few stones intended for kin.)

The handicraft of Pompe Stevens offers only glimpses into the black community of colonial Newport because this section remains a social and cultural filter of white attitudes and values. The fact that Pompe Stevens left no evidence of African culture on the gravestones in the Common Burying Ground is attributable in large measure to the dominance of the European craft tradition practiced by Newport artisans.[18] The Stevens shop and John Bull taught their slaves, servants, and laborers the proper colonial conventions. Variation in image and style, especially for artifacts on public display, occurred only within a given pool of conventions; cultural deviation from the pool itself was extremely unlikely. Thus it was that Pompe Stevens acquiesced to the public design of early New England stonecarving.

In the final analysis, it is the existence of these gravestones in conjunction with external documentation that might eventually lead to a reconstruction of black community life in colonial Newport. If the stones by themselves remain obdurate, then let us turn to the lives that preceded and succeeded them in an alien land. Despite the verbal culture of early New England, blacks in their inferior social status generally remained outside written documentation. The fragmentary nature of historical evidence has led historians to attempt to synthesize a general view of black life in New England.[19]

Yet in their broken eloquence, these gravestones call for a recognition of the textures and sensibilities of black communal life in eighteenth-century Newport. While such a project is beyond the limits of this essay, and quite conceivably beyond the limits of available evidence, we have tried to move from given names on the gravestones to other shards scattered in files at the Newport and Rhode Island Historical societies. With a name a life becomes possible. Unfortunately, most names have remained buried. We have managed, however, to recover a few that offer tantalizing glimpses into black lives in eighteenth-century New England.

Phillis Lyndon Stevens surfaced in the diary of Ezra Stiles, minister of the Second Congregational Church in Newport. The Reverend Stiles delineated her Christian evolution as he catechized her in the mysteries of the Christian faith and then baptized her during the month of March 1771, when she is "admitted . . . into full Communion." On January 3, 1773 Stiles recorded that he had "baptized Prince a negro Infant of Br. Zingo & Sister Phillis—Communicants in my Church."[20]

Three months later came the sad news:

March 9, 1773. This day died Phyllis a Negro Sister of our Church: I hope that she had chosen the better part. Her Husband Brother Zingo, upon becoming religious and joyning my Church, had an earnest Concern for his Wife and Children, and labored greatly to bring her into a saving Acquaintance with her Redeemer; and I doubt not his Endeavors and prayers were blessed to her saving Conversion. She was brought hither out of Guinea 1759 aet. 13 or 14, and has lived in Gov. Lyndons Family ever since. She was always free from the common Vices—and especially since her profession has walked soberly & exemplarly. She expressed her Trust in the Merits of the Redeemer, & died with a good hope.[21]

Her carved portrait soon appeared in the Common Burying Ground.

As a minister who came to oppose slavery, Stile's compassionate account focuses upon her spiritual development. Another glimpse of Phillis Lyndon Stevens is offered in the account books of Caesar Lyndon, an educated servant of the Governor. Caesar was the Governor's secretary and purchasing agent, no doubt a highly privileged position among the blacks of Newport, and certainly in vivid contrast to the harsh rural existence of Maroca, Mingo, and Hannibal, the slaves of Narragansett's Reverend MacSparran. Caesar nevertheless grew his own vegetables, slaughtered animals, and engaged in barter with the townspeople. He also had extensive cash accounts with Neptune Sisson and other blacks, to whom he loaned money. His life was hardly sybaritic, yet there was a measure of affluence, so that he could look after the silver buckles and leather britches of his own wardrobe, and note that "Phillis had her gown" at a cost of thirty-two pounds. There was also some leisure time. On a Tuesday, August 12, 1766, Caesar noted "a pleasant ride out to Portsmouth" for a picnic. He was accompanied by Sarah Searing, Neptune Sisson and his wife, Zingo Stevens and Phillis Lyndon, Boston Vose, and Prince Thurston. He also listed food purchased "for ye Support of Nature": "a Pigg to roast," wine, bread, rum, green corn, sugar, butter, and coffee.[22]

These simple pleasures were augmented by whitewashing the bed chamber of Sarah Searing, then painting the woodwork blue. On October 6, 1767 the Reverend Stiles "lawfully married" Caesar and Sarah. (Caesar noted that Zingo and Phillis were married by the Reverend Edward Upham, who served as minister of the First Baptist Church, which Josias Lyndon attended.) And there was despair: "Our little Darling Pompey was born ye 2nd Day of May 1763 taken ill in the night Thursday with the Bloody Flux September 5 1765 and died Wednesday Morning after 1/4 after 9 o'clock being the 11th of said Sept. 1765."[23] The child's gravestone was carved and signed by Pompe Stevens.

Let us leap ahead some 120 years, and consider George Champlin Mason's *Reminiscences of Newport.* He describes Mintus, the "last colored undertaker" of Newport, decked out in a "bell-crowned hat" and "blue swallow-tail," which scraped the ground as he led a funeral procession. Mintus emerges as a comic figure:

> It took Mintus some time to organize a funeral; but when everything was ready, he gave the signal to move, by walking ahead of the hearse in the middle of the street, one hand under his coat-tail, and taking long strides which carried him some distance ahead of his charge; then he turned his head, and, jerking his thumb over his shoulder, exclaimed in a hoarse whisper, "Come along with that corpse!" This was repeated from time to time till they reached the grave, where Mintus sought to do everything "decently and in order"; which meant with him as much pomp and ceremony as he could muster.[24]

Mason is hazy on dates, but we can assume that he is describing a mid-nineteenth-century practice apparently in decline.

Contrast Mason's benign but condescending description with the views of Caesar Lyndon, one of the founders of Newport's Free African Union Society. This association had its beginnings in the black church and sought to develop a back-to-Africa movement. Otherwise it engaged in mutual self-help.[25] In 1790 and again in 1794 Lyndon's group tried to regulate conduct at black funerals.

Unlike Caesar's journal entry of his child's death, the language of this decree of the Free African Union Society was formal and even stilted as only decrees can be. Nevertheless, the public and private statements were in accord. The decree recommended that members "dress themselves and appear decent on all occasions, that so they may be useful to all and every such burying ... that all the Spectators may not have it in their power to cast such Game contempt, as in times past...."[26] Here was recognition of hostility among Newport's white population and of the need to assume a dignified public appearance to protect the integrity of private grief.

Given the deep-seated tensions between masters and slaves in eighteenth-century Newport, white hostility can be reasonably attributed to a fear of blacks in public congregation, extending even to funerals. (The civil codes aimed at regulating the social behavior of blacks further testify to this fear.) There is also evidence to suggest that early funeral rituals held by blacks given their latitude had a celebratory quality that disturbed white New Englanders.[27] Since funerals were civil events with profound spiritual implications, unregulated black funerals with singing and dancing undermined both the social as well as spiritual order of the dominant community. The subsequent regulation of black funerals was a way to assert spiritual and social hegemony over a subordinate population.

The situation, however, was hardly a straightforward exercise in social dominance—or compliance, for that matter. The ironies and ambiguities that were generated and felt by all parties might be viewed as paradigmatic of cross-cultural discourse under the circumstances of slavery. While the outward appearance of a black funeral left unregulated may have appeared "heathenish," white funerals no less than black were essentially celebratory in function, serving the emotional needs of the surviving community. Ironically enough, as the eighteenth century wore on, the white population of New England could not maintain a simplicity of funeral rites as mandated by their colonial legislatures. Funerals became increasingly ostentatious and elaborate displays of conspicuous consumption. The regulation of black funerals thus imposed a double standard on the community and tacitly signalled the failure of masters to curb their own excesses.[28]

The decree of the Free African Union Society may well have been intended to forestall white scorn and violence. Given the social and political circumstances, that was a prudent measure. But the decree, written as it was by an acculturated Caesar Lyndon, may have also been intended to bring Afro-American funeral rites within the prevailing norms of white new England propriety. That this was done under the aegis of a Free African Union Society has an obvious irony—but with a double edge, resonating as it does under the ambiguity of signs. Caesar Lyndon may well have seized upon acculturation as a strategy to deflect repression and violence. Rather than simple compliance to white norms, then, his decree may have set the stage for Mintus and the safe expression of private feelings in a public arena controlled by whites.

How, then, should we interpret Mason's Mintus? Several possibilities emerge. Had Mintus become a buffoon for the amusement of white spectators, or was Mason's account reflexively stereotypical in a failure to recognize Mintus as a community leader? In either case, had African funeral customs been sacrificed in tacit exchange for the public exercise of funeral rites? Or was the behavior of Mintus and his fellow mourners still sufficiently (though subtly) out of tune with the dominant social norms that white spectators—in their ignorance and ethnocentricity—could only be amused in watching what they mistakenly assumed to be an ignorant parody of proper behavior?

The situation dramatizes that double consciousness posited by W. E. B. Dubois, that dual existence first imposed by an alien culture and society but then necessarily nurtured for survival, that learned ability to keep an eye on others as blacks went about their own business. The graveyard to which Mintus led his community gave final testimony of kidnapped Africans becoming Afro-Americans. The stones themselves but hint obliquely at the struggles of those blacks even after death to gain a final place of rest.

Notes

1. See Alden G. Beaman, *Rhode Island Vital Records,* New Series, II: *Births 1590–1930 from Newport Common Burial Ground Inscriptions* (East Princeton, Mass.: Rhode Island Families Association, 1985), p. ii.

2. Robert S. Franklin, "Newport Cemeteries," *Special Bulletin of the Newport Historical Society* 10 (December 1913), p. 29.

3. According to Winthrop D. Jordan, "In the northern cities and towns at least, Negroes were often, probably usually, interred in a separate section of the burial ground, and in this matter alone separation was occasionally written into law" (*White over Black: American Attitudes toward the Negro, 1550–1812* [Chapel Hill: The University of North Carolina Press, 1968], p. 132). Such legislation does not seem to have been the case in Newport.

4. For an excellent account of the Rhode Island slave trade, see Jay Coughtry, *The Notorious Triangle: Rhode Island and the African Slave Trade, 1700–1807* (Philadelphia: Temple University Press, 1981). For studies of blacks in Newport, Rhode Island, and New England, see William Dawson Johnston, "Slavery in Rhode Island, 1755–1776," *Slavery in the States: Selected Essays* (New York: Negro Universities Press, 1969); Lorenzo Greene, *The Negro in Colonial New England, 1620–1776* (Port-Washington, N. Y.: Kennikat Press, 1966); and Edgar J. McManus, *Black Bondage in the North* (Syracuse: Syracuse University Press, 1973). For a related community study of Providence, Rhode Island, see *Creative Survival: The Providence Black Community in the 19th Century* (Providence: The Rhode Island Black Heritage Society, 1980). For a recent study of blacks in early New England from the perspective of folk culture, see William D. Piersen, *Black Yankees: The Development of an Afro-American Subculture in Eighteenth-Century New England* (Amherst: The University of Massachusetts Press, 1988).

5. James MacSparran, *A Letter Book and Abstract of Out Services,* ed. Daniel Goodwin (Boston: D. B. Updike, 1899), p. 40.

6. MacSparran, *A Letter Book,* pp. 15, 29, 52, 54, 56, 63.

7. Ibid., p. 52.

8. Ibid., p. 45.

9. Ann Tashjian used a Bronica with 120 film to photograph the markers. Enlarged contact prints have been made for study purposes. These images are coded according to coordinates from a 1903 map of the graveyard that can be found at the Newport Historical Society. Corresponding texts (vital statistics and other statements comprising the epitaph), along with dimensions of the marker and its material, are currently recorded on 3 by 5 cards and will eventually be entered on computer to facilitate whatever demographic analysis might be teased from the data.

10. According to Piersen, "The continued use in New England of Gold Coast day names (names given to record the day of birth) reinforces the probability of important ties to the Fanti-Ashanti cultures of West Africa. Children's day names like Quashi for Sunday or Quamino for Saturday were used by New England masters who appear to have recognized them because of the commonness—a recognition more general among slaves then masters elsewhere in the New World" (*Black Yankees,* p. 7).

11. Piersen suggests that free blacks took the surnames from the given names of their fathers or matrilineal surnames derived from their mothers in conforming with an African sense of matrilineal kinship (*Black Yankees,* pp. 35, 92).

12. *In Small Things Forgotten: The Archaeology of Early American Life* (Garden City: Anchor Press, 1977), p. 64.

13. Piersen claims that only "a tiny minority" of Afro-Americans were religiously converted because "the Christianity [that the Yankee masters] offered was self-serving and neither emotionally nor intellectually satisfying to most Africans and Afro-Americans" (*Black Yankees,* pp. 60–61).

14. For an account of the Stevens shop, see Harriette M. Forbes, *Gravestones of Early New England and the Men Who Made Them, 1653–1800* (New York: Da Capo Press, 1967), pp. 90–97; see, too, Esther Fisher Benson, "The History of the John Stevens Shop," *Newport Historical Society Bulletin* 112 (October 1963).

15. Harriette Forbes was perhaps the first to attribute the Phillis Lyndon stone to John Stevens III. See *Gravestones of Early New England and the Men Who Made Them,* p. 96.

16. After much thought, we have come to see the provenance of the Phillis Lyndon Stevens stone to be problematic. Because of the vagaries of stonecarving it is not impossible that Stevens III carved the stone after gaining proficiency in carving the Mercy Buliod Stone. However, we are much less certain on the matter than we were in 1974 when we agreed with Forbes in *Memorials for Children of Change: The Art of Early New England Stonecarving* (Middletown: Wesleyan University Press, 1974), pp. 139–40.

17. Pompe Stevens is identified as a stonecarver in Sue Kelly and Anne Williams, "'And the Men Who Made Them': The Signed Gravestones of New England," *Markers* II (1983), p. 94.

18. For an excellent account of African survivals and acculturation in the antebellum South, see John W. Blassingame, *The Slave Community* (New York: Oxford University Press, 1972). Closer to home, William Piersen takes the same approach in *Black Yankees:* "Far more than we might have imagined, during the eighteenth century the region's black population maintained African values and approaches to life—especially in the free hours they shared together" (ix-x). He does not, however, examine gravestones, even though he discusses funeral rites. For trade and craft roles taken by blacks in the North, see Lorenzo Greene, *The Negro in Colonial New England, 1620–1776,* pp. 100–123.

19. Piersen concedes: "Because evidence that illuminates New England's black folk culture is sparse and (at least as I collected it) wildly eclectic, conclusions about the details of black life cannot be finely drawn" (*Black Yankees,* x).

20. Ezra Stiles, *The Literary Diary of Ezra Stiles,* ed. Franklin Bowditch Dexter, 3 vols. (New York: Charles Scribner's Sons, 1901), vol. 1, pp. 95, 97, 329.

21. Ibid., p. 355.

22. Rhode Island Manuscripts, vol. X, pp. 82A, 83B, 83A (Rhode Island Historical Society). Although Caesar Lyndon's written legacy is more account book than diary, it may well be one of the few surviving diaries written by an Afro-American in the eighteenth century.

23. Ibid., p. 84C.

24. *Reminiscences of Newport* (Newport: Charles E. Hammett, Jr., 1884), pp. 106–7.

25. For a complete account of the records of the Free African Union Society, see William H. Robinson, ed., *The Proceedings of the Free African Union Society and the African Benevolent Society* (Providence: Urban League of Rhode Island, 1976).

26. William H. Robinson, *Black New England Letters* (Boston: Boston Public Library, 1977), pp. 14–15.

27. According to Piersen, "At first, slave funerals and burials were conducted by Yankee blacks much as they had been in Africa. Since it was believed that the dead would return to the ancestral continent, the original style and meaning of the ceremonies continued" (*Black Yankees*, p. 77).

28. For a historical analysis of Puritan funerals, see *Memorials for Children of Change*, pp. 13–33.

8

Navajo, Mormon, Zuni Graves:
Navajo, Mormon, Zuni Ways

Keith Cunningham

The Navajo have a phrase they use frequently, which they translate into English as "the Navajo Way," and they say it in English as in Navajo: all in capital letters and underlined. They apparently use this term to refer to their core complex of traditional beliefs and values which make them Navajo and which motivate and direct their behaviors from the cradleboard to the grave. "Way" is a very useful word for the study of culture. In terms of deathways, "way" involves funerary practices, cemeteries and gravestones, and the eschatology which reflects and directs these.

The Ramah Cemetery at Ramah, New Mexico, is presently the major burial ground for both the extensive Mormon and Ramah Navajo communities in the area. The VanderWagen Cemetery, located approximately twenty-five miles east of Ramah, is presently the major burial ground for the Zuni: two cemeteries, three ways, three eschatologies. This essay follows the model established by Dickran and Ann Tashjian in their classic work, *Memorials for Children of Change,* wherein they insist upon interpreting "carved gravestones as works of art within their cultural context" and needing to "make sense out of the objects as they were significant to those who made and used them."[1] It describes the three ways and eschatologies—Navajo, Mormon, and Zuni—in cultural context, and tries to make sense out of the three sets of graves in terms of the cultures which create and utilize them.

Located approximately a quarter of a mile due south of the Mormon community of Ramah, New Mexico, and approximately in the center of the traditional Ramah Navajo homeland is a city which serves the dead of both groups and which speaks to and of the living of both groups. Some twenty-five miles east of the Ramah Cemetery, due south of the community of

Zuni inhabited by the Zuni Indians, is a Zuni village of the dead. Individuals who come to reside in these cities of the dead come from different cultures after, and accompanied by, different funerary practices.

The Ramah Navajo are a part of the Navajo Nation and the Navajo culture. The vast majority of the Ramah Navajo are the descendants of seven families who separated from the main group returning to the Navajo lands from their captivity and imprisonment by the federal government at Fort Sumner in 1868. Though a part of the Navajo tribe, the Ramah Navajo have long lived somewhat isolated from the majority of the group and are generally recognized by scholars as a subgroup within the whole.[2]

Navajo funerary practice has been described by a number of the informants from whom I collected data in the Ramah area and in a variety of authoritative sources written over a long period of time.[3] Although it is clear there are differences in the descriptions across the space of the reservation and the time period of the observations, the accounts are similar in basic outlines.

It was contrary to the Navajo ideal for a Navajo to die inside a home, and such a death was considered unfortunate both for the one who died and for the ones who remained. Navajos who died outside of homes were prepared for burial by specially designated relatives and were interred by the same relatives or by others. Burial took place as soon as possible, usually within a day, in an isolated spot. The actual grave was often a rock crevice or gully and was covered by a high mound of earth which included rocks, branches, or poles. In the past, some of the deceased's favorite or most valuable possessions were buried with the body, and food or water was left by the grave. A common practice was to take the deceased's saddle, slash it, and leave it beside or on top of the burial mound. Occasionally a single pole marker was erected near a grave or broken dishes were placed on top of it. There were typically no gravestones or memorial markers.

There were special funerary procedures for a Navajo who was unfortunate enough to die within a home. The practice was to board up all windows and doors and make a new opening in the north wall. Mortuary preparation was basically the same as for a person who died outside of a home, and burial was most often also similar, with the body being taken out of the home through the opening in the north wall. In some cases bodies were buried within the home in which they had died, and the structures were abandoned, pulled down, or, less frequently, burned. According to tradition, not only was the hogan in which death had taken place abandoned or destroyed, but the entire remaining settlement was sometimes moved to a new location. The abandoned or deserted death hogan is called in Navajo *hook´eeghan,* or home without a hearth. The persons who performed the preparation and the actual burial underwent complicated ritual cleansing for four days. Far from being a city of the dead visited by the living, traditional Navajo burials, thus, were abandoned buildings or isolated graves scattered on the landscape, and the strong feeling was that all mention of graves, the dead, or death was to be avoided.

Primarily because of their longstanding interest in self scrutiny, Utah Mormons, members of the Church of Jesus Christ of the Latter-Day Saints, are among the most widely recognized and frequently studied of Anglo-American cultural groups in terms of both their history and their traditional art, including gravemarkers. Mormon groups residing outside the state of Utah, however, have less frequently been the subject of research and are less well known.

The Ramah Mormon community came into being as a part of the general Latter-Day Saint southern expansion in the late nineteenth century. The first Mormon settlement in the Ramah area occurred in 1876. This first settlement was abandoned in 1880 after its members had been decimated by a smallpox epidemic, but the settlement was reestablished two years later at its present location.[4]

Mormon traditional lore and folklife, particularly folk song[5] and legend,[6] has been frequently studied. Mormon custom in general has been treated in Mormon histories[7] and autobiographies,[8] and traditional Mormon eschatology has been thoroughly described by apologists.[9] Little scholarly attention, however, has been directed toward Mormon custom and even less to the traditional customs of Mormon groups living outside the boundaries of Utah. I have been involved in extensive field collecting among White Mountain, Arizona, Mormons, a group with the same general history and development as the nearby Ramah group, since 1969. As a part of the social interaction involved in extensive field research, I have fought back tears at a number of Mormon funerals in the White Mountain area and have heard several accounts and tape recordings of others.

Mormon preparation for burial across the entire geographical range of American Mormonism is almost always performed by a professional mortuary or funeral home, and the basic practices, including having the corpse on display for visitors at the funeral home, are well within the mainstream of the Anglo-American way of death.[10] Funeral services and interment traditionally take place three days after the death of the individual.

Rural Arizona or New Mexico is not Salt Lake City, and funerals in these areas are a distinctly Mormon folk event. Funeral services, usually held within a stake center or ward building, are one of the most important and best attended community events in these rural Mormon communities. There is usually "special music" by a local group and/or soloist as a part of the service, but in marked contrast to what has been described in the Midwest as the "town and country soprano," whose function is to "augment grief." Here the special music is most often, literally and figuratively, up-beat. The spoken portions of the service are delivered by family and friends of the deceased and are determinedly cheerful and positive. The recollections and remembrances about the deceased are persistently sanguine and include traditional jokes and humorous anecdotes calling forth laughter as a response from the audience. The entire service is highly personal and centers upon the individual. Foibles as well as strengths may be the subject of anecdotes, but the emphasis is on the individual and his state of grace.

The indoor service, as is also true of Anglo-American funerals in general, is often followed by a graveside service. The actual preparation of the grave and interment are performed by professionals from the memorial home and/or the cemetery, although in many small communities the cemetery is operated by the ward or stake, and church members perform the "opening" and "closing" of the grave.

Because the Zunis were first contacted by Coronado in 1540, the written record concerning the Zuni begins much earlier than is true of most other North American Indian groups. The Zuni history is indeed an ancient one and involves over 400 years of observations by priests, adventurers, travelers, and historians.[11] In the course of this scrutiny, Zuni funerary practices have been well described over a long period of time by many observers.[12] Several of my visits to the village of Zuni have occurred just after or before burials, and family members have described contemporary Zuni funerary practices to me.

Zunis traditionally inter a corpse the day after the person dies. There is an all-night ceremony before burial which the Zunis call in English a "wake." The body is cleansed and laid out in a home, most often the home of the deceased, and family and clan relatives remain with the body during the night. Ritually prepared food is brought by traditionally designated individuals and given to the dead during the night, and a window is left open in the home. Early the next morning the corpse is taken to the place of burial and interred. Traditionally in the past some of the deceased's most valuable and/or favorite possessions (usually jewelry) were buried with the body, and food and water were left by or on the grave.

And so the Zuni come from their homes in their village to their homes in their village of the dead. And so the Ramah Mormons come from services at their church's stake center or ward building to interment in their church's cemetery. And so the Ramah Navajo come to a contemporary Navajo burial. As they come from different cultures after, and accompanied by, different funerary practices, so they come to different cities of the dead.

Lying just south of the Mormon community of Ramah, New Mexico, and in the center of the traditional Ramah Navajo homeland, is a city which serves both groups (fig. 8.1). The cemetery has no sign or marker but is

Figure 8.1. Ramah Cemetery, Ramah, New Mexico
(Photograph Kathryn Cunningham)

called the Ramah Cemetery, the Ramah Community Cemetery, or simply the Cemetery by the Mormons in the area and the Mormon Cemetery by the Navajos. It is located on a knoll surrounded by farm and ranch land to the east and north and bordered by a cattle feedlot and barn on the south; a road runs along the west side. The cemetery is enclosed by a fence marking its boundaries, but (particularly when compared with modern, mainstream American cemeteries featuring perpetual care, carefully manicured landscaping, and lawns) looks even less controlled than the ranch lands around it where the grass and weeds are kept short by grazing animals. There is a flagpole approximately in the center of the cemetery, but there are no large memorial statues. The ground is covered primarily by native grasses and weeds. Because of the ecology of the area, the mounded graves return very slowly to the natural level of the earth and require even longer to acquire a covering of vegetation, but then disappear completely if they do not receive minimal care. The grass's work is done slowly but thoroughly in the American West. The result is that graves which are twenty or thirty years old often look as though they were made very recently, while some are impossible to discern with any degree of certainty.

The cemetery was initially established as a Mormon burial ground, but today (as Navajos are very fond of observing) it is divided into two sections. The entire western half and the northeastern quarter contain Anglo-American Mormon graves, while the remaining southeastern quarter contains Navajo graves. The cemetery has a unified appearance when viewed from a distant perspective, but the differences between the two sections are so pronounced upon close inspection that it seems to be two separate burial grounds separated by an invisible line.

The Navajo section contains seventy-one graves which can be positively identified by their appearance. The bulk of the Navajo graves have no permanent markers of any kind (fig. 8.2). There are a few fairly recent and obviously commercially manufactured markers, plus one gravestone of the sort traditionally used across America to indicate the grave of an individual who served in the United States Armed Forces. The rest of the graves are either totally unmarked or are indicated by small plaques furnished by mortuary homes. Some of the plaques are thin metal plates which are lightly incised by handheld electric engraving machines, while others are heavy paper which have been written on with felt-tipped markers and covered with transparent plastic. These markers are used in most areas of America for temporary identification until permanent markers are put in place. In the Navajo section of the Ramah Cemetery, however, the temporary markers remain even though weathering quickly makes both kinds illegible. A few of the graves have been decorated with artificial flowers which are stuck into the mounds, and some have vases in various states of

Figure 8.2. Typical Navajo Grave in Ramah Cemetery
(Photograph Kathryn Cunningham)

dissolution suggesting previous decoration, but most are undecorated. The simple metal markers give the names and dates of birth and death of the deceased. The graves are individual. There is no indication of any attempt to bury family members side by side or close together. All the graves are approximately the same distance apart and are laid out in what is basically a straight line. The headstone or other marker and the grave are placed so that the main side of the marker and the head of the deceased point toward the West, and the deceased would face East if sitting or standing.

The Mormon section of the cemetery has basically the same sort of natural landscaping as the Navajo side, but the markers, the plots, and the information they convey are very different. There are 209 graves in this three-fourths of the cemetery. The memorial markers in the Mormon section are both more numerous and at the same time more varied than those in the Navajo section and include both homemade and commercial markers in a variety of styles, forms, and materials from different time periods.

The memorial markers which appear to be handmade objects include relatively early ones of rather crudely shaped and incised native sandstone and a much more recent one which is a carved, highly varnished, large pine board. The commercial markers range from early stone slabs such as those featuring carved lambs for children's graves, a form and use traditional all across America, to very recent pictorial markers which include an actual picture of the deceased as a part of their design and contemporary sand-blasted stones which allow very intricate and exact representations of floral motifs and even recognizable representations of Mormon temples at Mesa, Arizona, and Salt Lake City, Utah. One group of four stones in the cemetery is of particular interest to the student of folk art. The four stones were obviously handmade from red sandstone found in the general area. Three of them are in the general shape of hearts and are covered with unusually deeply incised roses (fig. 8.3). The fourth is a rectangular pillar of the same red sandstone again decorated with unusually deeply incised flowers. The four stones, three of which were together in a family plot, date from the same general time period, have what appears to be the name of the maker (or company) incised on the side of the base, and seem to represent a revival of folk art memorial marker carving on the Mormon frontier. The stones represent a high degree of artistic achievement, and it is disturbing that one of them disappeared form the cemetery between February and August of 1987.

While the graves in the Navajo section are individual, the Mormon section graves are often arranged in groupings based on family relationships. The plots are indicated by joint stones for husband and wife (including one which details a wife buried elsewhere and one which has a place for the death date of the wife who apparently planned later interment

Figure 8.3. Morman "Hearts and Flowers" Folk Gravestone, Ramah Cemetery, Ramah, New Mexico

(Photograph Kathryn Cunningham)

beside her husband) and by a number of multirow plots which include children and parents. As in the Navajo section, the headstones and the graves are placed so that the principal side of the stone and the head of the deceased point toward the West, and the deceased would face East if sitting or standing.

There is much more information about the deceased given on the memorial markers in the Mormon section than is included upon those in the Navajo section. Mormon markers very frequently indicate the dead's relationship to the living and occasionally give information about their lives. A few include epitaphs suggesting the possible existence of a folk verse tradition, for example: "The lightning came from the sky/ Took our dad we know not why/ So tall handsome strong and young/ His story half written his song half sung."

Approximately twenty-five miles east of the Ramah Cemetery, lying due south of the community of Zuni, is a Zuni village of the dead. It has no sign, but when asked, the Zuni call it the VanderWagen Cemetery and credit its establishment to a trader named VanderWagen who was important in their dealings with Anglo-American culture in the past (fig. 8.4). It is located on the side of a hill near the valley floor, across the road and south of the village's water storage tanks. It is surrounded by hills, one of which includes in its contours forms which Zunis, undoubtedly correctly, identify as ruins of a prehistoric village.

This is the second major cemetery of the Zuni historic period. When the Spanish missionaries came to Zuni in the sixteenth century, they brought with them the Spanish Catholic funerary tradition which viewed cemeteries as holy ground. The Zunis adopted the tradition, called *camposanto* in the Southwest,[13] and continued to so view and utilize the Mission courtyard long after the Mission had been abandoned. This system of utilizing a very limited space for burials, plus the fact that over a long period of time corpses were interred in blankets rather than coffins, meant that digging new graves often turned up old bones. The opposition of the Dutch Reform Church at Zuni to the *camposanto* system may well have been a major factor in the establishment of the VanderWagen Cemetery.

There are many more graves in the VanderWagen Cemetery than in the Ramah Cemetery. It is a Zuni belief that it is wrong to count certain kinds of objects or events, including stars and graves, and their village of the dead is the most rapidly growing of the three under discussion, so we may note only that there are somewhere between 500 and 600 graves here. The graves' decorations and memorial markers are more varied than is true of either of the major sections of the Ramah cemetery. There are the familiar military stones marking the graves of Zunis killed in each of the three whiteman's wars in which the People of the Middle Place have partici-

Figure 8.4. VanderWagen Cemetery, Zuni, New Mexico
(Photograph Kathryn Cunningham)

pated: World War II, Korea, and Vietnam. There are a few recent, obviously commercially manufactured, memorial stones and a much larger number of stones from a wide spread of time which appear to be handmade objects. Some are painted sandstone, some are shaped and incised sandstone, some are sandstone which is both painted and incised, and there is one cinder block patio paver which has been painted and pressed into service as a stepping stone from this world to the next.

One very recent stone in the cemetery is a unique object of folk art (fig. 8.5). Native sandstone was primed with a dark background color and then used as a canvas for a hauntingly beautiful painting. The painting shows a deep canyon with a figure seated at the top playing a flute while facing toward an eagle which is flying upward. The blending of iconographies in the painting is complex and fascinating. The figure is a familiar, stylized Plains Indian as portrayed in Anglo-American culture, recognizable as such by the feathers in his hair. The flute, the canyon, and the impossible background colors of the Southwest sunset are ethnographically, geographically, and climatologically accurate and Zuni (one thinks, of course, of the hump-backed flute player figure so widespread in Southwestern Native American iconography). The disproportionately large figure of the eagle draws upon images found in both Anglo-American and Native American cultures and gains significance from its bicultural meanings. The stone is a painting of power.

Simple wooden boards or slabs with names carved and/or painted upon them, and similar wooden crosses are also very common markers here. Unique to this village of the dead, however, are the number of Zuni pots on the graves. Some include death dates and serve as markers. Some are traditional designs which may be intended to function as decorations. Some may fulfill a function not readily apparent to non-Zuni observers. The Zuni graves in the VanderWagen Cemetery very often include a combination of the markers and decorations noted above and artificial flowers.

The arrangement of the Zuni village of the dead upon the land is markedly different from the plan of the Ramah Cemetery. Ramah is set upon the crest of a hill; the Zuni village of the dead, like the Zuni villages of the living, is set on the side of a hill. There are no real family plots in the VanderWagen cemetery although relatives who die at the same time may very well be buried side by side. Unlike the practices observed at the Ramah Cemetery, graves at VanderWagen are very frequently enclosed by any of a number of kinds of fences and are not in parallel lines or rows. The graves are relatively close together, and there is very little empty space in the entire cemetery. In direct opposition to the pattern seen in both the Navajo and Mormon sections of Ramah, the Zuni graves at VanderWagen are oriented so that the principal side of the stone and the head of the deceased

Figure 8.5.　Painted Zuni Gravestone, VanderWagen Cemetery, Zuni, New Mexico
(Photograph Kathryn Cunningham)

point toward the East, and the deceased would face West if sitting or standing.

Ramah Mormons and Zuni have their "ways," and they both, like the Navajo, invoke them frequently. Just as Ramah Navajo, Ramah Mormon, and Zuni funerary practices, graves, placement of graves, markers, and decorations are very different, so are the eschatologies which create them and which they image.

Freud defined religion (by which he seemed to have meant primarily a belief in immortality) as the universal obsessive-compulsive neuroses of mankind; Marx damned it as the opiate of the people; Niebuhr praised it as a citadel of hope built on the edge of despair.[14] In their traditional way the Navajo build no citadels; neither do they take opiates; nor do they believe in the future of an illusion. The Navajo are unusual in the long history of mankind in that they have no concept of personal immortality. Their eschatology affirms the mortality of man and the immortality of evil.[15] In Navajo traditional thought *ch'iidii,* a Navajo word often loosely translated into English as ghosts, are the evil which live after men, while the good is at best set free when their bones are interred. At the moment of death of a young child (Navajo ethnotheologies disagree as to the maximum age) or a very old man who has lived a blameless life and walked in the way of beauty, the good that was in them is set free to journey to the North to a vaguely defined ancestral land of shades. At the death of all other Navajos, the good that was in them which goes North is much less important or significant than their evil or disharmony. The latter becomes a *ch'iidii,* which for the People are the cause of illness and misfortune in the land of the living.

Traditionally, therefore, Navajos shun dead bodies and live much of their lives attempting to control and confuse the *ch'iidii* and the ugliness and disharmony they bring to the way of beauty and harmony. The old Navajo custom of burying jewelry with its owner is believed to aid and speed the deceased (as is the presentation of food and water), but the custom serves other uses as well. Jewelry is very important in Navajo culture. Stones speak, and no stone speaks as loudly to the Navajo as turquoise. Turquoise and bear claws have power of their own and when skillfully worked with silver to form a massive brooch, necklace, or bracelet worn by an elderly Navajo, their power becomes the wearer's, and the wearer's power becomes theirs. The jewelry (or other important possessions of the dead) may attract their *ch'iidii* and is extremely powerful in and of itself. When Navajo bury jewelry with its owner, it is buried for the living as well as for the dead.

The fact that Ramah Navajo are buried together in the Ramah Cemetery is unusual in the long run of Navajo history because of the power of the *ch´iidi.* Do changing mortuary practices indicate changing ways? Yes and no. A Manx folklorist has concluded that when the fairies on the Isle of Man encountered the Methodists, they just went away.[16] Many of the Navajos buried at the Ramah Cemetery are Mormons as well; for them in their lifetimes the *ch´iidi,* like the Manx fairies, may well have lost their power. There is, however, a story frequently recounted by both Navajos and Mormons which in general outline tells of Navajos who claim their dead were Mormon so that the Mormons will bury them and save the family from an unpleasant and possibly dangerous task. Some of these Navajos, too, undoubtedly lie at Ramah wearing uneasy crowns. All the Navajo at Ramah, furthermore, have non-Mormon relatives, acquaintances, and clansmen. Just as the old Anglo saw affirms that there are no atheists in fox holes, so for some Navajos facing death the old, deeply ingrained *ch´iidii* belief probably lies close to the bone.

The Navajos are buried in the Mormon cemetery so that they would face East if they were sitting or standing either because they are also Mormons or because their families found this orientation easy to borrow since traditional Navajo burials could face any of the traditional six directions except down (though there was some statistically discernible preference for having the head point to the North).

Death for the Navajo involves a cause. The cause is felt by Navajos to be potentially dangerous to others. Spirits of the dead, except for very young children or very old, worthy adults, are furthermore dangerous in and of themselves. It was because of this dual danger that the Navajo traditionally avoided the dead; marked graves with high mounds, a slashed saddle, a solitary pole, or broken vessels; indicated hogans in which a death had occurred by boarding up windows and doors and making an opening in the north wall; and practiced ritual cleansing for those who performed funerary rites. The opening in the north wall and the slashed saddle were to facilitate the journey northward of the good within an individual which journeys, but they also served to warn the living of the *ch´iidii* which remain. The Ramah Mormon cemetery serves Mormon and non-Mormon Ramah Navajos by concentrating danger in one well-marked, easily avoided location. Ramah Navajo graves within the Ramah Cemetery are, by and large, viewed and treated by the Navajo in the same manner as Navajo graves elsewhere.

Across the invisible line in the Ramah Cemetery come the Latter-Day Saints, for that is what in the Mormon eschatology those buried there are. The Saints, according to Mormon belief, came into this world as willing preexistent spirits both to prepare the way for others and as a part of their own individual evolutionary perfection. Here in life they participated in the Restored Priesthood and began kingdoms on earth which are eternal and ever-expanding beyond earth. Here in death they lie awaiting the Resurrection and at the same time becoming kings of infinitely expanding kingdoms. They came to earth to be men; they left earth to be gods.[17] They lie so that they would be facing East if sitting or standing, in common with many other American Christians, so that they may face Christ when he appears or so that they face the rising sun.

The kingdom of Mormon eschatology is basically a family kingdom. In Mormon eschatology a man's descendants become the inhabitants of his kingdom, and his life beyond earth builds on the accomplishments of his life on earth. The identification of the Mormons at Ramah Cemetery is most often in terms of family and thus kingdom relationships.

Stones speak, and the Mormon faithful hear and heed their voices. Precise biographical information, of the sort typically found on Mormon gravemarkers, is essential for compiling genealogies and conducting temple work. The images of Mormon temples on stones customarily indicate that the people remembered by the stones had their earthly marriages conducted or sealed in the temple pictured. Photographs remember and honor the deceased, and the record of their earthly accomplishment indicates the foundation of their kingdom.

Funerary practices serve to reinforce the message that the Saints pass through this world on their way to evolutionary perfection. The funeral's emphasis to be of good cheer and think on positive things in the face of loss asserts the essential evolutionary Mormon message: "As man is God once was; as God is man may become."[18] Mormons say you should mourn when a baby is born and rejoice when a Saint dies. Though they admit the advice is hard to follow in times of loss, they bury their dead and mark their graves in terms of their way.

For the Zuni the dance is life and death is the dance. Life is the dance: the Zuni is never more Zuni than when he participates in the great cultural rituals of his people and, masked and costumed so that he is indistinguishable from his neighbors, becomes a part of a great line which stretches from prehistory to posthistory. To serve the common good and to serve it so well that one attracts no attention to oneself but is seen as the middle person in the middle place is the traditional aim and purpose of Zuni life.[19]

The Zuni village of the dead is on the side of a hill as is the Zuni village of the living; *Kolhu/Wala:Wa,* the abode of the dead to which Zuni spirits journey, is underwater on the side of a lake. All are middle places. *Kolhu/Wala:Wa* is to the West of the Zuni cemetery, and Zuni headstones and graves are placed so that the main side of the stone and the head of the deceased point toward the East, and the deceased would face *Kolhu/Wala:Wa* if sitting or standing.

And death is the dance, too. The living serve the People according to the Zuni way and so, too, do the dead. On a simple, literal, direct level the living speak of their dead as a blessing and tell how the grief and shock of their passing improved and ennobled those they left behind. On a more ethereal plane the dead also bless the living according to the Zuni way. They dance in their spirit village, and their dance brings rain.[20]

Zuni funerary rites and practices, including offering ritually prepared food and leaving a window open at the wake, are designed to facilitate the spirit's journey to the spirit village to dance for the People for all eternity. The old Zuni custom of burying jewelry with its owner likewise serves to aid and speed the deceased on their journey; but, as with the Navajo, the custom serves other purposes as well. Jewelry is very important in Zuni culture. Much of the most elaborate and valuable of the Zunis' jewelry is worn infrequently, but it has tremendous ceremonial significance. During the great festivals and ceremonies of the People, jewelry becomes a major part of costume; masked dancers wear many pieces—their own and those loaned to them. In addition to ceremonially important jewelry, many Zunis have one or two small, dear pieces which they wear regularly. The pieces they wear and the pieces they share are, alike, a part of them. Mourning for the dead is as much a fact of life at Zuni as elsewhere, but grief is felt to be harmful and is discouraged. The deceased's possessions were buried in the past so that they would not remind the living of the loss and cause grieving.[21] When Zunis bury jewelry with its owner, it is buried for the living as well as for the dead.

The Zunis have often incorrectly been described as having a cult of the ancestors as a part of their religion because they have a ceremony of feeding the dead at regular and irregular occasions including Night Dances and Memorial Day. Although the feeding most often takes the form of burning food or placing it in or beside the Zuni River, the bowls on the graves are sometimes used for this purpose. Wherever the dead are fed, however, the emphasis in on the individual as a member of the People of the Middle Place rather than as an individual in isolation.

The Ramah Navajo is buried at the Ramah Cemetery as he lived: alone, separate, individual. The Mormon is buried at Ramah Cemetery as a family member and a future god whose descendants shall call him blessed. The Zuni in death, as in life, is in a Zuni village surrounded by his people achieving the ultimate Zuni goal of being one with them. Navajo, Mormon, Zuni graves: Navajo, Mormon, Zuni ways.

Notes

I wish to express my thanks to the Navajo, Mormon, and Zuni people for sharing their views of their graves and ways with me and to Jean Lewis Bratthauer for her special assistance.

1. Dickran and Ann Tashjian, *Memorials for Children of Change: The Art of Early New England Stonecarving* (Middletown, Conn.: Wesleyan University Press, 1974), pp. xiii-xiv.

2. See Stephen Jett and Virginia Spencer, *Navajo Architecture: Forms, History, Distributions* (Tucson: University of Arizona Press, 1981); John L. Landgraf, *Land-Use in the Ramah Area of New Mexico: An Anthropological Approach to Areal Study,* Papers of the Peabody Museum 62: 1 (Cambridge, Mass., 1954); and Ruth M. Underhill, *The Navajos* (Norman: University of Oklahoma Press, 1956).

3. See, for instance, Jett and Spencer, *Navajo Architecture;* Underhill, *Navajos;* and Leland C. Wyman, W. W. Hill, and Iva Osanai, "Navaho Eschatology," *University of New Mexico Bulletin, Anthropological Series* 4:1 (1942).

4. Landgraf, *Land-Use,* pp. 26–32.

5. See, for instance, Thomas E. Cheney, ed., *Mormon Songs from the Rocky Mountains: A Compilation of Mormon Folksong* (Salt Lake City: University of Utah Press, 1981) and Lester A. Hubbard, *Ballads and Songs from Utah* (Salt Lake City: University of Utah Press, 1961).

6. See Austin Fife and Alta Fife, *Saints of Sage and Saddle: Folklore Among the Mormons* (Salt Lake City: University of Utah Press, 1980) and Hector Lee, *The Three Nephites* (Albuquerque: University of New Mexico Press, 1949).

7. See Leonard J. Arrington and Davis Britton, *The Mormon Experience: A History of the Latter-Day Saints* (New York: Knopf, 1979); Thomas F. O'Dea, *The Mormons* (Chicago: University of Chicago Press, 1957); and B. H. Roberts, *A Comprehensive History of the Church of Jesus Christ of Latter-Day Saints.* 6 vols. (Salt Lake City: Deseret News Press, 1930).

8. Two representative examples are *The Life and Times of Joseph Fish, Mormon Pioneer,* ed. John H. Krenkel (Danville, Il.: Interstate Printers and Publishers, 1970) and Annie Clark Tanner, *A Mormon Mother: An Autobiography* (Salt Lake City: Tanner Trust Fund, University of Utah Library, 1973).

9. See William Edwin Berrett, *The Restored Church* (Salt Lake City: Deseret Book Company, 1956) and M. Lynn Bennion, *Mormonism and Education* (Salt Lake City: Deseret News Press, 1939).

10. Richard Huntington and Peter Metcalf, *Celebrations of Death: The Anthropology of Mortuary Ritual* (Cambridge: Cambridge University Press, 1979), pp. 184–212.

11. For an extensive bibliography, see C. Gregory Crampton, *The Zunis of Cibola* (Salt Lake City: University of Utah Press, 1977), pp. 161–94.

12. See, for instance, Elsie Clews Parsons, "A Few Zuni Death Beliefs and Practices," *American Anthropologist,* n.s., 18 (1916), pp. 245–56 and Matilda Coxe Stevenson, "The Zuni Indians: Their Mythology. Esoteric Fraternities, and Ceremonies," in *Twenty-Third Annual Report of the Bureau of American Ethnology, 1901–1902* (Washington: Government Printing Office, 1904), pp. 305–17.

13. See Sandra O. Cobb, "Early Las Vegas: An Interdisciplinary Approach," *El Palacio* 91 (Winter/Spring 1986), pp. 28–34.

14. See John Milton Yinger, *Religion, Society, and the Individual* (New York: Macmillan, 1957).

15. Wyman, Hill, and Osanai, "Navaho Eschatology."

16. Margaret Killip, *The Folklore of the Isle of Man* (Totowa, N. J.: Roman and Littlefield, 1976), p. 30.

17. See Berrett, *Restored Church,* pp. 544–78; Fife and Fife, *Saints of Sage and Saddle,* pp. 12–13; and O'Dea, *Mormons,* p. 128.

18. Fife and Fife, *Saints of Sage and Saddle,* p. 12.

19. See Ruth Benedict, *Patterns of Culture* (New York: Houghton Mifflin, 1934), pp. 52–119.

20. Evon Z. Vogt and Ethel M. Albert, eds., *People of Rimrock: A Study of Values in Five Cultures* (New York: Atheneum, 1970), p. 232.

21. Parsons, "Death Beliefs," pp. 252–54.

9

San Fernando Cemetery: Decorations of Love and Loss in a Mexican-American Community

Lynn Gosnell and Suzanne Gott

For many families in mourning, there exist few social rituals which provide a means for both the expression of grief and continuing love for family members. Grave decoration is one of the few widely practiced activities which offers a framework for such expression. Even when tending to a grave is primarily the responsibility of one individual, the task is usually accomplished in the name of family. When couples or families spend time decorating a grave at a cemetery this function is more apparent. Most social of all occasions are religious or locally recognized decoration days, when an entire "community of bereaved" may participate together in this ritual of remembrance and familial obligation. Through our research into contemporary grave decorating practices in San Antonio, Texas, we have come to view gravesite decoration as a highly symbolic visual process though which families continue to experience a sense of ongoing relationship with departed relatives.[1]

This study of a large Catholic cemetery serving the needs of an urban Mexican-American community focuses on the ephemeral objects that appear, disappear, and return throughout the calendar year. The various objects used in contemporary grave decoration—an array of natural and synthetic flowers, as well as homemade and commercially produced articles—are evidence of a dynamic and artful communication process based within family and community. In contrast, the permanent formal features of the cemetery, such as engraved markers and the large religious statuary depicting Catholic icons or Biblical themes, function as more static markers signifying consecrated burial ground. In our analysis, we will examine the widespread practice of grave decoration by concentrating on the material culture itself, taking care to illuminate both the social and cultural meanings assigned to and emerging from the objects at hand.

The decoration of gravesites in America, as elsewhere, is an activity influenced by religion and ethnicity, by regional geography and history, as well as by the general location of the cemetery within a rural or urban setting. In addition, many contemporary cemeteries specify the form and extent of permissible decorations for the burial site. While such regulations may reflect practical requirements of maintenance, it is likely they also reflect local attitudes about death and remembrance, and the proper visual forms for expressing these attitudes within the cemetery. In the rural Southwest, especially in communities that maintain ties with an immigrant or ethnic heritage, it is not uncommon to find grave decoration forming part of the complex of cultural identity.[2] Where the economics of perpetual care override local or individual attitudes toward death and mourning, twentieth-century urban cemeteries tend toward visual uniformity.

San Fernando Cemetery, however, is an exception to this tendency toward uniformity in urban cemeteries. Throughout the year, but especially during religious and secular holidays, including Halloween, All Souls' Day, Christmas, Valentine's Day, Easter, Mother's Day, and Father's Day, the visitor to San Fernando takes part in an energetic practice of grave decoration and visual display.[3] During these days, cars and trucks jam the narrow traffic lanes which provide access to each block of this ninety-three acre cemetery. Relatives crowd the burial grounds, bringing with them gardening tools, flowers, and other decorative materials. Vendors temporarily establish themselves across the street from the cemetery in a shopping mall parking lot. They sell fresh and artificial arrangements of all sizes and prices. Some people busily tend to a gravesite, while others take time to chat and remark on a particularly well-decorated burial site. Still others stand quietly, singly or in groups, near the grave of a loved one. Grave decorating days within San Fernando Cemetery are therefore marked by a lively social interaction between the living and a heightened interaction between families and their deceased loved ones.

Perhaps the custom of social interaction in this cemetery can best be understood by looking at the history of the surrounding Mexican-American community. This popular expression of familial devotion is firmly rooted in the particular historical context of its geographical surroundings. San Fernando Cemetery lies within the loosely defined boundaries of San Antonio's Westside, approximately a fifty-square-mile area sliced away from the city's heart by that most concrete of urban barriers, the freeway. This obvious physical separation from predominantly Anglo neighborhoods and businesses has contributed to a cultural milieu that is distinctly "mexicano," especially in terms of its expressive traditions[4]. The roots of this community's distinctive character are, of course, much older than the presence of a highway, and much deeper than mere physical isolation.

Although these roots extend back in time to San Antonio's founding as a mission settlement on the northern frontier of New Spain in 1718, much of the Westside's physical and cultural appearance is the product of immigrant movement during this century. A large population of Mexican citizens fled north across the border states as a result of the economic, political, and religious turmoil of the Mexican Revolution. This great wave of refugees joined a well-established flow of immigrants drawn to the United States for work in agricultural, railroad, and mining operations—industries that depended heavily on this temporary work force but paid little compensation. San Antonio received a large proportion of all classes of this immigrant population, with most Mexicans settling in the area west of the downtown railroad depot[5]. This settlement pattern was partly the result of compatriots seeking out one another, but was also a reflection of Anglo-American efforts to segregate the growing number of Mexican arrivals.

The physical isolation of the Westside contributed to the city's failure to provide basic city services; by the 1930s this area was characterized by substandard housing and tremendous health problems related to poor living conditions. Developing class differences, as well as those inherent among the immigrants, weakened some of the cultural homogeneity of the Westside. Some groups in more flexible economic positions—the professional, technical, and managerial Mexican workers—tended to form enclaves away from the poorest sections or to move out to other parts of the city[6]. The cultural as well as physical separation of the Westside discouraged or slowed acculturation for those who could not afford to leave the barrios. For all immigrant Mexicans, the pressure to assimilate which came from public education, the media, and contact with the wider Anglo population was offset by the steady "flow of legal and undocumented immigrants and by the fact that they [the immigrants] represented not an isolated cultural group, but the northernmost tip of an Indo-Hispanic population"[7].

Although there is religious diversity among San Antonio's Mexican Americans, this population continues to display a strong allegiance to the Catholic faith. Ever since its original settlement by Franciscan priests in the eighteenth century, San Antonio's history has been and continues to be intricately connected with its religious life. This is especially true in the Westside, where the Archdiocese of San Antonio established Our Lady of Guadalupe Church to serve the people "in the western part of the city" in 1910. Up until this time the old San Fernando Cemetery, an eleven-acre site established in the mid-nineteenth century, was one of the examples of the Catholic presence in the western area of the city[8]. Many parishes grew up to accommodate the burgeoning Spanish-speaking population and soon there was a need for more burial space. As a result, the Archdiocese purchased a vast ninety-three-acre rectangle further west of downtown for a new San Fernando Cemetery. Although the old San Fernando continued to be used for burials, the new cemetery, with its wide green expanse, tall cypress trees, and well-tended grounds, proved more inviting to most families of the Westside parishes as a place to inter their loved ones.

Accounts of burial customs from the immigration period survive in San Antonio's principal Spanish language newspaper of this period, *La Prensa*, and in the memories of some of the older residents of the Westside. Most of this information concerns the intensive grave decorating activity on November 2, All Souls' Day, the official Catholic holy day of remembrance and obligation toward the faithful departed. For example, in 1925, an article in *La Prensa* reported that a great many people visited and decorated the graves in the morning and evening. The writer observed thousands of persons of all classes traveling to the cemetery to pay tribute to family and friends buried there. The presence of a priest in the cemetery on this day was a practice documented in *La Prensa* and remembered by elderly Mexican Americans. Up until the post-war period, oral and written reports of cemetery visitation closely resemble descriptions of Mexican cemetery traditions. Many of the elderly draw a distinction between the visit to the cemetery then and now: "Before we used to arrange all the flowers and take them to the cemetery. We used to take food and a little chair and stay there the whole day."[9] In contrast to the plastic and silk artificial flowers commonly placed on gravesites today, lighted candles and paper flowers are mentioned as decorating customs from "years back," objects no longer seen in San Fernando today.

Many scholars have documented the rituals and rich material culture associated with All Saints' and All Souls' Days, or *Dias de los Muertos*, throughout the Hispanic Catholic world[10]. Studies of the Mexican *Dias de los Muertos* highlight the use of elaborate visual forms for ritual communication, an approach related to our own research. Yet, the cultural distance of these Mexican Indian celebrations from contemporary Mexican-American life within San Antonio leads us to be cautious when drawing parallels between *Dias de los Muertos* traditions and decorating practices in San Fernando Cemetery. In our research we have observed an extensive decorating practice which continues throughout the year and is not isolated to All Souls' Day, although this day is perhaps the most widely publicized traditional decoration day. We might add that these decoration days include not only the "public" religious and secular holidays, but also the "private" decoration days specific to each family, such as birthdays and death anniversaries.

In contrast to older cemetery customs centered on a single annual decoration day, today in San Fernando one finds an ongoing cycle of re-membrance that incorporates readily available commercial materials as well as fresh flowers into a variety of visual displays of devotion and con-tinuing love. These rituals of remembrance combine elements of American popular culture and holiday items such as pumpkins, Christmas trees, and Valentine's Day cards with some of the elements used in contemporary *Dias de los Muertos* celebrations in southern Mexico. Our research over the past two years suggests that grave decorating within San Fernando is a vital, continually evolving activity, stylistically related to other expressive visual forms of San Antonio's Mexican-American Westside[11]. During reli-gious and secular holidays throughout the year, family members create decorative gravesite displays as a means of continuing to incorporate the deceased within the lives of surviving family members.

In this community, the practice of family-based grave decoration de-rives significance from its position within a larger complex of domestically based traditions found in the Westside, and in other areas in the United States where there are large concentrations of a Mexican American popula-tion[12]. In his study of folksongs of the border, Americo Paredes locates the "truly complete folklore performances" within the "intimate and extended family situations ..." of Mexican-American gatherings[13]. More recently, folklorists studying the folk art forms of San Antonio have asserted that "the family functions as the social group essential to the maintenance and trans-mission of all forms of Mexican-American traditional culture"[14].

Although it is mostly Mexican-American families from Westside par-ishes who use this cemetery, other ethnic groups with ties to the Catholic church also bury their family members here. San Fernando is predomi-nantly, but not exclusively, a Mexican-American cemetery, since within its gates one finds a number of Polish, German, Belgian, and Lebanese gravesites. Each parish once had its own burial area within the larger grounds of San Fernando, and in the older section there are rows of grave-stones with engraved names of other immigrant groups. We believe that the similarities between the decoration of the relatively small percentage of these gravesites with Mexican-American family graves can be understood as a pleasing and powerful community aesthetic structuring the practice of other Catholic families. Grave decoration in this cemetery is not the exclu-sive practice of a working class population, although the demographics of the Westside would certainly suggest that most of the families using this cemetery are either working or middle class. On decoration days, pick-up trucks as well as small foreign cars line up for a convenient parking place in a community practice of care and remembrance (fig. 9.1). If the people who now decorate gravesites do not live in the Westside, then it is likely their parents, grandparents, or in-laws still live there. In any case, their ties

Figure 9.1. San Fernando Cemetery, San Antonio, Texas
Cars line the cemetery's roadway on various decoration days throughout the year.
(Photograph Suzanne Gott)

to this area of rich Mexican-American cultural practices still continue, even if these ties now stretch as far as Northwest or Southside of the city or extend to the tops of highrise office buildings or the depths of corporate board rooms.

The grave decorations in San Fernando Cemetery are characterized by a strong preference for color and decorative patterning, the incorporation of personal written messages within the overall gravesite decoration, a dynamic use of mass-produced items, and the placement of conventional holiday decorations on the gravesite. The vibrancy of color apparent in both individual gravesites and in the cemetery as a whole is one of the most striking features during periods of intense decorating activity. Studies of other Texas Mexican cemeteries have remarked on this distinctive preference for colorful decorations[15]. This use of color is most obvious in the placement of bouquets of fresh or artificial flowers on the ground in front of the marker. The flower containers are often gallon-sized cans covered with shiny foil and weighted down with rocks. Large floral arrangements and wreaths or *coronas* are also popular. Sometimes the entire rectangular gravesite will be covered with a variety of floral arrangements and other decorative items, making the overall colorful hue of the cemetery change with each occasion. Thus, during the three-day decorating complex of Halloween, All Saints' Day, and All Souls' Day, from October 31 to November 2, San Fernando is marked by the orange of marigolds, a popular autumn flower as well as one traditionally associated with *Dias de los Muertos* observances. On Christmas the cemetery fairly sparkles with glittery silver and red tinsel. On Valentine's Day bright red hearts boldly accent individual gravesites, while one may observe a more subdued preference for pastel decorations and for white lilies on Easter.

The preference for orderly patterning is evident in the simplest as well as in the most elaborately decorated sites, as exemplified by the bilateral placement of flowers on either side of the gravestone. A common arrangement consists of the placement of fresh or artificial flowers in a row against the front of the marker or in a row down the middle of gravesite. It is not uncommon to see a group of five or six identical containers of flowers or upright wreaths arranged in this way (fig. 9.2). On many graves multiple containers of flowers form a geometric pattern on the burial surface. Still another common pattern is the arrangement of individual flowers or containers of flowers in the shape of a cross. This type of decoration is one of the more overtly religious that we have seen in the cemetery. The unmarked rectangular boundary of the gravesite may be outlined with ribbons, tinsel, or other materials. Like other types of decorations which we have observed, this patterning calls attention to the individual burial site, as well as enclosing the space in which memories are invoked. Some "ar-

Figure 9.2. Flower Wreaths in a Row
Floral arrangements are usually placed on gravesites in carefully ordered patterns.
(Photograph Lynn Gosnell)

rangements" may consist of only a single flower, decorative item, or container of flowers. Although lacking in complexity, such simple expressions of devotion are often quite poignant and serve as powerful images.

The incorporation of a variety of mass-produced paper, plastic, or styrofoam items into the gravesite decoration is another common practice. Brightly colored mylar balloons continue to be a popular item in the cemetery, on adults' as well as children's graves. Typically, a single helium-filled balloon anchored to the burial space or gravemarker can be seen bobbing and twisting in the wind. In addition to being intrinsically one of the more visually dynamic decorative items, these balloons often display personalized messages, picture cartoon characters, or contain some holiday greeting such as "Happy Easter" or "Happy Mother's Day." On Valentine's Day we also observed the frequent use of large red, heart-shaped mylar balloons. Large balloon hearts with smiling faces or those with extended inflated arms bearing messages such as "I LUV YOU SO-O-O MUCH" embody even more direct and personal communications to deceased loved ones (fig. 9.3). Items commonly associated with front yard display in the Westside may also be used for grave decorations. As with the mylar balloons, many of these objects, such as plastic whirligigs or foil pinwheels, incorporate movement into the burial space. One elaborate effort on Valentine's Day included a windsock hung from a tree branch above the gravesite. In addition, these moving objects may be placed in patterns outlining the edge of a grave or in a row down the middle of the burial site.

In a cemetery as large as San Fernando, where most gravestones are nearly identical in appearance, there is a strong tendency toward other means of personalizing the gravesite. One way this is accomplished is through affixing an enameled photograph of the deceased onto the stone marker. This custom of incorporating a visual image of the deceased within the burial space is an ancient one in Christianity[16]. The use of photography for this purpose is fairly recent and yet is common in the Southwest region of the United States. We have also observed the semipermanent placement of wooden crosses, with the name of the deceased carved or burnt into the wood, and set deep into the ground in front of the stone marker. On one occasion we noted the temporary placement of a homemade wooden cross which displayed family photographs of the deceased as well as an image of the Virgin of Guadalupe placed on a gravesite. Placing the name of the individual on ephemeral grave decorations draws special attention to the personal identity of the individual who is buried there. In addition to the ready-made decorations used in personalizing gravesites, large handmade signs bearing the name of the deceased may face outward from the grave. Such outwardly directed displays direct a heightened subjective presence of the deceased toward viewers passing by. Through the creation of these

Figure 9.3.   Valentine's Day Decorations
Brightly colored balloons and favorite indulgences of the deceased, such as a can
of beer, embody directly personal communications of love.
(Photograph Suzanne Gott)

highly visible and colorful signs, family members project vibrant evidence of the continuing presence of their departed loved ones in the world of the living.

The combination of color, pattern, and decorative images used to personalize the gravesite exemplifies the visual aesthetic present in the "everyday arts" of the Westside. In a recent study of artistic expression in San Antonio's Westside, Kay Turner and Pat Jasper characterize this aesthetic as one of "bold display; images, objects, and ornamentation are not absorbed into environments, but rather, they are pushed forward to catch the eye and to carry meaning."[17] Although grave decoration differs from the everyday visual expressions in the home, street, and yard, the periodic decoration days of San Fernando Cemetery provide another framework for expression of this visual style.

Within the personalized and often highly decorated space of the gravesite, there are a variety of communications directed toward the deceased. The most obvious communicative forms are handwritten greetings addressed to departed family members. These expressions are frequently written on enclosure cards prominently displayed in floral arrangements and contain such messages as "To our beloved grandmother with much love" or "To my Daddy whom I love very much" (fig. 9.4). Cards hidden from public view within envelopes suggest an even more private communication with the deceased. Notes may also be taped onto or tucked beside the headstone, as was one message we observed written in ballpoint ink on yellow notebook paper which contained the simple inscription, "I [heart picture] U." Standing wreaths or *coronas*, purchased at nearby vending stands or florist shops, almost always have greetings to the deceased printed or written in glitter or ink on the center. These standardized, commercially produced decorative materials are thus transformed into more personal expressions of greetings and love. The use of mass-produced signs with messages such as "Happy Mother's Day," or "Happy Birthday," are examples of conventional holiday greetings between the living, which are used more boldly in San Fernando Cemetery as communicative devices directed toward the deceased (fig. 9.5). Balloons with commercially printed holiday greetings may also be augmented with more personal messages written by family members with felt-tip markers. An even more directly personal gravesite communication which we witnessed featured a mylar balloon shaped like a big pair of red lips and bore the words "A Kiss for You!"

Messages in the form of handwritten notes, commercially produced greetings, or the smiles, hugs, and kisses offered by animated balloons are all communications of love directed toward deceased family members. In addition to these explicit forms of communication, objects may be placed on gravesites to express a sense of attendant interaction with the departed

Figure 9.4.   Communication with the Deceased
Handwritten messages are often tucked into floral arrangements.
(Photograph Lynn Gosnell)

Figure 9.5. Birthday Greetings
Commercially available signs are an important communicative element in
gravesite decorations.
(Photograph Suzanne Gott)

loved ones. Several graves exhibited decorating customs with roots in Mexican cemetery and altar traditions. Thus, the placement of an opened or unopened can of beer (usually next to more conventional decorations) was observed on several men's gravesites. Although food is rarely placed on graves in this cemetery, on Valentine's Day one family did leave a large bowl of food, a few cigarettes, and some coins on the grave of an elderly man. One woman told us that her son's part of grave decorating is bringing his grandfather's favorite hard candy to put on the grave. On various occasions throughout the year, we have seen candy placed on children's graves or even secured to gravemarkers with tape. Miniature toys, tea sets, or wrapped presents attest to the special consideration given to children's graves in San Fernando. Another interesting difference between children's and adults' graves is the frequent placement of large animated balloon figures such as smiling hearts or inflated rabbits facing *inward* toward the headstone rather than *outward* toward the visitor, indicting a particularly solicitous attention being directed toward the deceased child.

It is in the use of holiday imagery, suggesting a particular desire to include deceased family members within major holiday observances, that we see the most elaborate visual expressions of ongoing communication. Many decorative displays include various items, both homemade or ready-made, which are associated with particular holiday observances (fig. 9.6). Thus, real and plastic pumpkins add to the orange hue of the cemetery in November, miniature Christmas trees are common features in December, and, of course, hearts are prevalent on Valentine's Day. During Easter, the rectangular space in front of the stone bearing the deceased's name may contain plastic colored eggs, an Easter basket with chicks, or a styrofoam cut-out rabbit. Spring is also the time of San Antonio's annual Fiesta (a ten-day civic celebration in honor of Texas's independence from Mexico); and during the 1987 fiesta we observed a few graves with the popular confetti eggs broken on top of the stones. On Mother's and Father's Day there is less visual unity, but perhaps more use of balloons and greeting cards. Bright mylar balloons expressing holiday greetings are actually popular throughout the year. Dime store pictures of Halloween witches, or commercial greeting cards of all sorts are often worked into the grave decoration. In some of the newer cemetery blocks there is also a trend toward highly elaborate holiday decoration, in which the rectangular space in front of the gravemarker is cleared of all grass and then covered with a flamboyant array of decorative materials (fig. 9.7). This style of grave decoration is sporadic throughout the cemetery, but in one block in particular elaborate decorations are the rule rather than the exception.

The observance of major holidays in the cemetery allows families to observe, evaluate, and borrow decorating ideas from each other. One

Figure 9.6.　Holiday Decorations

Family members continue to include the deceased in the celebrations of the living through placing holiday items on gravesites.

(Photograph Suzanne Gott)

Figure 9.7. One of the Newer Blocks of San Fernando Cemetery
Highly elaborate gravesite decorations are a common sight in some of the newer
sections.
(Photograph Lynn Gosnell)

widow admired the homemade cross placed on a nearby gravesite and decided to find one for her husband's grave. Another woman stated that several decorators in a block had picked up ideas from observing an especially well-cared-for and decorated grave of a young man.

Children's graves, which tend to be grouped in one block together, receive particular attention on holidays. A special effort is made to provide the deceased child with holiday objects enjoyed by living children. On Halloween through All Souls' Day (October 31 through November 2) jack-o'-lanterns are the rule rather than the exception. On Easter, one sees large inflated rabbits on the graves. Some sites display carefully patterned arrangements of the traditional contents of an Easter basket, including small toy chicks and rabbits, real and candy Easter eggs. At Christmas, wrapped presents and tiny decorated trees are particularly poignant grave decorations.

In our description of the many shapes and forms of grave decoration at San Fernando cemetery, we have tried to suggest that one can observe in these ongoing practices an aesthetic style though which the bereaved express continuing affection and remembrance for deceased family members. Within the fluid boundaries of this stylistic framework, there is a great deal of individual choice and preference. For example, one does not merely place fresh flowers on the grave; one *chooses* fresh flowers over artificial. Similarly, one may prefer to artfully outline the grave with flowers rather than place all the decorative materials in the middle of the gravesite. This stated preference for one kind of patterning over another is common, although many grave decorations simply combine a variety of styles and imagery. As can be observed in front yard displays (another form of public yet personal visual composition) gravesite decorations embody their makers' creativity and project this creativity outward[18]. Economic, as well as aesthetic, factors figure strongly in people's preferences, and many family members state that artificial flowers are best because they last so much longer, thus extending the period of holiday wishes. In a similar manner, some people draw a distinction between "homemade and store-bought" decorations. It is not uncommon to find the sentiment that homemade is better, although the combination of both kinds of decorations is almost universal in San Fernando, and some gravesites contain only commercially purchased items. One woman stated that she makes Christmas ornaments for her mother's grave every year, in addition to placing two miniature artificial trees on the gravesite. Another woman whose extended family creates elaborate decorations on her deceased mother's grave expressed her preference for the homemade this way: "We usually make [the decorations] ourselves. To us it seems more personal, we're doing something for her. Now she's gone, right? We're still doing things for her."[19] Some people clearly prefer a more subdued gravesite decoration, while others think that the nontraditional materials in the cemetery are "a lot of fun." In some cases the choice to decorate or not may in fact be dictated by the deceased person's stated wishes while living. One woman was charged by her mother, "When I die you bring me flowers."

Within San Fernando Cemetery, the general style and popularity of gravesite decoration has been influenced by Mexican Catholic All Souls' Day traditions. However, grave decorating in this urban, Mexican-American cemetery has also been expanded and transformed into a vital, continually evolving activity distinctive in both its year-round practice and in its active incorporation of contemporary mass-produced forms. This practice is distinctive for its public, yet highly personal, expression of an aesthetic style present in the Westside, as well as for the emotionally meaningful framework decorating activity provides for directing communications of love toward the deceased. Therefore, while grave decorating in this particular cemetery is a more intensive and elaborate practice than is found in many contemporary American cemeteries, decorative displays within San Fernando can be understood as more highly marked examples of the widely practiced, yet extremely variable, activity of gravesite decoration as communicative practice.

For bereaved families with loved ones buried in San Fernando Cemetery, the grave decorating process provides one means of continuing to incorporate deceased family members within their ongoing lives. Through the use of holiday items and the inclusion of written messages and other means of communicative and attendant interaction, gravesite decorations provide dynamic, artful displays of remembrance and continuing love. While the flowers, objects, and decorative patterning used in gravesite displays within San Fernando Cemetery are communicative devices primarily directed toward the deceased, these decorations also face outward from the gravesite, directing a heightened and enlivened visual and verbal presence toward viewers passing by. This creation of highly visible, colorful grave decorations by grieving families therefore projects vibrant evidence of the continuing presence of departed loved ones in the world of the living as well as in the hearts of their family.

Notes

1. We would like to thank Richard Flores, Suzanne Seriff, and Kay Turner, and especially our teacher and advisor M. Jane Young for providing us with helpful insights during our research at San Fernando Cemetery and for commenting on various drafts of this paper. We would also like to thank Mr. Ernest Linares, Superintendent of Cemeteries for the Archdiocese of San Antonio, for providing us with pertinent facts on the history and operation of this cemetery.

2. The following (mostly journal-length) studies explore ethnic grave decoration in Texas: Sara Clark, "The Decoration of Graves in Central Texas with Seashells," *Diamond Bessie and the Shepherds,* ed. Wilson M. Hudson. Publications of the Texas Folklore Society 36 (Austin: Encino Press, 1972), pp. 33–43; Terry Jordan, *Texas Graveyards: A Cultural Legacy* (Austin: University of Texas Press, 1982); Beverly Kremenak-Pecotte, "At Rest: Folk Art in Texas Cemeteries," *Folk Art in Texas,* ed. Francis Edward Abernethy. Publications of the Texas Folklore Society 45 (Dallas: Southern Methodist University Press, 1985), pp. 52–63; John O. West, "Folk Grave Decoration along the Rio Grande," *Folk Art in Texas,* pp. 46–51.

3. Holidays that are noted for being "decoration days" in other parts of the country, Memorial Day and Veterans' Day, are not so intensively marked in San Fernando Cemetery as these secular and religious holidays.

4. See Suzanne Seriff and José Limón, "Bits and Pieces: The Mexican American Folk Aesthetic," *Arte Entre Nosotros/Art among Us,* ed. Kay Turner and Pat Jasper (San Antonio: San Antonio Museum Association, 1986), pp. 40–49, and Ricardo Romo, "An Insider's View of the Westside," *Arte Entre Nosotros/Art among Us,* pp. 50–59.

5. For an excellent general treatment of this period see Rodolfo Acuña, *Occupied America* (San Francisco: Canfield Press, 1972), esp. pp. 123–52, and David J. Weber, ed., *Foreigners in Their Native Land: Historical Roots of the Mexican American* (Albuquerque: University of New Mexico Press, 1973), esp. pp. 204–64. More recently, David Montejano's *Anglos and Mexicans in the Making of Texas, 1836–1986* (Austin: University of Texas Press, 1987) examines the political, historical, and economic frameworks that have shaped the relations of these two cultural groups.

6. Richard A. Garcia, "Class, Consciousness, and Ideology—the Mexican Community of San Antonio, Texas: 1930–1940," *Atzlan* 9 (1979), p. 31.

7. Ibid., p. 37.

8. Matthew James Gilbert, comp. and ed., *The Archdiocese of San Antonio: 1874–1949* (Archdiocese of San Antonio, 1949), p. 202.

9. Tape-recorded interview with MM by Lynn Gosnell, November 1985.

10. For discussions of the rituals practiced in Mexico, and in particular the city of Oaxaca, see Frances Toor, *A Treasury of Mexican Folkways* (New York: Bonanza Books, 1985); Robert V. Childs and Patricia B. Altman, *Vive tu Recuerdo: Living Traditions in the Mexican Days of the Dead,* Monograph Series 17 (Los Angeles: Museum of Cultural History, 1982); Judith Stroup Green, *Laughing Souls: The Days of the Dead in Oaxaca, Mexico,* Popular Series 1 (San Diego: Museum of Man, 1969); and Suzanne Seriff, *Laughing Death: A Critical Analysis of the Days of the Dead Celebration in Oaxaca, Mexico* (M.A. Thesis, University of Texas, 1984). Cf. James Griffith, *Respect and Continuity: The Arts of Death in a Border Community* (Nogales, Ariz.: Primera Alta Historical Society, 1985) for a view of All Souls' Day celebrations among Mexicans and Mexican Americans who share a border.

11. For a compelling argument stressing the need to emphasize cultural context in the presentation of "folk art" in the museum, see Kay Turner and Pat Jasper, "La Casa, La Calle y La Esquina: A Look at the Art among Us," *Arte Entre Nosotros/Art among Us,* ed. Kay Turner and Pat Jasper (San Antonio: San Antonio Museum Association, 1986), pp. 10–39. Also see Kay Turner, "Mexican-American Home Altars: Towards Their Interpre-

tation" *Atzlan* 13 (1982), pp. 309–26, and Seriff and Limón, "Bits and Pieces: The Mexican-American Folk Aesthetic," pp. 40–49.

12. Lynn Gosnell, *Grave Decorations in San Fernando Cemetery: Communicative Process and Aesthetic Form in San Antonio's Westside.* (M.A. Thesis, University of Texas, 1988.)

13. Americo Paredes, *A Texas Mexican Cancionero* (Urbana: University of Illinois Press, 1976), p. xxiv.

14. Turner and Jasper, "La Casa, La Calle y La Esquina: A Look at the Art among Us," p. 38.

15. Cf. Clark, "The Decoration of Graves in Central Texas with Seashells," and Jordan, *Texas Graveyards.*

16. Philippe Ariès states that the identity of the deceased was preserved in stone sarcophagi in ancient Rome during the fifth century. See his *Western Attitudes toward Death* (Baltimore: Johns Hopkins University Press, 1974), p. 8.

17. See Suzanne Gott, *"Affective Display": The Evocation of Emotional Experience through Foregrounded Visual Presentation* (M.A. Thesis, University of Texas, 1987).

18. Turner and Jasper, "La Casa, La Calle y La Esquina: A Look at the Art among Us," p. 18.

19. Tape-recorded interview with MM by Lynn Gosnell, November 1987.

10

Western Pennsylvania Cemeteries in Transition: A Model for Subregional Analysis

Thomas J. Hannon

This essay is the result of a long-term research project which has made intensive use of the cemetery landscape to reconstruct an aspect of the cultural history of the western one-third of the Commonwealth of Pennsylvania. It seems probable that the evolution of the cemetery and its transitional processes in that region are not markedly different from such processes elsewhere, except perhaps in terms of chronology or highly individualized regional nuances. Therefore, I am hopeful that the method employed here might present itself as a model which, with appropriate adaptation and modification, can be replicated anywhere in the United States.

David Sopher has referred to the cemetery as a formal positive expression of religion on the land. [1] That appraisal seems a valid one not only for cemeteries where religious affiliation is clear but also for those of a nonsectarian character. Further, the cemetery is a cultural landscape that, more than any other, represents the totality of the locale or region in which it is located. It is, as Richard Francaviglia has noted, an evolving cultural landscape. [2] The long-term perception that the cemetery is sacred or semi-sacred land has meant, in general, that it has avoided the disturbances which have so dramatically altered the landscape of the living.

The cemetery and the artifacts it contains are especially vital for the scholar engaged in regional study in Pennsylvania, given the fact that the Commonwealth has virtually no organized vital statistical records for the long period of settlement preceding 1893. These sites provide intact significant portions of the cultural-historical record needed by the researcher who is attempting to get at the roots of the characteristics of a region, or who desires to explain the transitions through which cultural regions have passed.

Western Pennsylvania, as defined here, includes the bulk of the Appalachian (or Allegheny) Plateau located in the western one-third of the Commonwealth (fig. 10.1). Although the southwestern portion of the study area, including Pittsburgh, was settled by people of white European extraction prior to 1775, as were a few localities in the southeast, the vast bulk of the region was not inhabited by people of European heritage until 1790 or later. The northeastern section adjacent to the New York border was not occupied by other than native Americans on a permanent basis until approximately 1820.[3] With the exception of Pittsburgh and the area immediately surrounding it, the entire region had an essentially frontier character until at least the 1830s. Indeed, a sizeable portion of the northeast still maintains a flavor of remoteness and is included in the Allegheny National Forest, with only a few small and scattered settlements found within its boundaries.

Despite early efforts by government and private individuals to grant free or low-cost land to former military personnel of the Revolutionary War and others interested in establishing homes in the region, settlement here was quite slow, even though Indian problems were largely resolved by the middle 1790s. The noted frontier historian Ray Billington has referred to this area as an eddy (or backwater) in the movement of settlers to the West in that it did not lie along the main routes of western migration, but served rather as a spillover for those moving across the natural corridor of New York or for those from eastern Pennsylvania who were using the Ohio valley.[4] Most of this spillover came originally from the latter group, those from southeastern Pennsylvania traveling through the Pittsburgh area and down the Ohio River. A secondary influx from New York State, representing New York and New England origins, was relatively minor in comparison, and confined itself largely to the north, including the areas surrounding present-day Erie and Meadville (fig. 10.2).

The bulk of the area, especially the southern two-thirds or more, was dominated ethnically by Scots-Irish frontiersmen, followed both numerically and chronologically by settlers of English and German heritage. That the Scots-Irish dominated through the first half of the nineteenth century is well illustrated in the number of Presbyterian churches found in the region in 1850. At this time, only Philadelphia County in Pennsylvania and two others—Hamilton County in Ohio and Washington County in New York—displayed densities of Presbyterian churches equal to or greater than the counties found within the study area of western Pennsylvania, and these were not contiguous with counties of equal density, as was the case here.[5]

Further evidence of the ethnic character of the region in the formative decades of settlement is found by examining a sampling of surnames taken from tombstones predating 1831 in sixty-four cemeteries in the region and

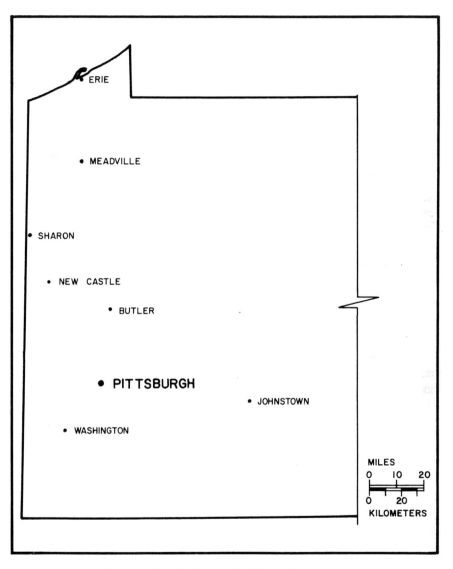

Figure 10.1.   The Study Area: Western Pennsylvania
(Diagram by Thomas J. Hannon)

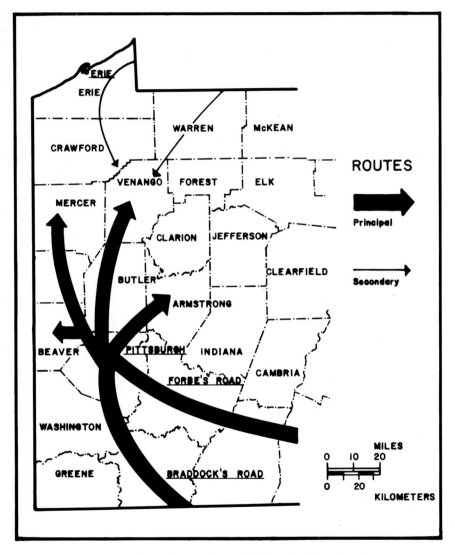

Figure 10.2.   Routes of Migration into Western Pennsylvania
(Diagram by Thomas J. Hannon)

comparing them against several surname lexicons. The precedent for this was established in 1932, when a committee of the American Council of Learned Societies made an attempt to reconstruct the ethnic character of the United States as it was in 1790 by analyzing surnames from the first Unites States Census. The committee compiled a list of the most commonly used surnames in 1863 in the United Kingdom (England, Scotland, Wales and Ulster), the present Republic of Ireland, and Germany, as well as a few additional countries which contributed small percentages to the ethnic mosaic of the United States. Names were analyzed in terms of ethnic origins and the technique was applied to the census of 1790. In addition, a list of what the committee referred to as "distinctive" names was compiled. These names, ten in total, had not been altered by generations and had not spread significantly to other countries before being carried to the United States by immigrants. The listing of "distinctive" names follows in the order presented by the committee:

1. Black	6. Cunningham
2. Blair	7. Maxwell
3. Boyd	8. McDougal
4. Campbell	9. Ross
5. Craig	10. Buchanan

An additional alphabetical listing of twenty-three names having origins in Scotland or Northern Ireland (Scots-Irish) that were common in western Pennsylvania in the early decades of white settlement follows:[6]

Anderson	Martin
Bell	Miller
Brown	Morrison
Clark	Patterson
Davidson	Robertson
Graham	Smith
Grant	Stewart
Gordon	Thompson
Hamilton	White
Hunter	Wilson
Johnston	Young
Kerr	

My own fieldwork in the sixty-four oldest cemeteries within the central portion of the area under study has verified the existence on gravemarkers of all the names appearing on these two lists. The stones bearing these names all predate 1831, a cutoff selected somewhat arbitrarily as the approximate end of the frontier period for much of the study area. I have compared this same group of names with modern era (1980s) telephone directories representing five urban communities in the area to determine the percentage they represent in the cumulative total of names in each community. Though by no means conclusive, this comparison provides some measure of the region's ethnic linkages with its past. The communities chosen were Butler, Erie, Meadville, New Kensington (a community on Pittsburgh's northeastern urban fringe), and Washington. These communities are well centralized on a line from north to south through the more densely populated portion of the study area, and, I feel, represent well the character of the region in ethnic terms. The results of this investigation follow:[7]

Community	Total Names in Phone Book	Cumulative of 33 Names Listed	33 Names as % of Total
Butler	43,488	1,656	3.5
Erie	100,104	3,748	3.7
Meadville	25,500	1,495	5.9
New Kensington	8,370	640	7.6
Washington	21,730	1,210	5.6

The same sources indicate that "Mc" prefixed surnames (excepting McDougal, which is on the first list), a strong indicator of Scottish or Scots-Irish tradition, represent rounded percentages of 4 percent for Butler, 2 percent for Erie, 2 percent for Meadville, 4 percent for New Kensington, and 3 percent for Washington.

It must be remembered that only thirty-three names, plus all "Mc" prefixed names, were used for this analysis; therefore, it is likely that the actual percentage of people of Scottish or Scots-Irish ancestry residing in the region today is actually much higher—most probably in the neighborhood of 10 to 15 percent of the total population. That estimate indicates that a surprisingly high percentage of the region's people claim Scottish or Scots-Irish heritage, despite the fact that the economic traditions of coal mining, oil production, steel, and other heavy manufacturing enterprises that followed the initial agricultural period attracted several ethnic groups from central, southern, and eastern Europe. These came in large numbers beginning in the last quarter of the nineteenth century. The picture in the modern era may be skewed a bit by the fact that some people of Eastern European descent Americanized their surnames and may have selected shortened names from among those found on the surname lists discussed previously.

In addition to surnames, cemeteries in the study area provide a lexicon of given names which may be reflective of ethnic and/or regional preferences through time. (Whatever the reason, it is clear that the choice of names given to children has undergone significant change in the past several hundred years.) Two cemeteries in the central part of the study area— Wolf Creek, approximately twenty-five miles northwest of Butler, and White Oak Springs, about eight miles southwest of that city—were chosen for specific investigation. Both are adjacent to active Presbyterian churches and both are old by the standards of the region. Wolf Creek's congregation was organized in 1807, while White Oak Springs was founded in 1815. In both cases, and clearly in most cases in western Pennsylvania, the cemetery predated the organization of the congregation, indicating a more immediate and practical need for a burial ground than for a church in the frontier period of settlement.

All given names were taken from readable tombstones through 1840 in each cemetery. Birth dates were used rather than dates of death. A few births were as early as the mid-1700s, indicating natality elsewhere (usually in the British Isles or southeastern Pennsylvania, since the earliest settlements in the vicinity of the churches named were made after 1790). The seven most popular male names and female names have been identified as follows and appear in order of total cumulative occurrence in both cemeteries:[8]

MEN

Name	Wolf Creek	White Oak Springs	Total
John	29	13	42
William	7	15	22
James	9	6	15
Thomas	12	2	14
Alexander	7	6	13
Robert	4	9	13
George	2	7	9
	70	58	128

WOMEN

Name	Wolf Creek	White Oak Springs	Total
Mary	20	10	30
Margaret	7	12	19
Jane	9	9	18
Elizabeth	12	5	17
Nancy	6	10	16
Sarah	5	7	12
Isabel(la)	2	5	7
	61	58	119

The total number of male burials in these two cemeteries for the period through 1840 was 202, while the total for females was 205. Therefore, the male names listed above accounted for more than 63 percent of the total names, while the female names listed accounted for 58 percent. One can infer the influence of the Bible here, especially the New Testament, in the time period considered in this analysis. Not listed because their numbers are relatively few are Biblical names that are rarely used today, names such as Abraham, Enos, Ezekiel, and Mordecai for males, and Eliza, Esther, and Rachel for females. Information gleaned from one area hospital indicates that Christopher, Michael, Jennifer, and Michelle presently enjoy great popularity as given names for newborns in a portion of western Pennsylvania.[9] None of these names are found on the lists of the two cemeteries cited previously, and, by the same token, a number of those which were once popular are rarely seen at all today in the area. Though the sampling presented here is small, it is intended to suggest the importance of the cemetery as a handy data base for inquiry into changing given name patterns.

The earliest burial places of the western Pennsylvania frontier are probably not unlike those of any other frontier in American history. Since remoteness and great distance between settlements of any sort was the norm in the early years of settlement, the isolated grave found along country roads or in the middle of the forest is not an uncommon feature, indicating, perhaps, that male family members were sent ahead from settlements in the east to clear the land for the family who would follow. The deceased was buried at or near the place of death and the grave marked in a crude manner. One can only speculate that the family's plans to settle nearby frequently did not materialize; however, a few isolated single burial places are marked by relatively elaborate (though often now tipped or broken) markers, indicating that someone long ago took pains to mark the grave in a respectable manner.

The first transition of any consequence that could be referred to as a cemetery or graveyard is the family burial ground. In the era before towns developed or church-related cemeteries were initiated, the family chose a burial place in a corner of the farmstead. In many cases the farm is now abandoned, the land turned over to strip mining or to some other endeavor in the sequence of occupancy, and the remaining cemetery, in overgrown condition, stands as mute evidence of what used to be.

Churches and adjacent cemeteries appeared in the Pittsburgh area and south and east of that community by the late colonial period. In the vast area north of Pittsburgh, however, church-related cemeteries did not initially appear until the late 1790s. As indicated previously, the church often postdated the cemetery with which it became associated. The morphology (i.e., physical form and structure) of the church cemetery is similar to the family burial ground in that the grid arrangement of European and coastal colonial cemeteries was adhered to on the frontier and continued to be the plan for new cemeteries in the area through the Civil War period (fig. 10.3). After the Civil War, especially in the 1870s, a new morphology came into vogue and most notably influenced the community, nonsectarian cemetery. This innovation, an outgrowth of the "Rural Cemetery" movement, will be discussed later.

With respect to specific location of cemeteries, whether of the family, church-related or community, nonsectarian type, the hilltop has been the clearly preferred site. One suggestion for the origin of this preference has been that is is related to a practice taken from the British Isles and transplanted here. Though it may also be argued that such selection represents a function of the undulating terrain of the region, my own observations made throughout the Northeast indicate a preference for the highest or next-to-highest elevation in local relief for cemetery location in the vast majority of areas, including those where flood threat is minimal. Joe T. Darden, in a study of the cemeteries of Pittsburgh, indicates that the phenomenon of high elevation has been a factor since the location of the first cemetery there.[10] Further, in an earlier study of Pittsburgh's cemeteries, C. W. Elkin has suggested that it had been the custom of the French, the Indians, and the English to bury their dead in elevated ground.[11]. A traditional explanation for this phenomenon is to see the preference for the hilltop site as a visible instance of our perception that a higher elevation is closer to heaven. However, from a more practical perspective it might also be noted that historically the hilltop often presented the least viable land economically—especially in a period when farming was the mainstay. My

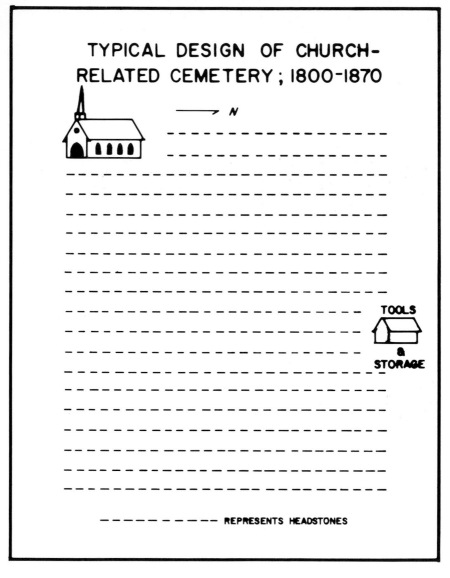

Figure 10.3.   The Grid Plan Cemetery
(Diagram by Thomas J. Hannon)

own observations in western and central Europe would seem to suggest little influence from that source, as none of the cemeteries which I examined there occupy the highest or next-to-highest elevations in local relief.[12] In addition, several topographic maps from widely scattered locales of France and northern Germany confirm that the cemetery is located in accord with the main pattern of settlement rather than in an isolated position on the highest elevation in local relief.[13] Although this is difficult to verify, the American colonists may actually have copied the hilltop site from the Indians and the idea then diffused to the frontier as it advanced westward. Despite the problem of ascertaining origins, the phenomenon itself is a clearly evident regional trait: my examination of fifty cemeteries in portions of six centralized counties in the study area immediately north of Pittsburgh has found that forty-one of them occupy the highest or second highest elevation in local relief.[14]

Closely related to the topic of site from the perspective of cultural geography is tombstone orientation. As the hilltop site has taken on a traditional element of the sacred with respect to land, the direction of the face of tombstones has done so with respect to artifact. In a pattern sustained by centuries of practice, deceased persons have traditionally been interred with their feet oriented in an easterly direction. Indeed, tombstone orientation is toward the east in forty-nine of the fifty cemeteries within the present study area. In addition, my investigation of cemeteries throughout the Commonwealth of Pennsylvania and the Northeast in general indicates that tombstone orientation is toward the east in the vast majority of instances. The exceptions to this rule are made in the "Rural Cemetery" movement of the 1870s in western Pennsylvania (and much earlier in the easter quarter of the Commonwealth), and the commemoral development of recent decades. The sacred is inherent in this practice, owing to the Christian belief that Christ will appear in the east on the last day and the dead will rise to face His countenance. An explanation that is somewhat more down-to-earth is that the forces of weathering are least severe from the east in these latitudes, thereby making an easterly orientation a wise choice if tombstone longevity is desired.

The earliest gravestones in Western Pennsylvania were often crudely cut, and the lettering was indicative of a very low level of literacy. This, of course, is as one might expect of the frontier, where schools were scattered and relatively few farmers placed a premium on education. It is not uncommon, therefore, to find gross spelling errors on markers up to about 1840 (fig. 10.4). After that date a more literate cadre of engravers had evolved in the area and errors are rarely found on stones from the middle 1800s onward.

Early markers were made of indigenous sandstone and appear as very

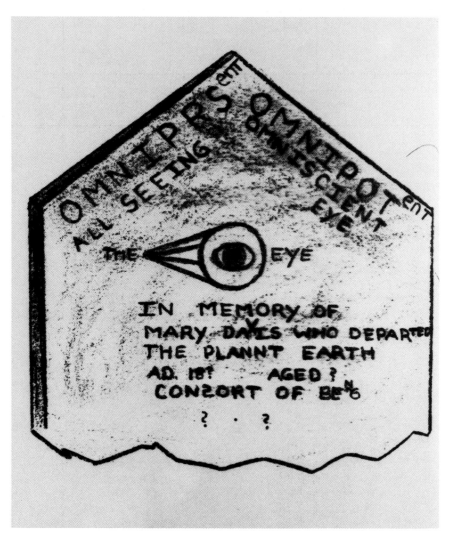

Figure 10.4. Dilapidated Indigenous Sandstone
The stone, too dark to photograph, had to be rubbed,
revealing several spaces and spelling errors. Question
marks are mine. The probable date is before 1820.
Plains U.P. Cemetery.
(Rubbing by Thomas J. Hannon)

dark brown or black. This was the material of preference until approximately 1840, when limestone and marble began to dominate the region (fig. 10.5). The transition from sandstone to marble may, in philosophical terms, reflect a movement away from the stark realities of death which were strengthened by the religious fervor of the "Great Awakening." That movement had serious impact upon the Pennsylvania frontier in the late 1700s and early 1800s up until the era of "Romanticism" with its emerging emphasis on emotion and its inherent belief in the goodness of man. This latter period was one of revolt against rationalism, when emotions won out over reason and intellect; and in that light it may be argued that the harsh realities of death represented by the dark sandstones of the early 1800s were transcended by light and the hope and joy of resurrection, factors suggested by the white limestone and marble gravestones dominant in the years following 1840.

Some relevant corollary inferences regarding this phenomenon can be made by comparing epitaphs of the sandstone era with those of the later 1800s. Epitaphs, to be sure, were not as common in the first half of the nineteenth century as they were to become later; however, what they lacked in frequency was compensated for by length. Their verses are stern and realistic, and they often speak of the departed in glowing, superfluous terms, thereby appealing indirectly to God for mercy. Consider the following example from the White Oak Springs cemetery:

IN MEMORY OF
MALCOLM GRAHAM
who departed this life August 30th, 1832
In the 78th year of his age

O ye whose cheek, the tear of pitty stains
Draw near; with pious reverence attend,
Here lies the loving Husband's dear remains,
The tender Father; and the generous Friend;
The pitying heart that felt, for human woe,
The dauntless heart, that feared no human pride,
The friend of man, to vice alone a foe,
For even his failings lean'd to virtues side.

Epitaphs of the later 1800s tend by contrast to be more succinct and philosophical in character. Furthermore, analogies and other figurative expressions were often the norm of the time, serving to diminish the gloom of death and the grave in deference to a joyous eternity. An 1892 example which illustrates this point is: "Awake from the Dream of Life"; while a

Figure 10.5. Typical Marble Tablet
This composition, as well as limestone, began to appear
as early as the middle 1840s in western Pennsylvania.
Slippery Rock Cemetery.
(Photograph Thomas J. Hannon)

rendition of 1894 presents the eloquent floral metaphor frequently seen on children's graves of this period: "Budded on Earth to Bloom in Heaven."

Coincidental with these philosophical transitions were new or improved means of transportation which also had an effect upon the type of material used in local gravemarkers. The middle 1800s to approximately the end of the Civil War, for instance, witnessed the increased usage of limestone. Although some of this was quarried locally, most had to be shipped in from central Pennsylvania. Marble began to gain in popularity in the late 1860s, and became the more popular of the two white materials in the 1870s and 1880s. The increased demand for both of these materials could not have been met without improvements in and extensions of rail service. That is especially true of marble, since the nearest source areas were several hundred miles from western Pennsylvania.

Changes in material were paralled by new tastes in monument size and shape. The late 1860s through the 1890s was the era of the obelisk and other types of huge monuments reflecting the revival of Neo-Classicism and the arrival of the Victorian era in western Pennsylvania. These were initially composed of limestone, and later of marble (in the 1870s and 1880s). By 1890, however, granite had begun to make minor inroads. Infrequently found in family cemeteries, the number of granite stones increased in the church-related graveyards. It was, however, in the emerging public or community, nonsecretarian cemeteries that granite found its greatest acceptance (fig. 10.6). Also during the period of the last quarter of the nineteenth century, the so-called white bronze monument made its appearance in western Pennsylvania. Examples of this type are noticeable not by their numbers but by their distinctive composition and design motifs. Many of the more elaborate versions were products of Monumental Bronze of Bridgeport, Connecticut. (See the essay by Barbara Rotundo in this volume.) These are more clearly in evidence in western Pennsylvania than in any other part of the Commonwealth; however, one rarely finds examples dated later than the first few years of the twentieth century (fig. 10.7).

Coincidentally complementing the Neo-Classical monuments and Victorian statuary of the last quarter of the nineteenth century was a new cemetery morphology alluded to previously—the "Rural Cemetery" movement. Although it involves a number of factors, this movement is most clearly tied to new concepts in cemetery design. In terms of location, these are usually (despite their title) urban cemeteries. The movement gained impetus in Britain and France in the latter half of the eighteenth century, though its roots lie in an even earlier era. Père Lachaise in Paris, founded in 1803, was the first of the landscaped garden cemeteries which characterized the transition. The movement diffused to the United States and had been initially employed in the creation of Mt. Auburn Cemetery in Cam-

Figure 10.6.   Marble Column and Granite Obelisk
These are representative of the revival of Neo-
Classicism in the late 1800s, granite replacing marble
and limestone around 1890. Butler North Cemetery.
(Photograph Thomas J. Hannon)

Figure 10.7.   White Bronze Monument
These became evident in western Pennsylvania during
the last quarter of the nineteenth century. Freeport
Cemetery.
(Photograph Thomas J. Hannon)

bridge, Massachusetts in 1831. Shortly thereafter, the concept was used at other sites, including Mt. Hope in Rochester, New York, and Laurel Hill in Philadelphia. The design would eventually permeate the American cultural landscape, with examples of this type of cemetery becoming popular in virtually every city in the United States. Gone in the designer's mind was the rigid grid plan of columns and rows discussed earlier in this essay; in its stead arose a circuitous form of winding streets and cul-de-sacs (fig. 10.8). The work of the landscape architect and nurseryman became all important, and no expense was spared in making these burial grounds showplaces to be enjoyed by the living. (See the essay by Blanche Linden-Ward in this volume.) Although several cemeteries of this genre have grown around older family, church-related, or public burial places in western Pennsylvania, one rarely finds examples of tombstones dating to a time period prior to the Civil War. From large to modest, examples of the rural cemetery type are found in every urban community of any consequence in the study area and all are beautifully maintained. Most notable, of course, is Allegheny Cemetery in the city of Pittsburgh, which has gained both regional and national acclaim as one of the most beautiful and interesting examples of the movement.

Imitating the basic morphology (though not the elaborate monumentation and landscaping) of the rural cemetery is the modern development of the 1950s and 1960s known as the commemoral.[15] More commonly termed Memorial Gardens or Parks, these sites continue to be extremely popular in the 1980s. Many of these commemorals have developed either within or on the expanding fringes of the rural cemetery.

The commemoral has done away with the elaborate upright marbles and granites of the rural cemetery in deference to flat bronze or granite markers that lie flush with the ground and allow very little space for personalization. Manicured lawns resembling astroturf are interrupted here and there by rhododendra, forsythia, junipers and other ornamentals. This type of cemetery was designed primarily for ease of lawn maintenance. However, several members of the Pennsylvania Monument Builders Association have recently suggested that, despite their original intent, they are more difficult to maintain than the more traditional cemetery because keeping the markers level is an almost continuous task. Within traditional cemeteries, where flat markers were also the vogue for a time, there is beginning to emerge a gradual shift back towards the use of more substantial monuments. Both of these factors suggest that the commemoral, in order to survive, might have to ultimately allow for the placement of upright markers. However, although such markers may indeed be gaining in popularity once again, it is doubtful that there will be a return to the classic character in evidence in the region several decades ago. The cost to the individual

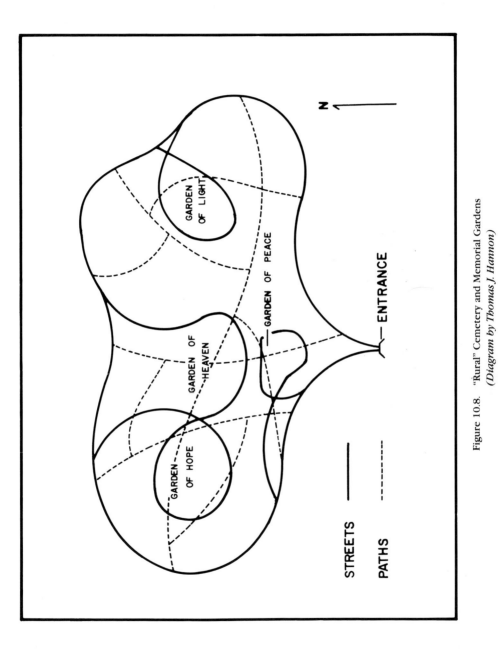

Figure 10.8. "Rural" Cemetery and Memorial Gardens
(Diagram by Thomas J. Hannon)

family would be prohibitive, for one thing, and entrenched cemetery ordinances governing monument size will most probably prevail. That there has developed a return to the concept of personalized gravemarkers in the past decade or so is, however, most obvious. (See the essay by Richard E. Meyer in this volume.) Granites of a variety of origins began to appear in western Pennsylvania in the middle 1970s depicting hunting or pastoral scenes, cheerleaders, pets and other aspects of life that were important to the deceased—or at least perceived to be important by survivors. It is not unusual to find motorcycles, campers, tractor trailers, golf scenes, baseball equipment, or other symbols of modern work and play. Couples frequently opt for entwined wedding rings, inside of which is engraved the tenure of their union on earth. This type of symbolism has all but totally replaced the traditional and purely religious lambs, anchors of faith, doves, roses, and statuary that lingered though the early to mid-twentieth century.

In summarizing, it should be stressed that cultural landscapes of all types are by nature transitory, primarily reflecting value systems, preferences, perceptions, and even marketing techniques of the changing times. The value of the cemetery as a cultural landscape lies in the fact that is is considered sacred or, at least, semisacred by the general public. Therefore, the cemetery, though it certainly reflects change, has been resistant to many of the alterations or destructive characteristics of other parts of the built environment. In that light, one can observe a preserved microcosmic representation of a region's history and characteristics in its cemeteries and gain important insights from which both specific information and informed inferences can be drawn.

As regions or smaller geographic units move through periods of cultural transition, the nature of these changes can often be read in the changing faces of their cemeteries and the artifacts they contain. As the present study has attempted to demonstrate, elements of particular importance in assessing these changes range from cemetery location and morphology to a whole host of factors involving the markers placed upon individual graves—spatial orientation, composition, size and design, epitaphs, symbolic visual adornments, and, of course, inscriptional data indicative of ethnicity and a large number of other cultural and statistical items. In western Pennsylvania, as elsewhere, these are severely endangered resources. It becomes imperative, therefore, that cemetery preservation and restoration and the recording of information from gravemarkers be actively pursued by civic organizations and historical societies in order to preserve for posterity the cultural information that is found there. Otherwise, the elements, time, and vandalism will have conspired to obliterate a valuable link to our past.

Notes

1. David E. Sopher, *Geography of Religions* (Englewood Cliffs, N.J.: Prentice-Hall, 1967), p. 32.

2. Richard V. Francaviglia, "The Cemetery as an Evolving Cultural Landscape," *Annals, Association of American Geographers* 61:2 (1971), pp. 501–9.

3. E. Willard Miller, *Pennsylvania: Keystone to Progress* (Northridge, Cal.: Windsor Publications, Inc., 1986), p. 14.

4. Ray Allen Billington, *Westward Expansion: A History of the American Frontier,* 3rd ed. (New York: Macmillan, 1967), p. 261.

5. See Edwin Scott Gaustad, *Historical Atlas of Religion in America* (New York: Harper and Row, 1962), p. 89.

6. Howard F. Barker, "Report of a Committee on Linguistic and National Stocks in the Population of the United States," *American Historical Review,* Annual Report 1 (1931), p. 209.

7. The following telephone directories were consulted: Butler (United Telephone of Pa., 1987); Erie (G.T.E. of Pa., 1986); Meadville (Mid Penn Telephone Corp., 1983); New Kensington (The Bell Telephone Co. of Pa., 1987); Washington (The Bell Telephone Co. of Pa., 1983).

8. William Helsel and Thomas J. Hannon, *Butler County Cemetery Inventory* 2 (Butler, Pa.: Butler County Historical Society, 1983), Wolf Creek Cemetery, pp. 1–12; and William Helsel and Thomas J. Hannon, *Butler County Cemetery Inventory* 4 (Butler, Pa.: Butler County Historical Society, 1984), White Oak Springs Cemetery, pp. 1–15.

9. Ms. Sandra Brown, R.N., head maternity nurse at Grove City (Pa.) Hospital, provided this information in a telephone interview on December 7, 1987.

10. Joe T. Darden, "Factors in the Location of Pittsburgh's Cemeteries," *The Virginia Geographer* 7 (1972), p. 4.

11. C. W. Elkin, "Remarks on Some Old Cemeteries of the Pittsburgh Region," *Western Pennsylvania Historical Magazine* 37 (1955), p. 97.

12. See Thomas J. Hannon, "A Comment on Cultural Sublety," *Academy Notes,* The Cultural Studies Academy 8:3 (Slippery Rock, Pa., 1973), p. 8.

13. Topographic Sheets of Parts of France include: Briançon Gap, Sheet 15 0, Scale, 1: 100,000; Grenoble, Sheet 14 N, Scale, 1:100,000; Mortagne Nogent-Le-Routrou, Scale, 1:100,000. German topographic sheets include: Cuxhaven, Sheet K 3, Scale 1:100,000; Lubeck, Sheet K 5, Scale 1:100,000.

14. Thomas J. Hannon, Jr., "Nineteenth-Century Cemeteries in Central-West Pennsylvania," *Proceedings of the Pioneer America Society* 2 (1973), p. 29.

15. Figure 10.8 illustrates the landscape concept of the memorial garden superimposed upon that of the rural cemetery.

Business and Pleasure

Business and Pleasure

There is an economic side to American cemeteries and gravemarkers, often overlooked by those of us who spend the bulk of our time pondering the origins of symbols and ritual practices or larger landscape features. Stonecarvers—today we would call them monument dealers or "memorialists"—have always had to maintain a delicate balance between artistic creativity and practical business sense, but it is almost exclusively the former quality which we have tended to emphasize in our academic studies. Barbara Rotundo's essay chronicling the history of the Monumental Bronze Company of Bridgeport, Connecticut provides a fascinating historical view into the business side of American monumentation, illuminating at the same time our understanding of these peculiar zinc gravemarkers which dot the landscapes of many older American cemeteries. In a time when large public parks and greenspaces for leisure activity have come to be an expected component of urban settings, it may come as somewhat of a surprise to learn that these functions were once provided by cemeteries. Such, however, is the case, as demonstrated by Blanche Linden-Ward in her detailed accounting of the rise of the "Rural" cemetery movement in America and its historic role in shaping some characteristic features of both urban land-use planning and landscape architecture.

11

Monumental Bronze:
A Representative American Company

Barbara Rotundo

Studies in the material culture of nineteenth-century America usually concern artifacts that have become obsolete because they no longer fulfill a
need or because alternative products are cheaper and/or more efficient.
Often such artifacts had a long history of folk use that predated industrial
mass production. Yet some, equally obsolete today, developed only after
modern industry made their manufacture possible. Sometimes, as in the
case of cast-iron buildings and building facades, the product had faults that
were corrected by an improved product—structural steel. But this essay
concerns an artifact that has many desirable traits, has never been improved
upon, yet has not been manufactured for more than fifty years: white bronze
grave markers. Just one firm, the Monumental Bronze Company of Bridgeport, Connecticut, manufactured these metal memorials. Despite restricting
its production to this unique product, Monumental Bronze epitomized
small industries in the American economy in its rapid expansion during the
post-Civil War era, its need to adapt to new conditions in the twentieth
century, and finally, in its closing during the Great Depression of the 1930s.

Although called white bronze, the metal in the monuments is actually
pure zinc, a nonmagnetic metal that is heavier than iron, but not so heavy
as lead. Zinc develops a protective coating of zinc carbonate when exposed
to the air;[1] that coating makes the characteristic bluish-gray color. (In Salt
Lake City, however, it is almost white.) White bronze "stones" were placed
in cemeteries all over America from the mid 1870s to World War I. Other
manufacturers also used white bronze an an attractive, elegant trade name
for zinc. A Monumental Bronze catalog gives this explanation: "The material
(being of a LIGHT GRAY COLOR) is more pleasing to the eye in the form of
STATUES and MONUMENTS than is the DARK or ANTIQUE BRONZE (which is an

amalgam of zinc, tin and copper), and this improvement in . . . color justly entitles our goods to their TRADE NAME of 'White Bronze.'"[2]

Zinc was not new in the nineteenth century. Early Romans, Chinese, and East Indians had all used zinc. However, the industrial science and technology of the nineteenth century provided the capability for smelting nearly pure zinc and for producing hollow statues and other decorations on a mass scale. Sand casting was the method used to make the markers that are the subject of this essay, and the manufacturer proudly announced that it used the purest zinc available, more than 99 percent pure.[3] By the 1880s a number of companies were turning out white bronze urns, eagles, civic monuments, architectural details, and even cigar-store Indians for an age that loved ornament and believed that more was better. Perhaps the best known company was Mullins of Salem, Ohio, whose catalogs can still be found in libraries and museums across the country (although they, too, have ceased production). But only Monumental Bronze of Bridgeport and its subsidiaries produced gravestones.[4]

The story told by the Reverend Samuel Orcutt in his history of Bridgeport, published in 1887,[5] is probably the best we can do for early facts about the company. A man named M. A. Richardson, dismayed at the condition of many cemetery stones in his charge in Chautauqua County, New York, experimented with stone china and galvanized iron in his attempt to find a permanent and attractive material. Settling finally on zinc, he took a partner, C. J. Williard, in 1873. They then contracted with two different foundries, but neither of these could produce a satisfactory product. At that point, the two men hired an experienced molder and built what Orcutt calls a shanty with a furnace. Inside of three weeks they had produced models that met their standards, to the astonishment of those who had failed. However, they were unable to attract the capital necessary to build a factory and produce the monuments on an economically feasible scale. They next made a contract with W. W. Evans, cashier at a large locomotive company in Patterson, New Jersey. He received exclusive manufacturing rights and agreed to sell his products to Richardson and Willard's agents at assigned prices. (Orcutt explains that before the Evans contract, Willard "made a trip into the country," returning with about thirty orders.) Evans soon gave up and early in 1874 sold his rights to Wilson, Parsons and Company of Bridgeport, who were already in business as an iron foundry. The Bridgeport firm succeeded where the others failed, and white bronze monuments had at last found a permanent home. The names of the originator, M. A. Richardson, and the other pioneers never appear again.

On the other hand, there were still some changes both in the manufacturing process and in the men in charge before the incorporation of the company that would send its product across the continent. In the early days of industrial expansion pioneers needed little capital to start up production of new products. Partners were added one year and dropped the next since no one investment was very heavy. The early manufacture of white bronze monuments followed this pattern exactly. Because Wilson, Parsons and Company already had a foundry building at Barnum and Hallett Streets, its main expense in 1874 would have been the payment to W. W. Evans. This should not have been very large, considering the history of failures. Daniel Schuyler soon joined, apparently replacing Parsons since the firm continued as Wilson, Schuyler and Company until 1877. At this point the name of Parsons returns, but a different man bears it. This Parsons had been a contractor with Wheeler and Wilson Sewing Machine Company, the largest sewing machine company in Bridgeport when that city was an important center of the industry[6] From 1877 to 1879 the white bronze company was known as Schuyler, Parsons, Landon and Company. Finally, in 1879, it incorporated as Monumental Bronze. What happened to Wilson? Where did Landon come from? How can we distinguish one Parsons from another? Orcutt's three-paragraph account is the only history of this venture, and no historian can find the internal records of the company. However, by turning to city directories we can find some answers and make some guesses.

Beginning with the first volume in the Bridgeport Public Library, 1880, the advertisements, the business listings, and the residential listings yield bits of information. For instance, in 1880 three companies—Wilson, Parsons & Company, Pembroke Iron Foundry, and Monumental Bronze—were listed at Barnum and Hallett Streets. The Parsons who was a partner of Wilson was Robert E., whereas Asa A. was president of Monumental Bronze. The logical conclusion is that Robert E. involved himself in 1874 but after that stayed with the iron foundry work. The two men may very well have been related since their companies shared a building. Furthermore, in 1882 and 1890 R. E. Parsons is listed as secretary for Monumental Bronze though he still ran Pembroke Iron Foundry at the same address. The two businesses, iron and white bronze, continued manufacturing at Barnum and Hallett until 1892, when Monumental Bronze moved to a building at Howard and Cherry Streets, a large factory if the engraved vignette can be believed and if the building still standing there dates from 1892, which seems likely. Pembroke remained at the same old address, but even after the move the directory lists a shop belonging to Asa Parsons at Barnum and Hallett that advertises "sharpening files by sandblasting." The sandblasting has significance because it was a unique step Monumental Bronze added in the manufacturing of zinc artifacts.

As for Landon, who was part of the white bronze company in 1877 through 1879, he appeared with Wilson, Parsons in 1880, and the very next year the company was Parsons and Landon, while at the same time continuing as Pembroke Iron Foundry. The omnipresent but nearly anonymous Wilson may well be the "gentlemanly superintendent" who was described by a visitor to Detroit Bronze in 1882 or 1883.[7] The account credited Mr. Wilson with "nine years experience in the business" and gave him full credit for the impressive factory, work force, and product. Since Monumental Bronze did not set up the Detroit subsidiary until 1881, Wilson could only have acquired his experience back in Bridgeport.

These names and dates may be confusing, but such a review seems necessary to convey the idea of the constant shifting. It is important to understand the flexibility, resulting in part from the small scale of the operation but also from a completely unregulated economy. The management hierarchy could remain fluid because all the officials were nearly equal in experience, ability, and perhaps in money invested in the enterprise (not large sums, either). In this business, all the men obviously had experience in metal-working, though not with zinc in particular. The two important men to follow are Asa Parsons and E. N. Sperry. Parsons was president of Monumental Bronze from 1879, when it was incorporated, until 1903. A large white bronze memorial marks his grave in Mountain Grove Cemetery, Bridgeport. Sperry first appears in 1883 as Superintendent of Agencies. He became Vice President in 1884, Treasurer in 1890, and in 1903 assumed the presidency. At that time he probably bought Parsons' shares since when the company closed its doors in 1939, the Sperry family owned nearly all of the stock. In 1901, two years before E. N. Sperry became president, the directory lists Ralph N. Sperry as clerk. Ordinarily the directory did not list clerks at Monumental Bronze, but Ralph was the son and heir, not an ordinary clerk. It was this Ralph Sperry who dissolved Monumental Bronze in 1939, asserting it was no longer profitable because of "the constantly increasing tax burden and government restrictions." By that time the company had long ceased advertising white bronze monuments, and no field reports mention markers that would have been erected after 1914. According to the press release at the time of the closing,[8] the plant had been taken over by the government during World War I for the manufacture of gun mounts and ammunition. Apparently, after the war was over fashions had changed; there was no demand for white bronze monuments, and the firm turned to producing castings in any nonferrous metal. Their ads in the city directories mention automobile and radio parts. The president blamed the government, but there were undoubtedly other major factors to consider, particularly technical obsolescence and a discouraging decline in business (again, typical problems besetting many small companies that never recovered from the Great Depression). From 1930 on the company had not even placed a small advertisement in the annual Bridgeport directory, suggesting they were not exactly expanding their business. They continued, however, to cast the tablets that made it possible for additional family members to be added to a monument after their deaths. In fact, C. A. Baldwin, who was secretary of the company when it was liquidated, became president of a company with a different address that continued to supply the tablets.[9]

Although we certainly do not need to know all the technical details of manufacturing white bronze monuments, some notion of the manufacturing process helps explain the changes made after production began in 1874 and establishes the background for the distribution system that evolved. There are three contemporary accounts that give information in addition to the catalogs and city directories. The earliest is a single surviving issue of *White Bronze Advocate* from 1883. Next chronologically was an unsigned article in *Scientific American* in 1885, and finally an article in a metal-industry publication in 1910.[10] The first step in the manufacturing process, as in any kind of casting, was the model, in this case a wax model. The company employed an artist full-time to make these wax models and offered the service of producing busts and bas reliefs from portraits or photographs (figs. 11.1 and 11.2). All the model-making was done by the artist in Bridgeport.[11]

A plaster cast was made of the wax model, and the cast was then used to make a plaster duplicate of the wax model. From this second plaster cast they made the sandcastings that became the monuments. The final plaster cast was cut in pieces so that the white bronze pieces were comparatively small and simple, allowing each casting to have sharp details. The pieces were fused together, apparently an innovative technique at that time. Rather than soldering the pieces together with a solder that was an alloy, Monumental Bronze workers clamped the pieces together and poured pure, hot zinc into the joints. Since the heat melted the surface of the cast pieces, they were truly fused together and became inseparable. Usually the bottom section of a monument was cast with four inner tabs with holes in them. These tabs were supposed to have pegs through the holes, the other ends of the pegs being sunk into the cement or granite foundation, just as granite monuments should be pegged to their bases as well as secured with mortar. Sometimes sections of tall monuments were bolted together through such tabs on the bottom of the upper and the top of the lower section. In the *White Bronze Advocate,* James L. Young, characterized as a very successful sales agent, described the best way to mix cement to make a foundation for a monument. This comes as close to an answer as we'll probably find to the question of who put these monuments in place: if customers needed such

Figure 11.1. White Bronze Bust Created from a Portrait or
Photograph
(Photograph Barbara Rotundo)

Figure 11.2.   White Bronze Bas Relief Created from a Portrait or
Photograph
(Photograph Barbara Rotundo)

advice about pouring foundations, they probably put up their own monuments. The large ones must have presented a problem. How ironic if they had to turn to the stone monument dealers for professional help.

Earlier I noted that the product changed between the first sales and the incorporation of Monumental Bronze. The casting and fusing actually remained the same; the modification came at the end of the manufacturing process and involved the treatment of the surface of the white bronze. There are three monuments I have seen from the 1877–79 period just before incorporation. Each happens to be a symbolic statue of Faith. Faith at Graceland Cemetery, Chicago, stands with one arm and her eyes raised to heaven, the other arm clasping a cross. In Bellefontaine Cemetery, St. Louis, an identical statue of Faith is rimmed with round holes where a vandal used her for target practice. In Spencertown, New York, a third Faith clasps a bible instead of a cross. On two of these it is possible to read the name Schuyler, Parsons, Landon and Company lightly etched on the metal base. After Monumental Bronze was incorporated, the name of the company, whenever it appeared—and there is no discernible pattern in the limited number of markers that do have the name—stands out clearly in neat raised letters (fig. 11.3). Those earlier statues have a smooth, dark-gray surface, while the later ones have a porous finish with the typical blue-gray color. The new production process involved sandblasting the fused cast, thereby causing the surface to resemble stone rather than metal and lightening the color. (Though it still does not resemble granite, as the advertising copy claimed, the two are closer in color when both have been darkened by heavy rain.)

As a first step in expanding its successful business, Monumental Bronze established a subsidiary in Detroit in 1881. If the earlier guess about Wilson was correct, the management of the parent company sent out an experienced man to guide production, but the list of officers of Detroit Bronze appearing in the city directory does not include Wilson. Instead, in Detroit as they were to do in setting up later subsidiaries, officials in Bridgeport looked for men of established standing in the local business and financial communities. Perhaps these figureheads received a salary, perhaps they received stock in the company, perhaps they received a percentage of the total sales for their subsidiary, but rarely did they seem to take an active part in producing white bronze monuments. In Detroit, for instance, the first president was a partner in a meatpacking firm, while two years later the president was an officer of the Michigan Gas Light Company. Frequently these officers continue to give only their original business affiliation for use in the city directory. Sometimes even the president does not list his connection to the white bronze company. The Detroit city directory reveals that one J. H. Eakins had been selling white bronze monuments as early as 1879,

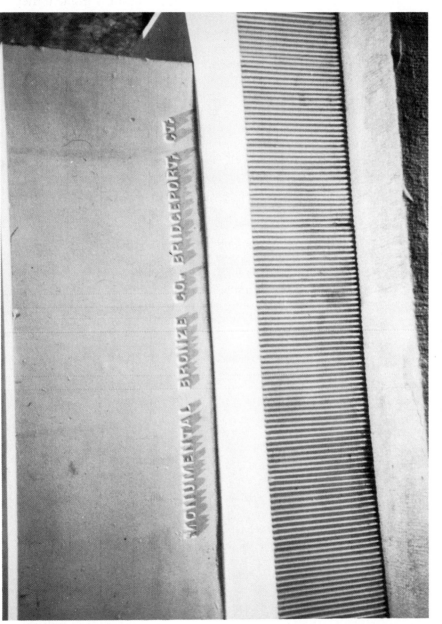

Figure 11.3.   The Monumental Bronze Name on the Base of a Marker
The company name stands out clearly in neat raised letters.
(Photograph Barbara Rotundo)

and a history of Detroit published in 1884 credits the incorporation of Detroit Bronze to Eakins, yet Eakins was never an officer of the company or its subsidiary.[12] Perhaps the sales by Eakins persuaded Bridgeport to choose Detroit for its first finishing and distribution center in the West. Something happened, however, because in 1886 the city directory no longer lists Detroit Bronze and the company never again appears in Detroit. The *White Bronze Advocate* in 1883 had divided the country in two and had given Detroit jurisdiction over Michigan, Indiana, Kentucky, Tennessee, and "all States West" (though Bridgeport kept Texas). We may never discover why operations ended in Detroit, but the places that picked up the western business are obvious. In 1885 or 1886 the appropriate city directories listed American White Bronze in Chicago, St. Thomas White Bronze in Ontario, and Western White Bronze in Des Moines. Confirming the directories, the *Scientific American* article in 1885 reported "art foundries" in Chicago, Detroit, Des Moines, and St. Thomas. Writing his Bridgeport history two years later, Orcutt described subsidiaries in Chicago, Des Moines, St. Thomas, and New Orleans, thus confirming the closing of Detroit, but making the sole reference to New Orleans appearing anywhere, a reference that I believe is an error.[13] Philadelphia White Bronze would not be included since it did not appear in Philadelphia city directories until 1897. The mystery about Philadelphia White Bronze is why its catalog makes no mention of Monumental Bronze or any of the other subsidiaries. It advertised stones identical in style and the company name was cast in the same raised block letters. Since the president of Philadelphia White Bronze, H. C. Gara, was before and after the company's existence also the president of Gara, McGinley and Company, manufacturers of zinc cornices, he probably had a different contractual arrangement with Bridgeport. Because Gara already had the plant and the foundry experience, they did not need to set up a subsidiary, but instead could offer him a franchise to make their product.[14]

This brings up a question that has no definitive answer as yet: was the casting, the heavy manufacturing, done at the subsidiaries or just the finishing? Certainly the newspaper reporter describing what he saw in Detroit indicated that only fusing and sandblasting took place there. Yet the *Scientific American* article stated that a fountain shown as an illustration "was cast at the Detroit foundry." The article was very generalized and did not include any eyewitness reporting. In fact, it read as though it were a reworking of a company press release without acknowledgment, a not uncommon practice in the nineteenth century. Perhaps the company spokesman wrote that the fountain was made in Detroit, meaning it was fused and finished there, but the editor understood the words to mean it was cast in Detroit.

The thickest white bronze catalog I studied contained 120 pages of models. Each page had from four to sixteen different models, with each coming in at least two sizes. Multiply that large number by the pieces into which each monument was cut for casting, and you have an incredibly large number of casts to duplicate and send out to each subsidiary. It would certainly have been more efficient and far less expensive to do all the casting in Bridgeport. Would the fact that the factories were called "art foundries" also suggest that the heaviest and dirtiest work were done elsewhere? Or is it another attempt, like the renaming of zinc, to add elegance to the product? Another point to consider is that the officers of the subsidiaries, with the exception of Philadelphia, had no experience in the foundry business, unlike the officers in Bridgeport. Although the question remains without a definitive answer, I am convinced that the original casting was done entirely in Bridgeport.

A brief review of the histories of the subsidiaries not yet discussed will show characteristics they had in common and that presumably were traits that Monumental Bronze sought. American White Bronze first appeared in the Chicago directory in 1886 with Homer N. Hibbard as president. Hibbard's personal occupation was "registrar in bankruptcy." In 1887 he became president of the newly formed Fort Dearborn National Bank, capitalized at $500,000. An American Bronze catalog (the "White" was dropped in 1888) pictured a large memorial (wider than it was tall and called a sarcophagus in white bronze catalogs) standing in Oak Woods Cemetery, Chicago, with HIBBARD in large letters on its side. The print beneath the picture identified Homer Hibbard as president of Fort Dearborn National Bank. This dates for us the otherwise undated catalog as coming between the summer of 1888 and April 1889, because in April the bank suffered "severe reverses" and Hibbard resigned. He was not accused of any wrongdoing and was exonerated because he lacked experience in the "vicissitudes of banking."[15] (It seems as though a registrar in bankruptcy should know a great deal about the vicissitudes of a free economy even if not specifically about banking.) Monumental Bronze kept Hibbard as president except for 1892, when the president was Paul Cornell, Jr., who had served among the other officers in other years. Cornell was also memorialized by a large white bronze monument in Oak Woods Cemetery. The fact that Hibbard continued suggests that Bridgeport was looking for popular and respected men as figureheads, not financial or engineering wizards whose good judgment was crucial. Other companies also sought out Hibbard after 1889. He was president of Chicago Electric Service in 1894 and secretary of Green Mountain Mining Company in 1897. He dropped from the Chicago directory in 1898, and American Bronze dropped from the directory in 1909, having existed for about twenty-three years.

The Des Moines subsidiary was the Chicago branch's closest internal competitor for longevity. It began the same year—1886—but dropped a year earlier than Chicago. Des Moines is an exception to my generalization about figureheads. In its first directory listing, Western White Bronze had H. A. Coffin, treasurer of Iowa Loan and Trust, for its president. That sounds like the usual practice, but the next year Coffin became vice president and Henry Galley was the president. The previous year, Galley's personal listing had been "works Western White Bronze." That does not mean he had worked as a laborer in the foundry, but it certainly means that he spent his working time at Western White Bronze, unlike the figureheads. From 1888 until 1900 Galley continued as president, while Coffin dropped from the directory. Then in 1901 Galley had only a residential listing with no occupation—and a Walter Coffin was listed as president. Was Walter the son of the late H. A. Coffin? If he had been listed earlier as boarding at H. A. Coffin's residence, we could assume a relationship, but there was no such listing. However, in 1901 Walter was president of the bank that H. A. Coffin had been treasurer of, a second coincidence that makes a family relationship seem even more likely. Furthermore, Monumental Bronze took a paternalistic view of its employees, and there are several instances besides the Sperry father and son of a family name being represented in consecutive generations—a circumstance that is not unique to the United States or to the nineteenth century.

The St. Thomas White Bronze Company began production in 1883 and ceased about 1900. This subsidiary always had a manager as well as the usual figurehead officers from various businesses and professions. In 1884 the city directory listed Henry B. Pollack as manager and at his home address listed also a Charles Pollack, "pourer at St. Thomas White Bronze," a single instance of a family member working in the factory. In 1890 a local newspaper[16] published an account of St. Thomas White Bronze when the manager was J. J. Blackmore, "who also travels for the Company." Assuming "traveling" had the same meaning in Canada as the United States at that time, the manager was a salesman for the company rather than a director of production. The article stated that the company had employed twenty-five to thirty hands during the year and talked in general terms about "new and taking designs" and the fact that "great care is needed in casting owing to the great shrinkage that takes place in this metal when cooling." Then it stated in more specific terms: "The works do not contain a great amount of machinery, most of the labor being hand, but it is very careful work. The room in which the designs are kept is an interesting place, there being several hundred of every conceivable form, nearly every emblem known being represented." The account gives the impression that casting took place in St. Thomas, yet it did not provide a description of the casting process at the same time that it gave the direct personal reaction to the room filled with models. We still lack convincing proof that the casting was done in the subsidiaries. In 1886, as the popularity of white bronze was reaching its greatest height, the paper reported negotiations with a firm in New Brunswick for supplying the maritime provinces. These plans never developed further because all signed Canadian white bronze monuments, from Nova Scotia to British Columbia, came from St. Thomas, Ontario.

The matter of territory is another unanswered question in the organization of Monumental Bronze. Since Canada had passed laws enforcing "buy Canadian" late in the nineteenth century, St. Thomas had unquestioned rights to its territory. The *White Bronze Advocate,* as mentioned earlier, showed Detroit and Bridgeport dividing the United States between them. In 1886, when Detroit was closing down, the Des Moines city directory stated that Western White Bronze controlled Iowa, Missouri, Kansas, Colorado, Nebraska, Wyoming, and Dakota. Such a jurisdictional division makes sense, yet the evidence in cemeteries does not support a rigid division. In two adjoining towns in western New York, the more easterly has a monument signed American White Bronze, Chicago, while the one further west has the signature of Monumental Bronze, Bridgeport. Similarly, field reports from northern Iowa indicate as many markers from Chicago as from Des Moines.

The truth of the matter is that the salesman or agent was all-important in the marketing of white bronze monuments. Neither the main plant in Bridgeport nor the foundries of the subsidiaries sold to customers. The role of the foundries was to fill the orders of the agents. The advertisements placed by the subsidiaries in the various city directories usually urged people to become agents. Sometimes they were merely institutional, boasting about the durability of the product, but they never gave an address where monuments could be purchased because every single monument was made to order. Customers could not walk into a salesroom to look over the designs. They had to judge the final product by monuments already erected in cemeteries or from the illustrations in the catalogs. The final pages of the longest white bronze catalog directly address possible agents, listing all the advantages, including "No investment of capital is needed." They point out white bronze has a product for everyone, with prices ranging from $2 to $5,000. Markers that could take a full name began at $4, with one for full name and dates at $6. The catalog also reminds future agents that there will always be a market for white bronze so long as people continue to live and die.

Most agents, in modern terms, were moonlighting; but judging by the markers they left behind, very few of them made any money. This system undoubtedly explains why most cemeteries contain only one or two examples of white bronze, and rarely does one have as many as a dozen among the hundreds or thousands of marble and granite monuments. Distribution, or sales providing the distribution, was the greatest marketing problem Monumental Bronze faced. Each agent probably started off with enthusiasm and visions of wealth, but after a year or so when he had sold only one or two, he lost all his drive. There seems to have been an unspoken boycott of white bronze markers by marble and granite dealers. I know of just two exceptions: a dealer in Cedar Rapids, Iowa, sold both marble and white bronze monuments,[17] and the catalog of the Philadelphia White Bronze Monument Company includes testimonial letters from two men who liked the white bronze but handled marble and granite monuments. The catalog make much of the fact that the marble dealer in Potsdam, New York, had just sold a white bronze monument to a customer. The very emphasis implies the rarity of the act.

There is a popular belief that Sears Roebuck sold white bronze. The one specialized Sears catalog that has been reprinted shows only what it calls blue marble and white marble, the blue being a limestone that is the cheapest in the catalog and costs about $4 for a marker comparable to the $6 marker made of white bronze. It may be that since Sears and white bronze agents sold out of catalogs, people have confused the content of the catalogs. Certainly Sears was the competitor in terms of providing inexpensive gravemarkers. The marble dealers would have been especially jealous of the comparatively modest prices for white bronze statues and other intricate work.

If a cemetery has more than a dozen white bronze monuments, we may safely conclude that there was a successful agent living nearby in the nineteenth century. Without knowing the commission paid, we cannot judge precisely how successful, but few if any would have been able to support a family on their earnings from white bronze. Again, the experience is typically American. The belief in the American dream of streets paved in gold and riches for everyone rarely worked out in the lives of real men and women. The optimists who thought they could make a fortune selling white bronze—or any other product—almost inevitably met with disappointment. The realists who wanted to supplement their regular income or added white bronze to a business they were already running found their expectations fulfilled, but only for a while. Of the half dozen agents whose names and addresses in city directories make it possible to follow their lives, not a single one retired from work or died while he was still selling white bronze. All changed to some other business or dropped white bronze from the lines they were carrying.

The agent in Syracuse, New York is typical not only of other agents, but also of the pattern followed by the subsidiaries: constantly changing personnel, changing addresses (this discussion has spared the reader those except for the major move in Bridgeport), and the activity limited to a restricted number of years. In the Syracuse city directory for 1875–76, Wilson and Blye were oil can manufacturers. In the 1877–78 edition Wilson and Blye added zinc monuments to their directory listing. By the 1881–82 directory they have broken up: Newell E. Wilson stays with zinc monuments and oil tanks while Alphonso Blye puts simply "oils" after his residential listing. In 1883–84 Wilson is the second-listed partner of a new firm, Van Antwerp & Wilson, selling zinc monuments. The following year Sylvester Van Antwerp returns to the trade he practiced before joining Wilson, tinsmithing, while Wilson lists his occupation as "flour safes and zinc monuments." In 1886–87, which would have been his tenth anniversary with white bronze, Newell Wilson lists only "wirework and vases." No other agent is listed for either zinc or white bronze. For some reason Wilson never used the trade name of white bronze—perhaps because he came to zinc from tin and thought in terms of handling metal rather than of fancy words or aesthetic considerations. One might speculate as to whether he might have used the term if he had sold more monuments. Is there a possibility that the Superintendent of Agencies visited Syracuse from Bridgeport and discovered to his horror that Wilson was selling "zinc monuments" and ordered him to stop? The only excuse for imagining this scene is that 1886 is very early to drop white bronze. Judging from the hundreds of monuments I have seen, I would say that sales reached their peak about 1888 and were beginning to taper off by 1892.

Wilson died in 1890 and is buried in Oakwood Cemetery, Syracuse, but does not have a white bronze monument. Neither does Alphonso Blye, who died in 1891 and was also buried in Oakwood.[18] I mention these two omissions because often people, noticing that a cemetery has only one white bronze, ask if the salesman put up one for himself as a kind of demonstration but failed to sell any others. This might have happened somewhere, but the Syracuse story shows that it is not necessarily so. On the other hand, it may be that bank presidents, generals, and industrialists received some kind of discount when they put up conspicuously large white bronze monuments, which were then put in catalogs as illustrations accompanied by letters of praise from the owners. There is no evidence suggesting that an agent or the first person to put up a marker in a cemetery received any concession or monetary reward. Perhaps being considered prominent was reward enough for the purchasers of the conspicuous monuments. For instance, P. W. Gates, whose monument is the largest white bronze in Rose Hill Cemetery, Chicago, was very proud of his successful business. The letterhead on which he wrote his commendation specifies that Gates manufacturers "The Greatest Rock and Ore-Crusher on Earth." Yet there must have been weak moments when Mr. Gates realized that he was pretty small compared to the men who were building empires from the stockyards or combining railroad lines to cross the continent. If he had been asked at such a moment whether he would buy a monument to be used as an illustration of a purchase by a prominent man, he might have been warmly reassured and quickly signed an order for an even larger monument than he'd been planning.

Certainly the people who bought white bronze memorials were not avante-garde tastesetters. The models offered in the white bronze catalogs were very conventional and imitated all the popular styles that people would have seen in marble or granite. They ranged from rather plain tablets and small lambs to obelisks with inverted torches and flaming urns or statues of classically draped Faith with her bible. It was even possible to combine these and more to produce an explosion of statuary like that illustrated from Patchogue, Long Island (fig. 11.4). Fraternal emblems and long-cherished religious symbols like the cross entwined in ivy showed in sharp detail on even small stones (fig. 11.5). The base often imitated natural stone (fig. 11.6), though real granite did not always have the smooth margin that white bronze required to ensure a smooth joint. Some people objected to the artificiality of having metal imitating stone, but that argument obviously involves taste rather than logic. The argument loses all rational effectiveness with a visit to any Victorian cemetery full of stones shaped like trees, lifelike flowers cut into the stone, and granite monuments ornamented with rustic letters formed as though from twigs. (All of this occurred in white bronze, too; see figure 11.7.) In one sense, all memorials are artificial. Even a field stone with no name on it must be in a particular spot to serve as a distinctive reminder. As the words tell us, art is full of artifice. Our preconceptions cause us to admire certain things as natural while we dismiss others as artificial.

One imitation that could be executed in white bronze but not in stone is a revealing example of differing definitions of "natural." The century plant (looking very much like a yucca)[19] was as popular for planting in cemeteries as weeping trees in the last century, and the plants have lasted as well as the trees. Every cemetery that dates from the nineteenth century contains a century plant or two. The folk belief that the plant bloomed once in a century, making it last "forever" in comparison to other flowers, would give it appropriateness as an immortal flower. Victorians were also fond of the exotic. The discovery that this "imported" plant, a native of the hot, arid southwest, could survive northern winters gave it an additional symbolic value. The thin, sword-shaped leaves obviously could not be copied in stone, but they were easy to imitate in white bronze (fig. 11.8). In fact, the small print below the catalog illustrations for these objects says they were molded from life. That makes a good argument for claiming they were

Figure 11.4. A Combination of Conventional Elements
An explosion of statuary from Patchogue, Long Island.
(Photograph Richard Welch)

Figure 11.5.　Ivy-Covered Cross
Emblems and symbols stand out in sharp detail.
(Photograph Carol Perkins)

Figure 11.6.   White Bronze Base in Imitation of Natural Stone
(Photograph Barbara Rotundo)

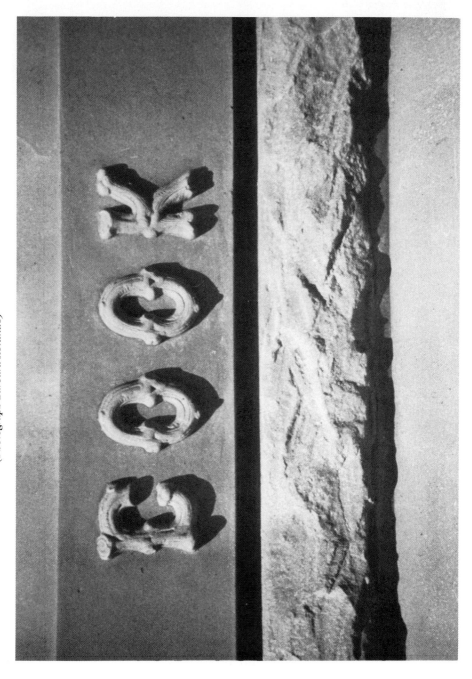

Figure 11.7. White Bronze Ornamented with Rustic Letters in the Form of Twigs
(Photograph Barbara Rotundo)

Figure 11.8.   White Bronze Century Plant
              The thin, swordlike leaves of the century plant could
              not be copied in stone.
              (Photograph Barbara Rotundo)

more natural than, say, the sheafs of wheat so often copied in marble and granite. But arguing about such matters leads us into philosophy, far from white bronze.

I have seen each of the three century plant models offered by white bronze more than once, and all were in good condition. The tip of only one leaf on a single plant had been broken off. Admittedly, all the examples I have seen were on tall plinths or the tip of an obelisk. Vandalism is not new. Our great grandparents were prudent enough to keep temptation out of the reach of adolescents, even if they didn't call them adolescents. For instance, within ten years of its founding in 1831, Mount Auburn Cemetery near Boston discussed hiring a guard to prevent the vandalism that was beginning to occur. Antisocial vandalism, damage caused by ignorance or carelessness, and official sweep-away-the-obstacles clean-up have been problems in burial grounds for centuries. It is not an increase in such happenings that has focused modern attention on cemeteries; this attention is due to the growing interest in preserving our artistic and architectural heritage.

And what about preservation? What is the condition of these century-old white bronze markers? Have the claims for durability held up? Given the strong language of their claims, the people associated with Monumental Bronze should have expected some problems. Readers who think Madison Avenue hyperbole is a modern phenomenon have never looked at nine-teenth-century hype. Of course, Monumental Bronze learned it from the master himself—Phineas T. Barnum. Barnum made Bridgeport his home and was an active and supportive citizen. He even wrote an enthusiastic letter about white bronze to help his fellow citizens, but his monument in Bridge-port's Mountain Grove Cemetery is granite.

One of the problems in meeting exorbitant claims for durability is that vandals can damage anything if they try hard enough. The most unsightly damage by vandals to white bronze is the removal of the tablets, leaving a hole in one or more sides (fig. 11.9). These tablets were not fused to the monument because they had to be removable for the addition of names and dates as family members died. If properly attached with the ornamental, unslotted screwheads, they require a really dedicated vandal to remove them. The gaping holes left by the missing tablets have given rise to several bits of folklore. A recurring tale, told to me on numerous occasions by people from different parts of the country (each apparently thinking their local white bronze monument was unique), is that bootleggers used these hollow stones to hide their liquor. If this were true, the smaller ones couldn't have held enough bottles to repay their efforts. In any case, the larger, taller ones would have had their space preempted by another bit of lore—the notion that these had removable plates so that caretakers could

Figure 11.9.   White Bronze Monument with Tablets Missing
Tablets needed to be removable for the addition of
names and dates as family members died. Unfortunately,
vandals can also remove them.
(Photograph Barbara Rotundo)

store rakes, brooms, etc. in them. It may, in fact, be true that workers use them for this purpose today, but it was certainly not the intended reason for the removable plates or the hollow space.

So far as damage by weather and pollutants like acid rain is concerned, time has upheld the glowing testimonials by chemists about the durability and imperviousness of zinc.[20] The details of letters and emblems are as sharp as ever and the blue-gray surface is unblemished. The white bronze memorials compare very well with granite and are in much better condition than the best of the marble, which corrodes so easily.[21]

There is an exception to the unblemished appearance of zinc that chemists and geographers working together might be able to explain. The white bronze monuments that I observed in Detroit cemeteries were often defaced by a black stain. This was not a stain upon the surface coating, but it had eaten through the coating so that an exploring finger moved into a depression in the metal as it reached the edge of the black area. Why this should happen in Detroit and nowhere else must be due to a particular pollutant, and it must be a strong one and too heavy or too evanescent to be conveyed by winds to other localities. A trade secret of Monumental Bronze that apparently will remain a secret was the makeup of the "film" that they brushed over each of the monuments after the sandblasting. They told the reporter on the Detroit visit quoted in the *White Bronze Advocate* that they were simply hastening the formation of the coating that would develop naturally from the atmosphere. Whatever the chemical reaction caused by the brushing, it produced an excellent protective coating everywhere except in Detroit.

The most damaging weakness of zinc is its tendency to creep, a word that becomes clearer in meaning as we look at what actually occurs. Creeping causes the most problems in large monuments of vertical design. Since there are hundreds of zinc Civil War monuments standing around the United States in town squares and other conspicuous public locations,[22] creeping represents the most serious preservation or restoration problem. Civil War soldier statues are the one product that Monumental Bronze produced in real competition with the Mullins Company of Salem, Ohio. As Stephen Davis has pointed out in an article on war memorials, Monumental Bronze supplied both Union and Confederate soldiers.[23] One story I've heard that may be apocryphal concerns a southern town where the people waited breathlessly for their soldier monument to be lowered from its high column for repairs. Having learned the statue came from Connecticut, they were afraid it would have Union insignia. But everyone was happy; he was a true Confederate soldier. At any rate the weight of the zinc at the top of the monument or statue puts pressure on the metal lower down and causes it to move very, very slowly. This is creep. This pressure and resultant movement means there is rarely a straight base line on a monument of any size. Sometimes the movement has also caused tiny cracks where the metal stretched too far and broke. The weight from above can cause any monument to creep, even those that are much smaller than the soldiers, who stand six feet, eleven inches tall in the shortest model. From all reports the only satisfactory way to prevent this creeping is an inner armature to support the weight. This preservation work, as is usually the case, costs many times the initial purchase. About 1882 the catalog offered the soldier for $450. (The substitution of a personal head sculpted from photographs would raise the cost to $600.) Recently, Bruce Holstrom, the dedicated president of Oak Woods Cemetery, Chicago, received an estimate of $10,000 for putting a framework inside a large white bronze monument that is nowhere near so complex a design as the standing soldiers. Sometimes in addition to a wavering baseline, the slow movement of the metal tips the figures forward. Their backs are still ramrod straight, but the whole body leans forward at an unnatural angle. The worst cause of creeping that I have seen involved more than tipping, for the upper part of the monument had sunk into the lower part, bending the lower section out of shape and causing irreparable damage. One point to make clear to people who hold responsibility for misshapen monuments is that the creeping is so slow that there is plenty of time to consult experts, seek contractors with experience, and debate endlessly in committee meetings.[24]

Why did people stop buying white bronze monuments? (Creeping seems to be more recent than the turn of the century, when white bronze fortunes started to decline rapidly.) Monumental Bronze advertisements feature three arguments favoring the choice of white bronze for cemetery memorials, and for various reasons each of these lost its effectiveness. The argument for durability, which a century and more of weathering has proved valid, was weakened by the Barre Granite Associations' campaign for the Rock of Ages. That echo of the popular hymn and the reminder that stone had been the enduring material over the centuries overpowered the white bronze claims. Furthermore, the taste-setters never accepted zinc as an artistic material. Foundries that cast the work of artists in traditional bronze made fun of the presumption of calling zinc white bronze—though only tradition made bronze, an alloy of tin and copper, superior.[25] Some of the leading cemeteries (such as Mount Auburn in Cambridge and Spring Grove in Cincinnati) passed regulations against metal markers, undoubtedly concerned about the many unsightly cast-iron fences around cemetery plots whose owners neglected the necessary frequent painting to prevent rust and collapse. But like the artists, they exempted bronze—and put white bronze in the prohibited group.

The second point that white bronze advertisements made to attract customers also had an unexpected reaction. In comparable size and shape, a white bronze monument would always be cheaper than one of granite. This would seem to be a strong selling point, but think what we do with the words "cheap" and "cheapen." People who manage to buy something at well under the selling price are clever and receive congratulations, but people who accept an imitation or an alternate material to the "real thing" in order to save money are less likely to win social approval. If the taste-setters were not accepting white bronze, who was buying the many thousands of monuments that were sold? The answer seems to be that a cross section of Americans were in fact pleased with white bronze monuments, and buying one was a fashionable thing to do for about twenty years. The occupations listed in the city directories for men memorialized by white bronze ranged from laborer and baggageman through carpenter and clerk to men who owned businesses with a number of employees and surplus money to spend on full page advertisements annually for over twenty years.[26]

Progress was the third selling point urged on customers by Monumental Bronze. Americans in the 1880s and 1890s wanted to be progressive and like the idea of a manmade product that was more durable than what nature had fashioned. The advertisements appealed to all forward-looking citizens to take advantage of this technological advance. People in the nineteenth century believed fervently that all progress was good and that they really now had the power to shape a perfect world. There was nothing they couldn't accomplish with their modern knowledge. Cast metal monuments that were durable, inexpensive, and endlessly adaptable because of the wide choice of shape, emblems, and epitaphs seemed for a while to fulfill this happy belief. But fashion is fickle and things were bound to change. Not only that, something more basic than superficial fashion was also changing. Through their own experiences and through reading the muckrakers, people gradually began to lose their faith in the perfectibility of the world. The promise of progress no longer evoked an automatic positive response. Ironically, the very motive of the man who originally sponsored zinc for cemetery monuments—to improve on the natural substances already available—helped to defeat the product when society came to suspect the validity of claims to improvement and progress.

Monumental Bronze went out of business not because of obsolescence such as the carriage-makers experienced, nor because of monopolistic competition such as forced many other small companies to close. Nor was it because of taxes and government interference as President Sperry believed. Rather, it was a change in the underlying beliefs and attitudes of a whole society which ultimately doomed this typically American product. But the company left behind in cemeteries all over North America an attractive material representation of that nation-building belief that Americans could accomplish anything—even do better than Mother Nature herself.

Notes

Since the study of cemeteries has only in recent times entered the realm of academic writing, the dedication of amateurs in research and preservation work over past decades is an invaluable resource. The field reports of members of the Association for Gravestone Studies have enabled me to make general statements with real confidence because the evidence on which I base my conclusions is far greater than one person could gather. Space limitations prevent me from listing all the members of A.G.S. who have sent reports and pictures. To them I extend my thanks and acknowledge my indebtedness. In addition I want to express thanks to Margot Gayle, founder of the Friends of Cast-Iron Architecture, who gave me my first clues about published sources of information.

1. Most accounts say zinc carbonate: one essay says zinc oxide. Both coatings are possible according to Professor W. Feitnecht in his "Studies on the Influence of Chemical Factors on the Corrosion of Metals," *Chemistry and Industry* (September 5, 1959), pp. 1102–9.

2. I have studied the catalogs owned by Winterthur Museum, Metropolitan Museum of Art, and Dr. Harvey Blanchet, Medina, New York. Those from Winterthur are now available on microfiche from Clearwater Publishers, New York City.

3. Monumental Bronze chose its zinc supplier very carefully and published letters from chemists attesting to the purity. Carol Grissom, Senior Objects Conservator at the Smithsonian and the leading authority on the historical uses of zinc, says that the monuments are indeed made from a purer zinc than other cast zinc objects.

4. No scholarly research on white bronze or white bronze monuments has been published. Deborah Trask wrote an accurate and richly illustrated introductory essay, "White Bronze," *The Occasional* 8 (Spring 1984), pp. 32–41, and Kenneth Ames mentions the memorials in "Ideologies in Stone: Meanings in Victorian Gravestones," *Journal of Popular Culture* 14 (Spring 1981), pp. 641–56.

5. *A History of the Old Town of Stratford and the City of Bridgeport, Connecticut* (Fairfield County Historical Society, 1886), vol. II, pp. 813–14.

6. David W. Palmquist, *Bridgeport: A Pictorial History* (Norfolk, Virginia: Dominion Press, 1985), p. 45.

7. P. J. C. Macaulay, letter to *Hudson* (Michigan) *Post*, extracted in *White Bronze Advocate* 2 (January 1883). A single sheet of newsprint folded over, the *Advocate* is unpaginated.

8. *Bridgeport Post*, March 9, 1939; *Bridgeport Telegram*, March 9, 1939; *Boston Post*, March 11, 1939. All three clippings are in the Ebenezer Sanborn Phillips Scrapbook, Bridgeport Public Library, and all are obviously based on the same press release.

9. Ernest Knight, of Raymond, Maine, shared with me his copy of a letter from C. A. Baldwin dated June 9, 1941 and headed Memorial Bronze Company, Bridgeport, Connecticut.

10. Macaulay in *White Bronze Advocate*: "White Bronze," *Scientific American* (November 14, 1885), p. 309; A. B. Saw, "Ornamental White Bronze Castings: How They Are Made in an Eastern Foundry, Which Has Made a Specialty of Refined Zinc Statuary and Monu-

ments," *The Foundry* 35 (January 1910), pp. 191–95. Since there are no page numbers in the *Advocate* and the *Scientific American* article is all on one page, future references to those two will give just title in the text.

11. The cover of the November 14, 1885 issue of *Scientific American* has nine illustrations showing Monumental Bronze and its subsidiaries, including the artist's studio in Bridgeport.

12. Silas Farmer, *The History of Detroit and Michigan or the Metropolis Illustrated* (Detroit: Silas Farmer & Company, 1884), pp. 810–11.

13. There is no other reference to a New Orleans subsidiary, no listing in the city directory, and no signed monument. Since Monumental Bronze won medals in a New Orleans World's Fair, Orcutt may have been looking at that, or the company may have planned on a subsidiary that for some reason it never established.

14. My conclusions result from Ernest Knight's research at the Philadelphia Public Library. He should not be blamed for anything I have drawn from his findings so graciously shared.

15. *Industrial Chicago: The Commercial Interests,* vol. 4 (Chicago: Goodspeed Publishing, 1894), p. 192.

16. George Thorman, a member of the St. Thomas Public Library Board and an authority on local history, has sent me xerox copies of several clippings from a local paper and his notes, all of which supplement what I could find in the incomplete series of city directories. He found a reference to the foundations begun for the "moulding shops" on June 30, 1883. That certainly suggests that the actual casting may have taken place in St. Thomas, despite the lack of eye-witness observations in the later account.

17. Loren Horton, Director of the Iowa Historical Society, generously shared his research with me and told me about this agent.

18. I checked the names on all the white bronze monuments in Oakwood Cemetery, Syracuse, and then checked for the names of the three former agents in the burial records.

19. Despite studying the entries in several botanical reference books, I am unable to tell the difference between a yucca and a century plant, but I do know there's no cemetery symbolism in a yucca plant.

20. C. J. Slunder and W. K. Boyd, *Zinc: Its Corrosion Resistance* (New York: Jointly published by Australia Zinc Development Association; Indian Lead Zinc Information Centre; Japanese Lead Zinc Development Association; Scandinavian Lead Zinc Association; Zinc Development Association; Zinc Institute Incorporated, 1971), p. 10. This study commissioned by zinc producers indicates a continued wide use of zinc because of its capacity to resist corrosion.

21. Local sandstones vary in their resistance to weather and pollutants, but they had already begun to lose their popularity when white bronze became an alternative.

22. Monumental Bronze claimed thousands of Civil War soldiers had been sold. After several years of living with their claims and their prose, I'll settle for hundreds.

23. Stephen Davis, "The Confederate Monument and the South," *Journal of Popular Culture* 16 (Winter 1982), p. 16.

24. Carol Grissom at the Smithsonian is willing to give advice, and her definitive book on historical uses of zinc should be published soon.

25. The Albany Institute of History and Art has a letter from the Henry-Bonnard Bronze Company to the sculptor John Quincy Adams Ward which does exactly this. The letter was brought to my attention by Mary Deal, Akron, Ohio.

26. I looked up only the names of men since nineteenth-century city directories very rarely gave an occupation for a woman. (Sometimes, of course, I could get the man's name from a daughter or a wife's marker—"wife of. . . .") I checked Schenectady, Chicago, Syracuse, and Des Moines directories for the names I took from white bronzes in Vale Cemetery, Rose Hill, Oakwood, and Woodland respectively. Although approximately seventy-five names may not be a statistically valid sample, they gave a wide enough spread to prove the point.

12

Strange but Genteel Pleasure Grounds: Tourist and Leisure Uses of Nineteenth-Century Rural Cemeteries

Blanche Linden-Ward

When Cincinnatians opened their newspapers one early fall day in 1867, they must not have been surprised to read of "grave charges of conviviality in the cemetery." They knew that Spring Grove, like the other "rural" or garden cemeteries founded on the peripheries of American cities from 1831 into the 1860s, was more than a plain and simple burial place. These new institutions served as popular "resorts" or "asylums," frequently termed that by the genteel who favored their use for meditative promenades, considered acceptable and even desirable by the staunchest moralists or advocates of well-spent, edifying leisure time. In their mid-century heyday, before the creation of public parks, these green, pastoral places also functioned as "pleasure grounds" for the general public, often to the dismay of their founders. They became major tourist attractions, touted by guidebooks and travellers' accounts as *musts* to be seen by any stranger, American or foreign, visiting their vicinity.[1]

The first American "rural" cemetery and prototype of the others was Boston's Mount Auburn, founded in 1831. Mount Auburn's picturesque landscape, so unlike any existing graveyard or churchyard, was a scenic composition of winding avenues, paths, and ponds on hilly, wooded terrain with dramatic panoramic views over the entire metropolitan area (fig. 12.1). Although meant to appear naturalistic, the landscape was carefully designed and constructed by General Henry A. S. Dearborn, aided by Dr. Jacob Bigelow and other members of the Massachusetts Horticultural Society, following principles developed in eighteenth-century English landscaped gardens and then applied at Père Lachaise, the Parisian cemetery

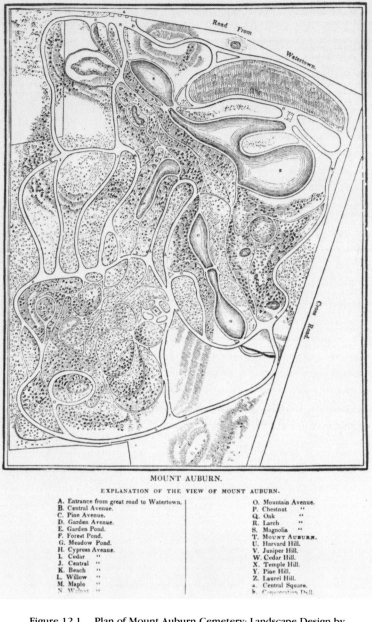

MOUNT AUBURN.

EXPLANATION OF THE VIEW OF MOUNT AUBURN.

A. Entrance from great road to Watertown.
B. Central Avenue.
C. Pine Avenue.
D. Garden Avenue.
E. Garden Pond.
F. Forest Pond.
G. Meadow Pond.
H. Cypress Avenue.
I. Cedar   "
J. Central   "
K. Beach   "
L. Willow   "
M. Maple   "
N. Walnut   "

O. Mountain Avenue.
P. Chestnut   "
Q. Oak   "
R. Larch   "
S. Magnolia   "
T. MOUNT AUBURN.
U. Harvard Hill.
V. Juniper Hill.
W. Cedar Hill.
X. Temple Hill.
Y. Pine Hill.
Z. Laurel Hill.
a. Central Square.
b. Consecration Dell.

Figure 12.1.   Plan of Mount Auburn Cemetery; Landscape Design by
Henry A. S. Dearborn
Map engraved by Alexander Wadsworth, 1832.
(Courtesy Mount Auburn Cemetery)

that attracted international renown after its 1804 founding. Like these precedents, already notable tourist attractions, Mount Auburn presented visitors with a programmed sequence of sensory experiences, primarily visual, intended to elicit specific emotions, especially the so-called pleasures of melancholy that particularly appealed to contemporary romantic sensibilities (fig. 12.2).[2]

Prime publicists of the cemetery, therefore, were ministers and moralists like William Ellery Channing and John Pierpont, religious liberals who argued that pastoral cemeteries served as schools of moral philosophy and catalysts for civic virtue. They urged youths, in particular, to visit Mount Auburn to learn from the exemplary lives of notables interred there and to be sobered by thoughts of the shortness of life. The young were to return home with new resolve to work hard and to do good (fig. 12.3).[3]

There was a distinct resonance between the landscape design of the "rural" cemetery and recurring themes in much of the literary and material culture of the era. The new cemetery epitomized the Whiggish sentimentality, melancholy, romanticism, and didactic moralism that characterized the poetry and prose of gift books, religious tracts, and even widely circulated newspapers and magazines like *Godey's Lady's Book*. Pierpont's popular inspirational verse, often referring to such a pastoral funerary setting, frequently occurred on those pages. The cemetery landscape also duplicated the allegorical funerary scenes of mourning pictures—stylized painted and embroidered compositions that became fixtures in many American parlors, often placed over hearths. The popular taste for the new cemetery echoed cultural trends and tastes shared by many Americans.[4]

Mount Auburn's founders intended to draw upon such sources for forms to make their new institution an attractive place with multiple cultural functions. In his consecration address, Judge Joseph Story anticipated that the cemetery would become a place where visitors might "indulge in the dreams of hope and ambition or solace their hearts by melancholy meditation." Dearborn, then President of the Massachusetts Horticultural Society, predicted that Mount Auburn would become "a holy and pleasant resort for the living ... one of the most instructive, magnificent, and pleasant promenades in our country. From its immediate proximity to the Capitol of the State, it will attract universal interest, and become a place of healthful, refreshing, and agreeable resort." Certainly, to that date, no other American cemetery had been designed to provide such diverse services and to fill such multiple functions.[5]

Mount Auburn was also meant to be an attractive place of history, an assemblage from the past of exemplary individuals, the accounts of whose virtues and accomplishments might be read inscribed on neoclassical stones. One writer in the *Christian Examiner* in 1836 believed cemeteries

Figure 12.2.   Forest Pond, Mount Auburn Cemetery
Engraving by W. H. Bartlett, ca. 1845.
(From the collection of Blanche Linden-Ward)

Figure 12.3.   Mount Auburn's Chapel
Engraving by James Smillie, 1847.
(Courtesy Mount Auburn Cemetery)

like Mount Auburn would stir "the sentiment of retrospection and reverence" for a common national past grounded in moralistic principles to be
emulated by future generations. The place would provide antidotes for the
disagreeable effects of the modern age, "the busy competition ... the hur-
ried, ambitious spirit" rampant in the most prosperous, bourgeoning cities
of the time, such as Boston.[6]

The didactic values of carefully designed, naturalistic landscapes were
recognized and discussed extensively on both sides of the Atlantic in the
decades preceding Mount Auburn's founding. When British moralist Henry
Tuckerman visited America, therefore, he approved of the way in which
"rural" cemeteries fostered "that association with the past essential to intel-
lectual dignity" that seemed to him to be fast disappearing in his age of
rampant change. Tuckerman looked to pleasant, pastoral cemeteries as
landscapes of the future, not just places of the past. Their attractiveness
would bring in precisely those members of the public who might be respon-
sive to their moralistic influence. Such places, theorists argued, would fos-
ter social stability and civility—what French philosophers had been describing as a "cult of ancestors." Alexander Everett, Bostonian and early
advocate of Mount Auburn, exclaimed, "How salutary the effect which a
visit to its calm and sacred shades will produce on souls too much agitated
by the storms of the world? It was surely fitting that Art and Nature should
combine their beauties to grace a scene devoted to purposes so high and
holy." Through the next four decades, other popular moralists echoed these
views, hoping to shape for the better "the moral taste and general sentiments of all classes" through the influence of the cemetery.[7]

Boston newspaperman Joseph Buckingham, advocate of the local "me-
chanics" class, agreed, offering Mount Auburn to the public as spiritual
medicine to assuage the ills of his age: "Reader! if you would have the
sympathies of your nature awakened, your earthly affections purified, your
anxieties chastened and subdued, go to Mount Auburn! Go not for the
gratification of idle curiosity, to comment with the eye of a critic upon the
forms of the monuments or the taste of those who placed them there. . . .
Go not there with cold indifference to shock the sensibility of the bereaved
with your antic and unseemly behavior. . . . But go to read and to learn the
lesson which you must transmit to those who come after you (fig. 12.4).[8]

Other writers prescribed the cemetery for acculturation of youth. In
her *Advice to Mothers,* Lydia Maria Child urged women to take their children on Sunday walks through the cemetery: "So important do I consider
cheerful association with death, that I wish to see our graveyards laid out
with walks and trees and beautiful shrubs as places of promenade." Mount
Auburn filled the bill; and, according to Child, deserved extensive emula-

Figure 12.4.   Visitors to Gossler's Monument on Yarrow Path, Mount Auburn Cemetery
Engraving by James Smillie, 1847.
(Courtesy Mount Auburn Cemetery)

tion across the nation. Indeed, illustrations of the cemetery from the mid-1840s show parents introducing toddlers to the place (fig. 12.5).[9]

Mount Auburn was meant to be a didactic, soothing, restorative place for all ages, all religions, and all classes—points emphasized by founders as well as by a host of publicists. Cornelia Walter, author of *Mount Auburn Illustrated,* published in 1847 with dozens of detailed engraved views of the wooded landscape, advocated "meditative wanderings" through the landscape on which one might "gain a lesson from nature." At the cemetery, visitors would "learn to conform [their] lives to the order of her [Nature's] works in view of both the present and future." Walter promised that "those periods of meditation derived from the enticements of Mount Auburn would remain constantly fixed in the recollection as bright oasises in the pilgrimage of life." The place appealed particularly to the pantheism and transcendentalism rising in vogue among the educated in that era.[10]

For instance, an impressionable schoolgirl like Mary Tyler Peabody gloried in the romantic melancholy she experienced at Mount Auburn. She wrote to her friend Miss Rawlins Pickman of Salem, Massachusetts in the fall of 1835 of wonderful emotions stirred by a Friday evening visit to the new cemetery: "How can I describe the feeling with which I looked again upon our gorgeous woods and heard the song of the wind in the pine groves? I should like to sleep there, with that beautiful soul sighing my requiem. Nothing that the hand of man has done is so interesting to me as the grave of a young wife, whose simple monument is surrounded by a railing and decked with beautiful flowers." Mary concluded, "I always feel as if I want to stay when I get there," echoing sentiments inspired by Keats and often repeated in popular, sentimental poems of the era.[11]

Similarly, a mill girl from Lowell exclaimed in print in 1840: "Mount Auburn! How soothing and tranquilizing is the remembrance of thy deep and quiet beauty! . . . As we stray through thy pleasant woods, we go back in imagination to our own homes and stand by the graves of our loved ones; and we remember the crushing weight of utter loneliness which preseed upon us as the green turf hid them from our view." The young woman, probably in her late teens or early twenties, valued the cathartic emotion stirred by a visit to Mount Auburn—a quintessentially romantic experience. The place served as an aid to mourning—not only for loved ones deceased but for a lost way of life missed nostalgically, particularly by Yankees in that era of immense social, cultural, political, demographic, and technological change. The mill girl, like many contemporaries, found at Mount Auburn an "asylum" from the industrialized workplace into which she was thrust, albeit willingly, but suffering cultural shock, confronting dramatic contrasts to the old places and way of life in rural New England towns and farms from which she and her coworkers came. Those yearning for a sense of family

Figure 12.5. William Ellery Channing's Lot at Mount Auburn Cemetery
Engraving by James Smillie, 1847.
(*Courtesy Mount Auburn Cemetery*)

or community lost or for the timeless rhythms of preindustrial, rural life found gratification at Mount Auburn, which, after all, drew its name from "Sweet Auburn," the fictitious but representative Irish village destroyed by estate building and enclosure acts in the eighteenth century and bemoaned by Oliver Goldsmith in his popular poem, "The Deserted Village."[12]

Such was the nostalgia shared by Caroline Orne, whose book-length poem, *Sweet Auburn and Mount Auburn* (1844), described how the "forest deep" two hundred years before had been transformed into the arcadic, rural landscape she recalled from her childhood on that western border of Cambridge, site of the cemetery, becoming a "City of the Silent ... sacred to the deepest affections." Orne's poem was meant to attract visitors to the cemetery, but she felt it necessary to add poetic, cautionary advice for good behavior:

> 'Tis holy ground—this City of the Dead
> Let no rude accents of untimely mirth
> Break the calm stillness of this sacred earth.[13]

Proper behavior was expected at the cemetery by its chief advocates, those already confirmed to gentility and strongly self-disciplined. Textile industrialist Amos Lawrence, who renounced drink, smoke, and theater as recreational pursuits in his youth, told his diary of many adult days of pleasant leisure spent at Mount Auburn. Charles Sumner, peace activist, abolitionist, and senator, used Mount Auburn as a retreat from the heat of national politics on the eve of the Civil War; and lore holds that a messenger found Franklin Pierce sitting under a tree in the cemetery when he came to notify the future President that the 1852 Democratic convention had nominated him compromise candidate. Bostonian George Ticknor Curtis had correctly observed in 1854 that Mount Auburn permitted people "to rid themselves of TIME among the final homes of those who have exchanged it for eternity."[14]

The author of Mount Auburn's first guidebook, *The Picturesque Pocket Companion and Visitor's Guide through Mount Auburn* (1839), aimed to promote such uses of the place, proclaiming rhetorically, "What object in or near Boston will be equally attractive?" That book was the first of many guides, some reissued annually in numerous editions, which furthered the fame of Mount Auburn and helped to program the visitor's experience there.[15] Similarly, *Dearborn's Guide through Mount Auburn ... for the Benefit of Strangers* was a slim, portable fifty-page booklet sold for twenty cents through the 1850s and 1860s (fig. 12.6). It contains a map, over sixty engravings of monuments and landscape, and a good deal of the secularized moral philosophy so popular at that time. The guide led visitors through the

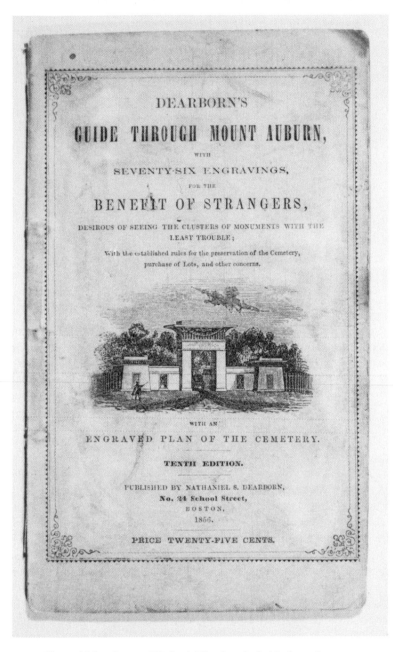

Figure 12.6.   Cover of Nathaniel Dearborn's *Guide through Mount Auburn,* 1856
(From the collection of Blanche Linden-Ward)

cemetery along a prescribed route, pointing out notable interments and monuments and providing short pieces of sentimental verse or pithy wisdom to set one's proper melancholy or sober frame of mind. Many of the moralistic poems have practical, hortatory messages reminiscent of Poor Richard's aphorisms, such as:

> Be wise to-day; tis madness to defer:
> Next day the fatal precedent will plead;
> Thus on, till wisdom is push'd out of life.
> Procrastination is the thief of time.

Or:

> At thirty man suspects himself a fool;
> Knows it at forty, and reforms his plan;
> At fifty chides his infamous delay,
> Pushes his prudent purpose to resolve;
> In all the magnanimity of thought
> Resolves and re-solves; then dies the same.

Poems in *Dearborn's Guide* urged wisdom, diligence, work, moderation, humility, stewardship of wealth, and other civic virtues. The *Guide* also provided an early example of the site-specific, self-guided, programmed tour.[16]

Dearborn's competitor, Levi Merriam Stevens, claimed his *Guide,* subtitled *A Handbook for Passengers over the Cambridge Railroad,* aimed "not to describe Mount Auburn as anyone *thinks* it should be, but to lead the visitor through the most interesting portions of the Cemetery, to call attention to EVERYTHING on the route worthy of observation, and thus enable him to view Mount Auburn as it IS—as Nature, Art, and Affection have made it." Stevens's seventy-five-page *Guide,* first published in 1856, provided detailed descriptions and engravings of major monuments and also emphasized moral lessons. Stevens asked, "To what better place can we go ... to cool the burning brow of ambition, or to relieve the swelling heart of disappointment? We can find no better spot for the rambles of curiosity, health, or pleasure; none sweeter for the whispers of affection among the living." Stevens urged people to visit Mount Auburn to "renew our failing resolutions for the dark and boundless future."[17]

Indeed, after only three years, according to Joseph Story, Mount Auburn became "a place of general resort and interest, as well to strangers as to citizens; and its avenues and paths, ornamented with monumental structures of various beauty and elegance, have already given solace and tranquilizing reflections to many an afflicted heart, and awakened a deep and moral sensibility in many a pious bosom." The 1857 *Boston Almanac* proclaimed it "one of the indispensables to a stranger sojourning in or near Boston, and few places present, within an equal space, either to citizens or strangers, a more varied combination of elements to attract attention and awaken thought." Strangers to Boston, in particular, proved anxious to see the remarkable place and to experience the emotions and associations it promised to arouse.[18]

The famous actress Fanny Kemble toured Mount Auburn in April of 1833 and described it as "a pleasure garden instead of a place of graves." The following summer, Swedish visitor Carl David Arfwedson saw the grounds and paraphrased Keats—"a glance at this beautiful cemetery almost excites a wish to die." That year, the Englishman Edward Abdy remarked that "parties of pleasure come hither from the city in great number," at a rate estimated to be over 600 a day. Others observed that "Daily, hourly, a line of carriages stands at its lofty gate, and countless guests pause at the solemn inscription . . . then enter to meditate among the unrivalled varieties of Mount Auburn." The young Englishman Henry Arthur Bright, close friend of Nathaniel Hawthorne, was surprised to find on his visit led by Henry Wadsworth Longfellow that "Cemeteries here are all the 'rage'; people lounge in them and use them (as their tastes are inclined) for walking, making love, weeping, sentimentalizing, and every thing in short." Such accounts of Mount Auburn functioned as publicity when published in national newspapers, travel accounts, and guide books; and they quickly won international acclaim for the cemetery.[19]

Foreign visitors proved the best publicists through example as well as testimonial. Sir Charles Lyell, a friend of Judge Joseph Story, first President of Mount Auburn, made sure to visit the cemetery on both of his trips to Boston from England in 1842 and 1849, and he published praise of the place in his travel narrative. Lady Emmeline Wortley also described the wonders of the landscape in her widely read book on the United States. Through mid-century, a host of notables made Mount Auburn as major an attraction as the Erie Canal or Niagara Falls on their Grand Tours of America. Charles Dickens and the Emperor Dom Pedro of Brazil acclaimed the importance of Mount Auburn. In October of 1860, cemetery trustees escorted Lord Renfew, Prince of Wales and future King Edward VI, to the cemetery, followed by a throng of celebrity-seeking Bostonians who watched the heir-apparent plant a yellowwood and purple beech in front of the chapel. Newspapers across the nation reported that Napoleon III "gave the palm to Mount Auburn for its natural beauty of position" and for the designed landscape he discovered there on his 1861 visit. One Boston newspaper justly bragged, "Every visitor goes to Mount Auburn as a matter of course."[20]

The English writer Harriet Martineau, who received a personally guided tour by Judge Story in August of 1847, judged Mount Auburn a particularly American phenomenon, indicative of New England's dominance in the national culture: "As might have been predicted, one of the first directions in which the Americans have indulged their taste and indicated their refinement is in the preparation and care of their burial places." Martineau attributed this tendency to "the pilgrim origin of the New England population, whose fathers seemed to think that they lived only in order to die." Hence, in America, thoughts of death filled "a large space in the peoples' mind," Martineau explained, having observed the resonance of ideas about death in the cemetery as well as in the rapidly developing mass culture.[21]

Despite the centrality of death in the culture of the era, Martineau saw evidence at Mount Auburn of a nascent trend in American mentality which social observers would later label the "denial of death." She wrote, "A visitor from a strange planet, ignorant of mortality, would take this place to be the sanctum of creation. Every step teems with the promise of life. Beauty is about to 'spring out of the ashes,' and life out of dust; Humanity seems to be waiting with acclamations ready on its lips, for the new birth. That there has been any past is little more than a matter of inference." Ironically, despite Mount Auburn's founders' attempt to create a usable, civilizing display of the past at the cemetery, they seemed, to Martineau, to have denied it.[22]

Martineau moderated her criticism of American culture precisely because she considered Mount Auburn representative of it and also "the most beautiful cemetery in the world" with an "air of finish and taste, especially in contrast to Père Lachaise," a major tourist attraction in Paris. Mount Auburn epitomized hope; the French cemetery, mourning. At Père Lachaise, Martineau observed, "there is no light from the future shining over the place. In Mount Auburn, on the contrary, there is nothing else." Mount Auburn appealed "to us, in whom education, reason, the prophecies of natural religion, and the promises of the gospel unite their influence to generate a perfect belief in a life beyond the grave." The place must, she speculated, appear much different to the doubtful, the agnostic, the atheist. Still, based only on the beauty of its naturalistic landscape, it was an appealing "mazy paradise, where every forest tree of the western continent grows and every bird to which the climate is congenial builds its nest." (Indeed, Mount Auburn continues in the late twentieth century to be both an arboretum and a sanctuary for birds in the Boston metropolitan region.) Martineau considered the cemetery as metaphor for both travel and life, presenting lessons of transience with which she, appropriately, chose to end her two-volume travel narrative of the United States.[23]

Americans from other cities and regions recognized the importance of Mount Auburn as prototype and inspiration for cemeteries which they would create as local amenities for themselves when they returned home from visits to Boston. Time and time again, cultural and commercial leaders from other cities visited Mount Auburn and went away determined to found their own voluntary associations, acquire charters, and lay out landscapes for their own garden cemeteries to serve both as showplaces of urbane taste and local accomplishments and as retreats for salutary recreation of their fellow citizens. Their own civic pride and localistic ambitions were roused on hearing that "neither care nor expense had been spared in efforts to enhance [Mount Auburn's] great natural advantages." They read in the *American Cyclopedia of Useful Knowledge* in 1835, as in travellers' accounts, that Mount Auburn was "justly celebrated as the most interesting object of the kind in our country," a place that attracted visitors from far and near, a place representative of local sophistication, an amenity that although technically private served many public functions. Other Atlantic seaboard civic leaders took such words as a challenge to create their own cemeteries in the attempt to rival Mount Auburn.[24]

The Philadelphia writer and horticulturist John Jay Smith provided the second example of America's "rural" cemetery movement when he created a joint-stock company to purchase a thirty-two-acre estate near his city, high atop the eastern bank of the Schuylkill River. Although the design by local architect John Notman was slightly more constrained and geometric than the freely flowing naturalism of Mount Auburn and although the site was half the size of the original, Laurel Hill opened in 1836 to vie with Mount Auburn for public recognition and popular acclaim. Smith acknowledged that "both are calculated to strike the imagination and make it in love with nature," although the landscape styles were markedly different from the start—Mount Auburn reflecting the more woodsy, irregular, naturalistic qualities defined as "picturesque" and Laurel Hill modeled after the newer taste for the more constrained parterres, terraces, and plantings of the "gardenesque" (fig. 12.7).[25]

Within a year of its founding, one local guidebook proclaimed Laurel Hill "one of the lions" of Philadelphia, and a number of subsequent publications featured it as being of major interest to tourists as well as to local urbanites desirous of finding a green place for well-spent leisure in easy access from the city. A commanding view up and down the river from the cemetery site and the ever-increasing number of finely sculpted monuments attracted Philadelphians like Sidney George Fisher, who enjoyed carriage rides through Laurel Hill. Nationally prominent landscape theorist Andrew Jackson Downing deemed it "a charming pleasure-ground" that

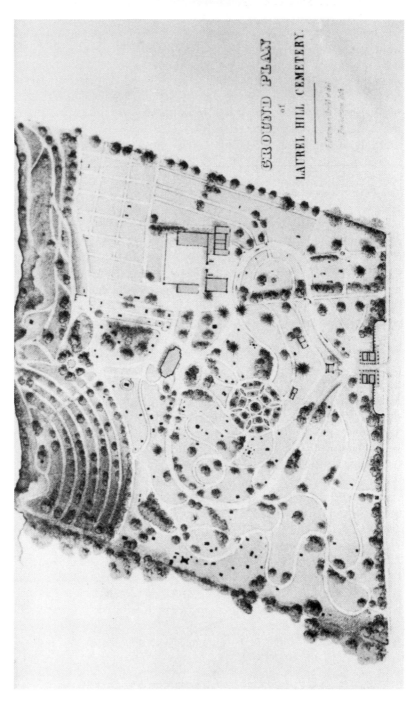

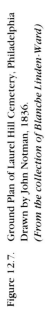

Figure 12.7.   Ground Plan of Laurel Hill Cemetery, Philadelphia
Drawn by John Notman, 1836.
(From the collection of Blanche Linden-Ward)

attracted at least 30,000 visitors between April and December of 1848 alone (fig. 12.8).[26]

In order to bring even more visitors to his cemetery, Smith purchased a sculptural group from the Scotsman James Thom for display under a Norman Gothic shelter just inside the gates. The theatrical scene depicts Sir Walter Scott's story of "Old Mortality," a man who traveled Scotland, recutting fading funerary inscriptions. Scott himself is present in the tableau. Smith anticipated that the display would prove "a great attraction," adding to "the novelty of a rural cemetery" to increase public demand for Laurel Hill lots (fig. 12.9).[27]

Both Laurel Hill and Mount Auburn provided models and impetus to spawn other similar cemeteries in short order. Baltimoreans observed that Mount Auburn and Laurel Hill by 1837 "already constitute the most attractive objects to the visitor" to their cities; and there was "scarce an inhabitant" of either area "who does not testify to the pride with which he regards the public cemetery in his neighborhood. No traveller with the necessary leisure on his hands is content to quit those cities without an excursion to Mount Auburn or Laurel Hill."[28]

Baltimoreans, proud of their recent ability to compete commercially with older cities to the north, determined to follow suit. Stephen Duncan Walker returned home from a New England trip to praise publically the many civic functions of Mount Auburn. He appealed to local pride to produce a similar institution: "Maryland has not been without her great men, names that would have adorned a Roman age, in her proudest era; but under our present [burial] system, where are they? ... They are scattered to the four winds ... here and there in obscure, isolated tombs, undistinguished and almost forgotten." Walker invoked the civic pride of the people of Baltimore to "collect their ashes ... prepare them a sanctuary ... study their virtues, [and] ... write anew upon our hearts and on their tombs a nation's epitaph!" But Baltimoreans, who had already pioneered in the civic venture of historic monument building, were motivated by more than a simple commemorative impulse or desire to create a museum of local history; they wanted to emulate the multifunctional example of the cemetery in Boston, "always in the lead in taste, literature, and refinement." They aimed to duplicate for themselves a Mount Auburn, "one of the most solemn, classic, and interesting scenes in the United States" at the same time as they created an open space for healthful recreation within a half-hour's walking distance from their city center, the market. Thus in 1838, they received a charter and laid out Green Mount as combined "rural cemetery and public walk," to be touted in local guidebooks as a "beautiful and romantic spot," a certain attraction for any stranger in town as well as for local residents.[29]

New Yorkers did not lag far behind in performing the newly perceived

Figure 12.8. Visitors to Laurel Hill Cemetery with View of the Schuylkill River Engraving by A. W. Graham after W. Croome for *Godey's Lady's Book,* ca. 1844. *(From the collection of Blanche Linden-Ward)*

The first object
attraction, on pass
through the gate,
the celebrated group
Thom, representing O
MORTALITY, HIS PON
and SIR WALTER SCO
The reader will find t
scene in Sir Wal
Scott's historical tale
"Old Mortality."
To the north of th
ort of "the Burns of Sculpture," is the GODFREY MON

Figure 12.9. "Old Mortality, Sir Walter Scott, and His Poney"
Statuary grouping by James Thom, just inside the
entrance to Laurel Hill Cemetery. Engraving from R. A.
Smith's *Illustrated Guide*, 1852
(From the collection of Blanche Linden-Ward)

civic duty of founding a "rural" cemetery as "pleasure ground" as well as exemplar of moral values. In 1839, the real estate entrepreneur Henry E. Pierrepont organized a voluntary association of civic leaders in New York City and Brooklyn to acquire a charter for a "rural" cemetery to be laid out on Brooklyn's Gowanus Heights, site of a Revolutionary War battle. The place commanded a stunning panoramic view over Manhattan Island, the harbor, and even the ocean. Major David B. Douglas, an engineer, laid out a landscape of rambling roads and ponds through the large and varied terrain in a fashion that more closely approximated that of Mount Auburn than of Laurel Hill or Green Mount (fig. 12.10).

Almost immediately, according to a local newspaper, visitors "began to be attracted from the city in considerable numbers daily." The press predicted that Green-Wood was destined to "become a popular and elegant place of resort, where some of the wild and lovely features of nature might be retained near the city." One New Yorker wrote in 1842, "We love to dally on the road, to pluck a flower here and plant one there, and while away a little of our time in the pursuit of pleasure among sanctified creations of nature"; and, after all, at that time, preserves of nature in the immediate vicinity of the burgeoning metropolis, in easy access of urban dwellers, were becoming increasingly hard to find. Green-Wood offered a convenient retreat or "asylum," a preserve of nature in a new suburb where a tight grid of streets had recently been laid to obliterate any of the remaining pastoralism of the area. As one journalist asked, "What merchant in New York—What professional man—What mechanic, but would feel better, physically and morally, to forget the season, the cares and toils incident to his pursuits, amidst the beauties of Green-Wood Cemetery?" Indeed, unless he was prosperous enough to own a country estate, there were few other ways in which even the urban merchant or professional—to say nothing of the mechanic or the unskilled worker—could have leisure access to the salubrity of nature in the vicinity of the city.[30]

Andrew Jackson Downing, who lived on a "rural" estate further up the Hudson River but who frequently worked in New York City, was tactful in comparing major cemeteries. He concluded, "We place Mount Auburn first, because to the inhabitants of Boston belongs the credit of first showing this country how beautiful and consoling a spot 'God's acre' may be made ... how soothing and benign the influence upon the living, rural beauty may exert even in the last resting place of the dead." Downing found Green-Wood in 1847, "not yet equal to Mount Auburn in monuments" or "in its interior of leafy woods and dells," although his criticism left New Yorkers with a goal towards which to strive. Downing considered Mount Auburn's salutary influence on taste to be national in scope.[31]

Green-Wood was one of the first of many American rural cemeteries

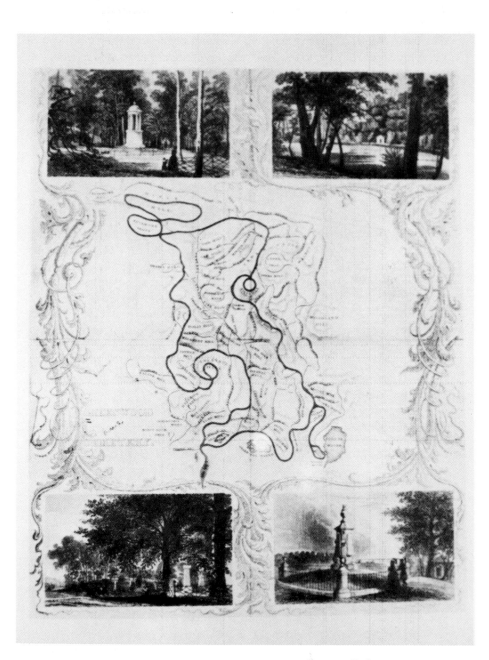

Figure 12.10.   Green-Wood Cemetery, Brooklyn, New York
Map and views engraved by James Smillie, 1847.
(Courtesy Mount Auburn Cemetery)

to be compared with Mount Auburn. National periodicals from the 1840s through the 1870s often contained articles by a new breed of American landscape connoisseur intent on weighing the merits of various cemeteries. A piece in the mass-circulating *Ballou's* in 1855 described Mount Hope, founded near Rochester, New York in 1839, as having such "wild and picturesque scenery" that it vied with Mount Auburn "in natural beauty." John McConnell, a Rochester architect, looked to Mount Auburn for inspiration in designing the Egyptian gateway for that cemetery in 1838. Indeed, all of Mount Hope's founders consciously referred to Boston's cemetery, rather than to Green-Wood, as a model.[32]

Such was also the case in Cincinnati in 1844 when Robert Buchanan, a successful merchant and leading force in forming the Cincinnati Horticultural Society, convened a meeting at his home to instigate a "movement for the procuring of grounds for a Rural or Public Cemetery." Buchanan admitted that "to our Eastern brethren we look for such instruction in the adornment of cemetery grounds" as was requisite for creating a picturesque, parklike institution in the new suburbs of his city, "a necessary distance from the annoyances which the smoke and turbulence and noises of the city industry and commerce might occasion." Cemetery founders sent the local architect, Howard Daniels, on a four-month excursion to study the design and organization of the best eastern cemeteries, and he returned to lay out the core of Spring Grove Cemetery so as to attract immediate acclaim by Cincinnatians as well as visitors (fig. 12.11).[33]

Spring Grove's development as a parklike space accessible to the city continued beyond the initial landscape design following the example of eastern models. In 1855, the Prussian landscape gardener Adolph Strauch became Superintendent and Landscape Gardener with the mandate from the Board to make the cemetery "the most interesting of all places for contemplative recreation" with everything in it being "tasteful, classical, and poetical." Following the design principles of his mentor, Prince Herman von Pückler-Muskau, the "great European park reformer," Strauch converted unused wetlands on the grounds into five acres of picturesque ponds, drawing inspiration form those designed by the English gardener Joseph Paxton in 1843 for Liverpool's Birkenhead Park, one of the first truly urban and public recreational areas in the world (fig. 12.12).[34]

Through the 1860s, the Cincinnati press acclaimed Spring Grove, "Our Beautiful Cemetery," for being "haunted at all seasons by hundreds of persons daily, by the sight-seer, and those who yearn for green fields, no less than by those who have a mournful reason to frequent and lingering visits." After two decades, it continued to be "steadily gaining in favor of the public." One journalist waxed poetic: "Words can not convey an adequate idea of the charms of Spring Grove in spring and summer. A broad expanse

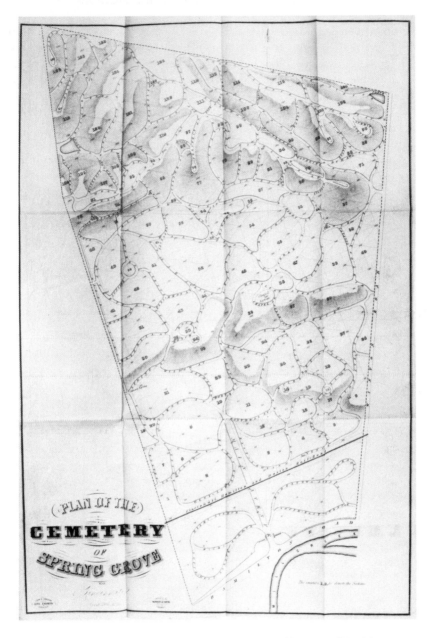

Figure 12.11.   Spring Grove Cemetery, Designed by Howard Daniels,
1845
Map from the *Annual Report* of 1852.
(From the collection of Blanche Linden-Ward)

Figure 12.12.   Geyser Lake at Spring Grove Cemetery, Designed by Adolph Strauch in 1855
Engraving of 1869.
(From the collection of Blanche Linden-Ward)

of undulating greensward, diversified by graveled walks, delights the eye. The placid waters of the lake, reflecting heaven's own blue, and bearing upon its bosom the snowy form of the graceful swan, is highly suggestive of peace and repose. All the bounties of nature and the works of art can not be comprehended in a glance." The tourist or urbanite would find much at Spring Grove to fill more than one day's visit and to bring him back again and again.[35]

Indeed, the pleasant, unprecedented parklike landscapes of these cemeteries more than the praise of urban boosters in the local press attracted throngs of visitors. Spring Grove's gatekeeper counted annually through the 1860s and 1870s attendance ranging from 86,000 to 160,000 coming in carriages, buggies, and on foot (presumably via public transportation), *not counting* mourners in funeral processions. John Jay Smith estimated 140,000 visitors to Laurel Hill in 1860 alone; and that year, a Bostonian remarked that "quiet, home-keeping citizens, even in Cambridge, may not be aware of the great number of persons who daily visit Mount Auburn." Throngs flocked to these cemeteries on holidays like the Fourth of July, New Year's Day, and, after the Civil War, the newly declared Decoration Day. Spring Grove's management followed the lead of the Boards of Mount Auburn and other eastern cemeteries in passing stringent regulations against picnicking or drinking or other "frivolous" behavior, precisely because members of the public insisted on trying to use these places as "pleasure grounds."[36]

Ironically, contrary to the moralists' predictions, visiting "rural" cemeteries had not calmed the souls of those whose behavior did nothing but bring the "storms of the world" into the pastoral "asylum." These places were meant for those already confirmed to gentility; but through mid-century, they attracted many others. After all, the young read of the "magic wilderness of [Mount Auburn's] beautiful and almost endless variety," in which "you are not only lost in astonishment at what you see, but are in danger of losing yourself among its mazes, through which you might wander for hours without finding a clue to an escape." The fantasy landscape, unequaled until the development of amusement parks, appealed to a sense of mystical excitement and even adventure, so much a part of romanticism. The attraction had special significance for proponents of transcendentalism and spiritualism. Yet recreation there had to remain quiet and passive, according to regulations. Still cemeteries could serve as favored trysting places for the young, as noted by Fanny Kemble.[37]

Many visitors to "rural" cemeteries, however, sought only present pleasures rather than the "pleasures of melancholy," lessons of moral philosophy, or simple transcendental appreciation of nature. Cemetery founders and lot owners complained after only two years that Mount Auburn was used "in a manner very different from what had been expected, destroying the solemnity and quiet" intended for the place. Visitors mutilated trees (especially given the propensity for whittling in that era), broke fences, gathered flowers, and trampled lots. In response, hand-lettered signs posted by management politely urged: "Visitors are desired to confine their walks to the avenues and paths and to avoid treading on borders." Or, "Pause—this is hallowed ground, sacred to the dead and the living. Pluck not a shrub—touch not a flower. Leave every thing in its beauty." Other notices commanded more forcefully: "Walk your Horse!"; or, as at Spring Grove, "No Fast Driving," but to no avail. Visitors on horseback were most disruptive and damaging, riding down narrow paths intended for contemplative strollers and tethering their mounts to trees and shrubs, damaging the plants. Such behavior could not be and was not tolerated.[38]

Eventually, the Massachusetts General Court gave cemetery regulations the force of law, with a $20 reward given for information leading to conviction of whittlers and those firing guns in the cemetery, offenses deemed misdemeanors with fines ranging from $5 to $50. Mount Auburn's President Bigelow concluded, "There is a class of persons ... by no means a small one, who can be made to respect the rights of their fellow citizens only by the enactment of a strict code of laws and the rigid enforcement of them." Directors of other cemeteries agreed and added additional prohibitions to curtail undesirable activities as the years progressed. By the 1850s, Laurel Hill forebade picnicking or bringing dogs to run through the grounds.[39]

Mount Auburn provided a model by obtaining such legislation and also by exerting internal control by requiring tickets for carriage entrance into the cemetery. Each lot owner received a "ticket" which functioned as a pass or membership card and permitted him to drive into the cemetery in a carriage containing as many family members or friends as desired. Out-of-town visitors of "respectable" appearance could easily obtain temporary tickets free of charge from trustees, from the cemetery office in the city, or from local hotels. Horseback riders were banned entirely from Mount Auburn until the 1860s, when special passes were issued to a limited number of well-known and well-behaved individuals upon payment of a "bonus" or annual fee for the privilege. Pedestrians had access at all times, although in the early years, trustees attempted unsuccessfully to ban their access on Sundays, the sole day of rest for the working classes—the day that had seen the greatest numbers of people at the cemetery.[40]

Again, other cemeteries followed suit. Free tickets to Green-Wood could be obtained from any undertaker in New York City, and those intending to tour Laurel Hill could obtain theirs without cost from Smith at the Philadelphia Library or from any other cemetery directors. Because Laurel

Hill was "so popular," Smith also employed two men who made a handsome income "by watching the numerous horses hitched outside" the gates by those who did not own lots and therefore could not ride into the cemetery. "Two other stalwart men were required to take tickets and keep out those not fortunate in getting admissions in the city." The practice of issuing tickets impeded loiterers or mere passers-by from entering on a whim, thus eliminating the sort of persons who tended to create disturbances.[41]

The intention was not to keep out those who did not own lots but to regulate their number and behavior. Mount Auburn banned omnibuses, charabans, and excursion wagons early on, but Spring Grove did not. By one account, wagons full of new German immigrants readily won access to the grounds. Mount Auburn's Board considered but rejected the idea of stationing carriages-for-hire at the gates to provide tours through the grounds for those arriving by foot or public transportation; trustees discovered early on that exclusivity of admission for carriages, most of which were driven into the grounds for recreation, provided an incentive to those who were able to purchase a family lot in order to get a ticket for the privilege. The leisure time promenade in the slow horse-drawn carriage, to see and to be seen traversing a particularly picturesque route, served as a major social and recreational activity through mid-century.[42]

Control of visitors on foot, however, became increasingly more difficult as improvements in public transportation brought more and more visitors to the cemeteries. Typically, because the cemeteries were major destinations on the urban fringe, new mass transit routes of horse-drawn street railways usually laid out their first routes to those destinations. In Boston, in 1834, 1838, 1856, and 1863, new omnibus, street railway, and then railroad lines were established to bring passengers—members of the general public who could not afford their own carriages or rental of one—to the very gates of Mount Auburn. There, trustees worried that "the grounds [would] be overrun by crowds of persons who [would] make it a resort of pleasure and amusement and thus disturb the sacred quiet of the place"; but they were powerless to stop the urban transportation revolution that made Mount Auburn, in particular, of all Boston sites of the times, accessible to the masses. The pattern was repeated in other cities as well. Steamboats plied the Schuylkill River between Philadelphia and the Laurel Hill Landing three and a half miles away, providing easy public access from the founding of the cemetery well through the 1860s, but by the 1850s, those without their own horses and carriages could also choose to take a "very airy and comfortable" passenger car along the Ridge Road to Laurel Hill. Access to Green-Wood in Brooklyn could be had from Manhattan by the South, Wall Street, and Fulton Ferries and then by public horsecar. A horse railway charging a fifteen-cent fare linked Cincinnatians to Spring

Grove in 1857; and the line was electrified in 1880 with the lowering of the fare to a nickel.[43]

Mount Auburn's trustees reacted to the public onslaught by hiring a watchman to supplement the gatekeeper's surveillance and to prevent "unseemly noises" not directly prohibited by the posted regulations; but incidents of vandalism and graffiti only increased through the 1840s and 1850s, despite the offering of cash rewards for identification of offenders and even state legislation deeming malicious damage of cemetery plantings or structures a misdemeanor. Finally, in 1857, the adjacent municipalities of Cambridge and Watertown agreed to deputize a number of Mount Auburn employees, authorizing them to wear badges on "suitable occasions" like holidays in order to assert their authority and to enforce the new laws.[44]

Yet, at the same time, trustees began to provide new amenities "for the benefit of outsiders" visiting Mount Auburn—for example, a pump house with fresh drinking water in a shady Victorian gingerbread gazebo just inside the cemetery entrance. In 1860, they reconstructed the interior of the Egyptian gate in order to provide a porch to shelter visitors waiting for rides. In 1861, privies or water closets were built near the front of the cemetery for ladies and children, despite opposition from some of the oldest trustees; and in 1869, a Reception House, selling refreshments and providing "respectable quarters" for those awaiting public transportation was constructed with costs shared by the cemetery and the Cambridge Horse Railroad. Following these examples, provisions for public comfort were installed in other cemeteries. In 1865, Spring Grove added several "summer houses" where "weary visitors may rest in the shade" as well as provisions for dispensing water and refreshments in the basement of the new chapel near the entrance.[45]

The vicinity of each "rural" cemetery took on leisure functions as well, and attempts by the Boards at Mount Auburn and Spring Grove to provide amenities for visitors may have stemmed from a desire to provide public services before, and to stem the rise of, competing businesses which themselves might have served as leisure-time attractions for the pleasure-seekers of the cities. After all, decades before development of the adjacent Fairmount Park in the 1870s, Laurel Hill became the focus of a recreational area enjoyed by Philadelphians, with taverns and social clubs dotting nearby hills for the enjoyment of visitors. The Lemon Hill "beer garden," for instance, served lager to thirsty visitors at tables on a lawn surrounding a rambling Victorian house.

In Cincinnati, Spring Grove Avenue, the boulevardlike toll road lined with silver-leaved poplars, built by cemetery founders to provide easy carriage access to the city, attracted crowds of those who liked to view the long, formal funeral processions, virtual parades sometimes a mile long, including marching bands and the ostentation of Victorian mourning trappings. By 1877, however, Spring Grove's Directors asked for state legislation to stop the most disruptive recreational use of the approach to the cemetery, the amateur and professional horse races held on the "speedways" or rolled dirt lanes flanking the 100-foot-wide avenue. The resulting law levied a $25 fine or ten days in jail for conviction of driving any animal past cemetery gates faster than six miles per hour.[46]

The immense popularity of "rural" cemeteries, however, eventually led to the breakdown of the restrictive ticket system for admission rather than passage of more comprehensively restrictive laws on a state or municipal level. At Mount Auburn, liberalized admissions for those in carriages began to appear in the 1850s. A younger generation of trustees determined to maintain only "a mild and reasonable enforcement of the rules," to provide public access, and yet to impede in an unobtrusive way the promiscuous use of the grounds as "a pleasure drive for all pleasure seekers who may chance to pass that way," perhaps en route to the recreational facilities at the nearby Fresh Pond Hotel. Conscious that Mount Auburn was "the pioneer of ornamental cemeteries—the delight and pride of our citizens and the admiration of strangers," trustees felt responsibility to make the place as accessible as possible to visitors of evidently proper intention since "its fame extends wherever Boston is known" and "all strangers visiting this part of the country should be desirous of seeing it."[47]

The fame of all of these garden cemeteries was so great by the late 1850s that a new sort of photographic entrepreneur began to provide means for the armchair traveller to have visual accessibility to these places from the comfort of his or her own parlor. Production of stereopticon cards—hundreds of different views mass-produced in thousands of copies each—satisfied the demand of the nontravelling public to see the landscape and monuments of Mount Auburn, Green-Wood, Spring Grove, and even many of their smaller imitators, to compare their attractions, and to make the sort of good use of leisure time advocated by moralists. The quantity of stereo cards of garden cemeteries produced through the last half of the century attests to the continuing popularity of these places among those who could not visit them personally or those who wanted souvenirs of visits made.

Andrew Jackson Downing wrote frequently of the great public appeal of garden cemeteries and "the gala-day of *recreation* they present. People seem to go there to enjoy themselves, and not to indulge in any serious recollections or regrets." Even the most genteel, moralistic, and exclusive of Mount Auburn's founders captured the spirit of urban boosterism sweeping the nation on the subject of garden cemeteries. They were proud to read reviews of their institution as "a becoming appendage, an interesting ornament of the town." Laurel Hill's directors were delighted to have their cemetery described as "a better arboretum than can be easily found elsewhere in the country." But the popularity of visiting garden cemeteries extended to many other places, examples created near cities and towns, large and small, across the nation from the 1830s through the 1860s. "The idea took the public mind by storm," Downing observed; and "Travellers made pilgrimages to the Athens of New England solely to see the realization of their long-cherished dream of a resting place for the dead." Downing judged "from the crowds of people in carriages and on foot . . . constantly thronging Green-Wood and Mount Auburn" that "it is plain enough how much our citizens of all classes would enjoy public parks on a similar scale." He asked his readers, "Can you doubt that if our large towns added pleasure grounds like Green-Wood (excepting the monuments) . . . that they would tend to soften and allay the feverish unrest of business which seems to have possession of most Americans, body and soul?" Public parks modeled after the cemeteries would provide much-needed places of leisure and recreation. Other Americans agreed. Henry Coleman exclaimed, "How happy would it be for thousands in our cities if they would yield earlier to these impulses [to enjoy rural scenery and life] and seek the country early for the living as they now seek it late for the dead." Downing took action by lobbying for creation of the nation's first urban, public "pleasure ground"— New York's Central Park.[48]

The New York art critic Clarence Cook similarly recognized the significance of "rural" cemeteries which, he notes, had become "famous over the whole country and thousands of people visited them annually. They were among the chief attractions of the cities to which they belonged. No stranger visited these cities for pleasure or observation who was not taken there, nor was it long before the smaller cities, and even towns and villages began to set aside land and to lay it out for the double purpose of burying ground and pleasure ground." In their mid-century heyday, "These cemeteries were all the rage." They were "so beautiful" in themselves and filled such a public demand for green open space that it was not at all surprising that people were slow to perceive that there was a certain incongruity between a graveyard and a place of recreation. "The truth is," Cook asserted, "people were glad to get fresh air, and a sight of grass, and trees, and flowers, with now and then a pretty piece of sculpture . . . without considering too deeply whether it might not be better to have it all without the graves and the funeral processions." Writing these words in 1869 in his introduction to an early history of the new Central Park, Cook realized the importance of the cemeteries as models for the institution and landscape of the public park.[49]

After the invention of the public park and the dissemination of the pastoral landscape without the graves to cities across the nation, the recreational popularity of "rural" cemeteries began to wane in the last quarter of the nineteenth century. Frederick Law Olmsted criticized "rural" cemeteries as the "constant resort of mere pleasure seekers, travellers, promenaders, and loungers" and refused to design many new ones. Instead, following the changing tastes and priorities of the late nineteenth century, Olmsted made his career designing similar landscapes, but, as Cook observed, "without the graves and the funeral processions." The New York Board of Park Commissioners made sure to rule early that Central Park would contain no graves or funerary monuments, although many of the monuments there resemble cenotaphs in a cemetery landscape.[50]

Other cultural forces contributed to the diminishing popularity of "rural" cemeteries through the last quarter of the century. The immense casualties of the Civil War shattered much of the sentimentalism and melancholy that permeated mass culture in the romantic age. Creation of museums of fine arts for display of high cultural artifacts, sculpture, and architecture formerly only seen by the public at cemeteries provided more desirable, accessible, and protected didactic institutions than the outdoor funerary landscape. Furthermore, at most "rural" cemeteries, with the notable exception of Spring Grove, accretion of fences, stones, curbs, and miscellaneous garden furniture placed on lots by proprietors obliterated the original pastoralism of the places, making them far less attractive and naturalistic. Yet even in Cincinnati, H. A. Ratterman wondered in 1905, "Why is Spring Grove no longer the attractive star of Cincinnati?" He surmised that new public parks and an extensive zoological garden provided alternative pleasure grounds, but he also complained that "the original landscape charm" of the cemetery had not been maintained. Ratterman did not realize that since the 1867 annual meeting, a growing number of Spring Grove lot holders had been calling for election of directors who would treat the cemetery simply as a place of burial and not as an arboretum.[51]

The number of recreational visitors to "rural" cemeteries declined markedly in the last decades of the century. Only a few Proper Bostonians, according to Cleveland Amory, continued to cultivate "the love of funerals and funeral going," with regular visits to Mount Auburn in between obsequies. James Russell Lowell insisted that a trip to Mount Auburn remained a necessary part of the ritual of elite Boston hospitality, *de rigueur* after a Beacon Hill dinner "with people you never saw before nor ever wish to see again." Lowell mused, "Your memory of the dinner is expected to reconcile you to the prospect of the graveyard." By then, however, nature had been greatly disfigured at Mount Auburn, and the original charm of the place had been obliterated by an accumulation of Victorian funerary artifacts, not to be restored to a parklike appearance until several decades later in the twentieth century.[52]

Only in the 1970s and 1980s, so it seems, have Mount Auburn and other major garden cemeteries begun to attract extensive public recreational and tourist use comparable to that of their heyday in the mid-nineteenth century. Perhaps restoration of the arboretumlike quality of the landscape by historically and horticulturally minded superintendents in certain locations has been a contributing factor. Today, an organization called the Friends of Mount Auburn, founded in 1985, sponsors a variety of lectures and tours that reemphasize the natural and artistic amenities the landscape still offers; and birdwatchers flock to the grounds, often before dawn, provided with keys to pedestrian gates locked at night.

A similar organization, the Friends of Laurel Hill Cemetery, was founded in the mid-1970s to encourage restoration and preservation of the original historic landscape of the Philadelphia cemetery, which had deteriorated over the course of the century because, unlike many of the cemeteries of its ilk and its era, it had a profit-making corporate structure without sufficient provision for endowment of perpetual care of the grounds. At other historic "rural" cemeteries, as well, superintendents note a marked increase in public recreational uses of the grounds in recent years. These developments are encouraging for historians, historic preservationists, and some cemeterians as well, who realize that such renewed public interest in the pleasurable aspects of such landscapes as Mount Auburn, Laurel Hill, Green-Wood, and Spring Grove may help to forestall the potential neglect that might develop if they, with burial space becoming exhausted, would no longer be places of vital use.

Notes

1. "Spring Grove Cemetery," [Cincinnati] *Commercial* (Oct. 6, 1867).

2. Blanche Linden-Ward, "Putting the Past in Place: The Making of Mount Auburn Cemetery," *Proceedings of the Cambridge Historical Society* 44 (1985), pp. 171–96; and "Putting the Past under Grass: History as Death and Cemetery Commemoration," *Prospects* (Annual of American Culture Studies) 10 (1985), pp. 279–314.

3. Also see Rev. John A. Clark, ed., *Christian Keepsake and Missionary Annual* (Philadelphia: William Marshall and Co., 1839); John Pierpont, "The Garden of Graves," in S. G. Goodrich, ed., *The Token: A Christmas and New Year's Present* (Boston: S. G. Goodrich, 1832), pp. 374–87. Clark made similar reference to Green-Wood Cemetery in *Gleanings by the Way* (Philadelphia: W. J. and J. K. Simon, 1842), pp. 188–91.

4. See "The American Cult of the Melancholy to 1825," in Blanche M. G. Linden, "Death and the Garden: The Cult of the Melancholy and the 'Rural' Cemetery," 2 vols. (Ph.D. diss., Harvard University, 1981).

5. Joseph Story, "Consecration Address," in *The Picturesque Pocket Companion through Mount Auburn* (Boston: Otis, Broaders, and Co., 1839), pp. 74–75; William Wetmore Story, ed., *The Life and Letters of Joseph Story* (Boston: Charles C. Little and James Brown, 1851), II, pp. 64–65.

6. "Mount Auburn," *The Christian Examiner* 26 (1836), clipping in the files of the Corporation, Cambridge; also see J. Brayer, "The Burial of the Dead," *The Christian Examiner* 31 (1842), pp. 137–64 and 281–307.

7. Alexander Everett, *An Address Delivered before the Massachusetts Horticultural Society at the Fifth Annual Festival, Sept. 18, 1833* (Boston: J. T. Buckingham, 1833); Henry Tuckerman, "The Law of Burial and Death," *The Christian Examiner* 26 (1836), p. 338; Wilson Flagg, "The Moral Influence of Graves," in Flagg, *Mount Auburn: Its Scenes, Its Beauties, and Its Lessons* (Boston: James Munroe and Co., 1861), pp. 36–38.

8. Joseph T. Buckingham, "Mount Auburn," *Mount Auburn Memorial* 2:1 (July 4, 1860), p. 3 (originally in the Boston *Courier,* Sept. 28, 1838).

9. Lydia Maria Child, *Advice to Mothers* (Boston: Carter and Hendee, 1831), p. 81.

10. Cornelia Walter, *The Rural Cemeteries of America: Mount Auburn Illustrated in a Series of Views from Drawings Taken on the Spot . . . with Descriptive Notices* (New York: R. Martin, 1847), pp. 5–7, 67, 95, and 113.

11. Mary Tyler Peabody to Miss Rawlins Pickman, Salem, Massachusetts (Oct. 9, 1835), Horace Mann II Papers, Massachusetts Historical Society, Boston.

12. Zillah, "Mount Auburn," *The Lowell Offering* 1:1 (1840), pp. 13–14. A young teacher visiting from the western frontier responded similarly: see "The Diary of Arozina Perkins," in Polly Welts Kaufman, *Women Teachers in the Frontier* (New Haven: Yale University Press, 1984), p. 69. Emily Dickinson also visited in 1846: see Dickinson to Abiah Root, letter 13 (Sept. 1846), in *The Letters of Emily Dickinson,* ed. by Thomas H. Johnson and Theodora Ward (Cambridge: Harvard University Press, 1958), vol. I, p. 36. Also see E. E. T., "Burial and Burial Places," *The Lowell Offering* series II, vol. 1 (1840), pp. 154–57.

13. Caroline F. Orne, *Sweet Auburn and Mount Auburn with Other Poems* (Cambridge: John Owen, 1844), pp. iii-v, 33, 43.

14. William R. Lawrence, ed., *Extracts from the Diary and Correspondence of the Late Amos Lawrence* (Boston: Gould and Lincoln, 1855), pp. 129, 175–76; G[eorge] T[icknor] Curtis, "Mount Auburn," *New England Magazine* 7 (Oct. 1834), p. 316.

15. Story, *The Picturesque Pocket Companian,* p. 208.

16. Nathaniel S. Dearborn, *Dearborn's Guide through Mount Auburn Cemetery* (Boston: N. Dearborn, 6th rev. ed., 1852), pp. 15–16. (Not to be confused, as has happened in print, with Henry A. S. Dearborn, who laid out the landscape design of the cemetery.)

17. Levi Merriam Stevens, *A Handbook for Passengers over the Cambridge Railroad* (Boston: Bricher and Russell, 1860), pp. 26 and 29.

18. Story, "Records of Committees," (July 19, 1834), 22 and (Oct. 17, 1834), 24, manuscript book in the offices of Mount Auburn Cemetery, Cambridge; Hammatt Billings, "Sketches at Mount Auburn," in Damrell V. Moore and George Coolidge, eds., *The Boston Almanac for the Year 1857,* no. 22 (Boston: John P. Jewett, 1857), p. 51; "Cemetery at Mount Auburn," *New England Farmer* 10:11 (Sept. 1831). Also see Henry A. S. Dearborn,

"Historical Sketch," *Transactions of the Massachusetts Horticultural Society, 1829–1838* (Boston: William D. Ticknor, 1847), pp. 77–79.

19. Fanny Kemble, (Apr. 15, 1833) *The Journal of Frances Anne Butler, Better Known as Fanny Kemble* (1835, reprint, New York: B. Blom, 1970), pp. 175–76; Carl David Arfwedson, *The United States and Canada in 1832* (1834, reprint, New York: Johnson Reprint, 1961), I, pp. 211–13; Edward S. Abdy, *Journal of a Residence and Tour of the United States of North America* (London: John Murray, 1835), I, p. 120; Caroline Gilman and Rev. S. Gilman, *The Poetry of Travelling in the United States* (New York: S. Gilman, 1838), p. 158; Anne Henry Ehrenpreis, ed., *Happy Country This America: The Travel Diary of Henry Arthur Bright* (Columbus: Ohio State University Press, 1978), p. 18.

20. Sir Charles Lyell, *A Second Visit to the United States of North America* (London: John Murray, 1849), I, pp. 14–16, 171–72; Lady Emmeline Wortley, *Travels in the United States . . . during 1849–50* (New York: Harper Brothers, 1851), pp. 47–48; [Marie T. Courcelles,] "Silent Cities," [Cincinnati] *Daily Enquirer* (Feb. 25, 1877). Other foreign acclamations of Mount Auburn included D. Ramon de la Sagra, *Cinco Meses en los Estados Unidos de la America del Norte desde el 20 de Abril al 23 de Sentiembre de 1835* (Paris: Pablo Renouard, 1836), p. 333.

21. Harriet Martineau, *Retrospect of Western Travel* (London: Saunders and Otley, 1838), II, pp. 227–33.

22. Ibid., pp. 231–33.

23. Ibid.

24. "Mount Auburn," in *American Cyclopedia of Useful Knowledge* (1835), clipping in the files of Mount Auburn Cemetery, Cambridge; Also see Billings, "Sketches," p. 51.

25. John Jay Smith, *Recollections of John Jay Smith* (Philadelphia: J. B. Lippincott, 1892), p. 103. See also R. A. Smith, *Smith's Illustrated Guide to and through Laurel Hill Cemetery* (Philadelphia: William P. Hazard, 1852), pp. 29–31; and J. J. Smith, *Guide to Laurel Hill Cemetery, Near Philadelphia* (Philadelphia: By the Cemetery, 1844), p. 14. Between 1844 and 1858, Laurel Hill Cemetery published and sold at its gate and in the city seven editions of these guides, each of which contained many illustrations. Thereafter, through the century, portions of the guides were reprinted in *Rules and Regulations* published by the Corporation. Laurel Hill was unlike most of the other garden cemeteries that were nonprofit, eleemosynary corporations. John Jay Smith admitted to profiting from the cemetery after losing his "patrimony in drugs and newspapers" in order to "retrieve [his] circumstances." Other initial investors also made money from development of the cemetery which nevertheless served as an urban amenity.

26. *A Guide to the Lions of Philadelphia* (Philadelphia: Thomas T. Ash, 1837), pp. 68–70; H. S. Tanner, *A New Picture of Philadelphia; or, The Stranger's Guide* (New York: The Map and Geographical Establishment, 1841), pp. 100–102; *The Stranger's Guide in Philadelphia and Its Environs, including Laurel Hill* (Philadelphia: Lindsay and Blakeston, 1852), pp. 216–28; Sidney George Fisher (Mar. 13, 1838), in Nicholas B. Wainwright, ed., *A Philadelphia Perspective: The Diary of Sidney George Fisher Covering the Years 1835–1871* (Philadelphia: Historical Society of Pennsylvania, 1867), pp. 46, 59–60; Andrew Jackson Downing, "Public Cemeteries and Public Gardens," *The Horticulturist* 4 (July 1849), pp. 9–10.

27. Fisher, Ibid. (Oct. 13, 1838), pp. 59–60.

28. J. J. Smith, *Guide,* pp. 12–14; *Second General Report of the Board of Managers of the Proprietors and Lot Holders of the Green Mount Cemetery* (Baltimore: John D. Toy, 1848), pp. 29–30. Also see A. D. G. [Clinton, N.Y.], "Rural Cemeteries," *The Horticulturist* 5 (1855), p. 279.

29. Stephen Duncan Walker, *Rural Cemetery and Public Walk* (Baltimore: Sands and Neilson, 1835), pp. 6–7; "Walk No. 2," in *The Stranger's Guide to Baltimore* (Baltimore: Murphy and Co., 1852), pp. 19–24.

30. [Brooklyn] *Star* (July 15, 1839) and (July 31, 1841); [New York] *Daily News* (Mar. 15, 1842). Major guidebooks to New York and its cemetery include Campeador, *Rambling Reflections in Green-Wood; with a Description of the Same in 1853* (New York: George W. Wood, 1853); *The 1866 Guide to New York As It Is, or Stranger's Guide to the Cities of Brooklyn and Adjacent Places* (New York: J. Miller, 1866; reprint, Schocken, 1975), p. 114; and John Mountain, *Visitor's Pocket Guide to Green-Wood Cemetery . . . How to Find the Most Prominent Points of Interest* (New York: Johnson, Wilson, and Co., 1873).

31. Downing, "Review: *Greenwood Illustrated,*" *The Horticulturist* 1 (July 1846–June 1847), p. 228.

32. Rev. Paracellsus Church, *An Address Delivered at the Dedication of Mount Hope Cemetery, Rochester, Oct. 2, 1838* (Rochester, N.Y.: David Hoyt, 1839), pp. 16–17; "Mount Hope Cemetery," *Ballou's* 9:24 (1855), pp. 376–77.

33. See Blanche Linden-Ward and David C. Sloane, "Spring Grove: The Founding of Cincinnati's Rural Cemetery, 1845–1855," *Queen City Heritage* (Cincinnati Historical Society) 43:1 (spring 1985), pp. 17–32.

34. [Adolph Strauch,] *Spring Grove Cemetery: Its History and Improvements* (Cincinnati: Robert Clarke, 1869), pp. 5–9. Also see "Pückler-Muskau and Alphand," in Norman T. Newton, *Design on the Land: The Development of Landscape Architecture* (Cambridge: Belknap Press, 1971), pp. 233–45.

35. "Our Beautiful Cemetery," [Cincinnati] *Commercial* 27 (Apr. 14, 1867); [Strauch,] "Superintendent's Report," in "Spring Grove Cemetery," [Cincinnati] *Enquirer* (Oct. 6, 1868); J. J. Smith, "Cemeteries," *The New Englander* 85 (1863), p. 606.

36. The total for 1866 was 85,770. "Spring Grove Cemetery of New Year's Day," [Cincinnati,] *Daily Enquirer* (Jan. 1, 1867); [Strauch,] "Spring Grove Cemetery: Annual Meeting," [Cincinnati] *Commercial* (Oct. 6, 1874); [Strauch,] "Superintendent's Report," [Cincinnati] *Commercial* (Sept. 30, 1876); "Mount Auburn," [Cambridge] *Chronicle,* reprinted in the *Mount Auburn Memorial* 1:45 (Apr. 18, 1860), p. 357.

37. [Fanny Kemble,] p. 176. See Mrs. C. H. Putnam [of New York,] "Letters from Home: Mount Auburn Cemetery," *Young Lady's and Gentleman's Parlor Album* (New York, ca. 1843), pp. 309–12.

38. "Proceedings of the Massachusetts Horticultural Society," *Transactions,* I, pp. 106–7; Story, "Report," (Sept. 1832), *Transactions,* I, p. 47.

39. "Proprietors' and Trustees' Reports," III (Mar. 4, 1861), pp. 171–75 (manuscript volumes in the Office of the Cemetery, Cambridge, hereafter abbreviated PTR); See "Regulations Concerning Visitors to the Cemetery," *Mount Auburn Cemetery: Visitor's Reference Book* (3rd ed., Boston: S. S. C. Russell, 1866), pp. 5–7.

40. PTR I (July 14, 1842), p. 82; II (Apr. 7, 1856), p. 76; III (Mar. 4, 1861), pp. 171–75; (Aug. 5, 1861), p. 212; J. J. Smith, *Recollections,* p. 255; R. A. Smith, p. 38.

41. Fanny Kemble Wister, "Sarah Butler Wister's Civil War Diary," *Pennsylvania Magazine of History and Biography* 102:3 (July 1978), p. 297; Fisher (Aug. 3, 1854), p. 330.

42. "Admissions to Spring Grove," [Cincinnati] *Gazette* (1865), clipping in the Newspaper Scrapbook, p. 4 (at the Offices of the Cemetery, Cincinnati); PTR I (July 14, 1842), pp. 84–86.

43. Fisher in Wainwright (ed.), *Philadelphia Perspective* (Aug. 3, 1859), p. 330.

44. PTR I (July 14, 1842), pp. 84–86; II (June 18, 1855), p. 44; II (Sept. 4, 1855), p. 46; II (Aug. 3, 1857), pp. 209–10; II (April 5, 1858), p. 244; III (Nov. 4, 1861), p. 247; "Records of Committees" (1832), p. 8; PTR IV (June 20, 1866), p. 77.

45. A. T. to the Editor, "Mount Auburn Cemetery," [Boston] *Evening Transcript* (Nov. 4, 1856); "Introductory," *Mount Auburn Memorial* 1:1 (June 15, 1859), p. 6; Billings, "Sketches," p. 52; PTR IV (Apr. 12, 1870), p. 323; "Skating," *Mount Auburn Memorial* 1:25 (Nov. 30, 1859), p. 197.

46. "Shall It Be a Race Course," [Cincinnati] *Gazette* (Feb. 20, 1878). Legislation was numbered S.B. No. 390. See related newspaper coverage on p. 36, Clippings Book.

47. The ticket system was enforced at Spring Grove through the 1860s.

48. Andrew Jackson Downing, "Public Cemeteries and Public Gardens," *The Horticulturist* 4 (1849), p. 10; Downing, "A Talk About Public Parks and Gardens," *The Horticulturist* 3 (Oct. 1848), p. 157. Also see George W. Curtis, ed., *Rural Essays* (New York: Leavitt and Allen, 1854), pp. 138–46; Downing, *Landscape Gardening* (New York: John Wiley and Sons, 1921), p. 371; Henry Coleman, "Mount Auburn," *Mount Auburn Memorial* 1:2 (June 22, 1859), p. 10.

49. Clarence Cook, *A Description of the New York Central Park* (1869, reprint New York: Benjamin Blom, 1972), p. 15.

50. Commissioners of the New York Central Park, *Annual Report of 1867,* quoted in Frederick Law Olmsted, Jr. and Theodora Kimball, *Forty Years of Landscape Architecture: Central Park, Frederick Law Olmsted, Sr.* (Cambridge: MIT Press, 1973), p. 486. See also Olmsted, Sr. to William Robinson (Spring 1875), to Jonathan D. Crimmins (Aug. 2, 1888), Deposition in the Case of Jacob Weidenmann, Mount Hope Cemetery (Feb. 1888); and "Park" in Charles E. Beveridge and David Schuyler, eds., *Papers of Frederick Law Olmsted: Vol. III: Creating Central Park (1857–1861)* (Baltimore: Johns Hopkins University Press, 1983), p. 357.

51. "Spring Grove Cemetery," [Cincinnati] *Commercial* (Oct. 6, 1867); "Conduct of Visitors of Spring Grove Cemetery," *Commercial* (June 22, 1868); H. A. Ratterman, "Spring Grove and Its Creator," (Mar. 4, 1905), p. 17, typescript at the Cincinnati Historical Society.

52. Cleveland Amory, *The Proper Bostonians* (New York: E. P. Putnam, 1947), pp. 253–57; James Russell Lowell, quoted in Martin Duberman, *James Russell Lowell* (Boston: Beacon, 1966), p. 192.

Bibliography

Richard E. Meyer

The decision to provide within this book a selective bibliography for the study of cemeteries and gravemarkers has been prompted by the simple fact that no truly comprehensive, multidisciplinary listing of this sort currently exists to assist those wishing to engage in this emerging field of study. Even at that, the present effort has its own self-imposed limitations, determined as much by considerations of space as by any standards of intrinsic merit. Excluded, for instance, are references to essentially genealogical compilations and listings, though such documents are available in abundance at community, county, and state levels nationwide and can often yield valuable insights to cemetery and gravemarker patterns in a given locale and over time. An exceptional model for the bibliographic consolidation of such materials on a statewide level is Anne M. Hogg, ed., *Virginia Cemeteries: A Guide to Resources* (Charlottesville: University Press of Virginia, 1986). Contemporary trade publications of professional organizations with direct bearing on the focus of this book contain numerous examples of well-researched and enlightening articles, and, though not represented in the listing which follows, two of these in particular—*Stone in America* (monthly trade journal of the American Monument Association) and *American Cemetery* (monthly trade journal of the American Cemetery Association) are well worth consulting. Finally, no bibliographic overview of published material in this area would be complete without specific reference to the important contributions found in the ongoing publications of the Association for Gravestone Studies: *Markers,* annual journal of the Association, and the quarterly *AGS Newsletter,* a splendidly edited document containing valuable information of all sorts, including critical reviews and essays.

In listing what seems to me the most reprentatively significant current scholarship on cemeteries and gravemarkers, I have adopted the expediency of arranging individual entries into ten separately labeled subcategories. This is admittedly a somewhat dangerous strategy, owing to the rather obvious fact that many entries defy such neatly defined categorization. Some easily qualify for more than one of the headings presented here, while others possess a scope which might arguably defy any attempt at standardized classification. Still, the strategy is based upon the assumption that such a breakdown is potentially more useful to the reader with specific interests than would be a simple, straightforward listing, and in assigning entries to particular categories I have tried to base my decisions on what appears to be the primary distinguishing characteristic or focus of that particular work. Thus, articles and books grouped under the first and largest category, Regional/Subregional Studies, seem most distinguished by their contributions toward an appreciation of the role cemeteries and gravemarkers may play in understanding the cultural values of a specific geographic area. The same logic was applied with reference to the other categories. Though not essentially scholarly in nature, a section has been provided for the listing of a number of useful cemetery guidebooks, and a final section presents a representative selection of general and correlative works on death and culture which are seen as particularly relevant to the study of cemeteries and gravemarkers.

Regional/Subregional Studies

Ball, Donald B. "Observations on the Form and Function of Middle Tennessee Gravehouses." *Tennessee Anthropologist* 2:1 (1977), pp. 29–62.

———. "Social Activities Associated with Two Rural Cemeteries in Coffee County, Tennessee." *Tennessee Folklore Society Bulletin* 41:3 (1975), pp. 93–98.

———. "Wooden Gravemarkers: Neglected Items of Material Culture." *Tennessee Folklore Society Bulletin* 43:4 (1977), pp. 167–85.

Baugher, Sherene, and Winter, Frederick A. "Early American Gravestones: Archaeological Perspectives on Three Cemeteries of Old New York." *Archaeology* 36:3 (1983), pp. 46–53.

Benes, Peter. *The Masks of Orthodoxy: Folk Gravestone Carving in Plymouth County, Massachusetts, 1689–1805.* Amherst, Mass.: The University of Massachusettes Press, 1977.

Byers, Laura. *'Till Death Do Us Part': Design Sources of Eighteenth-Century New England Tombstones.* New Haven, Conn.: Yale Center for American Art and Material Culture, 1978.

Cantrell, Brent. "Traditional Grave Structures on the Eastern Highland Rim." *Tennessee Folklore Society Bulletin* 47:3 (1981), pp. 93–103.

Combs, Diana Williams. *Early Gravestone Art in Georgia and South Carolina.* Athens, Ga: The University of Georgia Press, 1986.

Cooper, Patricia Irvin. "Some Strange North Georgia Tombstones," *Pioneer America Society Transactions* 5 (1982), pp. 27–36.

Corn, Jack. "Covered Graves," *Kentucky Folklore Record* 23:2 (1977), pp. 34–37.

Davis, Stephen. "Empty Eyes, Marble Hand: The Confederate Monument and the South." *Journal of Popular Culture* 16:1 (1982), pp. 2–21.

Deetz, James. *In Small Things Forgotten: The Archaeology of Early American Life.* Garden City, N.Y.: Anchor Press, 1977, pp. 64–90.

Dethlefsen, Edwin S. "Colonial Gravestones and Demography." *American Journal of Physical Anthropology* 31 (1969), pp. 321–34.

Dethlefsen, Edwin and Deetz, James. "Eighteenth-Century Cemeteries: A Demographic View." *Historical Archaeology* 1 (1967), pp. 40–42.

Duval, Francis Y., and Rigby, Ivan B. *Early American Gravestone Art in Photographs.* New York: Dover Publications, 1978.

———. "Openwork Memorials of North Carolina." *Markers* 1 (1980), pp. 62–75.

Edgette, J. Joseph. "The Wood Family of Philadelphia: Four Generations of Stonecarving." In *By Land and by Sea: Studies in the Folklore of Work and Leisure.* Edited by Roger D. Abrahams, Kenneth S. Goldstein, and Wayland D. Hand. Hatboro, Pa: Legacy Books, 1985, pp. 69–76.

Edwards, Lucy Ames. "Stories in Stone: A Study of Duval County Grave Markers." *Florida Historical Quarterly* 35:4 (1956), pp. 116–29.

Farber, Daniel and Farber, Jessie Lie. "Early Pennsylvania Gravemarkers." *Markers* 5 (1988), pp. 96–121.

Fife, Austin E. "Western Gravestones." In *Exploring Western Americana,* by Austin E. Fife, edited by Alta Fife. Ann Arbor, Mich.: UMI Research Press, 1988, pp. 195–213.

Fife, Austin and Fife, Alta. "Gravestone Imagery." In *Utah Folk Art: A Catalog of Material Culture.* Edited by Hal Cannon. Provo, Utah: Brigham Young University Press, 1980, pp. 136–49.

Forbes, Harriette Merrifield. *Gravestones of Early New England and the Men Who Made Them, 1653–1800.* Boston: Houghton Mifflin, 1927.

Florin, Lambert. *Boot Hill: Historic Graves of the Old West.* New York: Bonanza Books, 1966.

———. *Tales the Western Tombstones Tell.* New York: Bonanza Books, 1967.

Gillespie, Angus K. "Gravestones and Ostentation: A Study of Five Delaware County Cemeteries." *Pennsylvania Folklife* 19 (1969–70), pp. 34–43.

Gillon, Edmund Vincent, Jr. *Early New England Gravestone Rubbings.* New York: Dover Publications, 1966.

Graves, Thomas E. "Pennsylvania German Gravestones: An Introduction." *Markers* 5 (1988), pp. 60–95.

Hannon, Thomas J. "Nineteenth-Century Cemeteries in Central-West Pennsylvania." *Proceedings of the Pioneer America Society* 2 (1973), pp. 23–38.

Haseltine, Maury. "A Progress Report on the Pictorial Documentation of Early Utah Gravestones." In *Forms upon the Frontier: Folklife and Folk Arts in the United States.* Edited by Austin and Alta Fife and Henry H. Glassie. Logan, Ut.: Utah State University Press, 1969, pp. 79–88.

Huber, Leonard V., McDowell, Peggy, and Christovich, Mary Louise. *New Orleans Architecture, Vol. III, The Cemeteries.* Gretna, La.: Pelican Publishing Co., 1974.

Jack, Phil R. "A Western Pennsylvania Graveyard, 1787–1967." *Pennsylvania Folklife* 17:3 (1968), pp. 41–48.

Jeane, Donald G. "The Traditional Upland South Cemetery." *Landscape* 18:2 (1969), pp. 39–41.

Jeane, Donald Gregory. "The Upland South Cemetery: An American Type." *Journal of Popular Culture* 11 (1978), pp. 895–903.

Jeane, Gregory. "Rural Southern Gravestones: Sacred Artifacts in the Upland South Folk Cemetery." *Markers* 4 (1987), pp. 55–84.

Jordan, Terry G. "'The Roses So Red and the Lilies So Fair': Southern Folk Cemeteries in Texas." *Southwestern Historical Quarterly* 83:3 (1980), pp. 227–58.

———. *Texas Graveyards: A Cultural Legacy.* Austin: University of Texas Press, 1982.

Kahlert, John M. *Pioneer Cemeteries: Door County, Wisconsin.* Baileys Harbor, Wis.: Meadow Lane Publishers, 1981.

Kallas, Phil. "The Carvers of Portage County, Wisconsin, 1850–1900." *Markers* 2 (1983), pp. 187–202.

Kremenak-Pecotte, Beverly. "At Rest: Folk Art in Texas Cemeteries." In *Folk Art in Texas.* Edited by Francis Edward Abernethy. Publications of the Texas Folklore Society, no. 45. Dallas: Southern Methodist University Press, 1985, pp. 53–63.

Levine, Gaynell S. "Colonial Long Island Grave Stones: Trade Network Indicators." In *Puritan Gravestone Art II.* Edited by Peter Benes. The Dublin Seminar for New England Folklife Annual Proceedings, 1978. Boston: Boston University Press, 1978, pp. 46–57.

Ludwig, Allan I. *Graven Images: New England Stonecarving and Its Symbols, 1650–1815.* Middletown, Conn.: Wesleyan University Press, 1966.

McDowell, Peggy. "New Orleans Cemeteries: Architectural Styles and Influences." *Southern Quarterly* 20:1 (1982), pp. 9–27.

Mayer, Lance R. "An Alternative to Panofskyism: New England Grave Stones and the European Folk Art Tradition." In *Puritan Gravestone Art II.* Edited by Peter Benes. The Dublin Seminar for New England Folklife Annual Proceedings, 1978. Boston: Boston University Press, 1978, pp. 5–17.

Michael, Dorothy Jean. "Grave Decoration." In *Backwoods to Border.* Publications of the Texas Folklore Society, no. 18. Dallas: Southern Methodist University Press, 1943, pp. 129–36.

Milmoe, James. "Colorado Wooden Markers." *Markers* 1 (1980), pp. 56–62.

Milspaw, Yvonne. "Plain Walls and Little Angels: Pioneer Churches in Central Pennsylvania." *Pioneer America* 12:2 (1980), pp. 76–96.

Neal, Avon and Parker, Ann. "Graven Images: Sermons in Stone." *American Heritage* 21 (August 1970), pp. 18–29.

Nelson, Malcolm A. and George, Diana Hume. "Grinning Skulls, Smiling Cherubs, Bitter Words." *Journal of Popular Culture* 14:4 (1981), pp. 633–40.

Norris, Darrell A. "Ontario Gravestones." *Markers* 5 (1988), pp. 122–49.

Perret, Maurice E. "Tombstones and Epitaphs: Journeying through Wisconsin's Cemeteries." *Wisconsin Academy Review* 21:2 (1975), pp. 2–6.

Poulsen, Richard C. *The Pure Experience of Order: Essays on the Symbolic in the Folk Material Culture of Western America.* Albuquerque: University of New Mexico Press, 1982, pp. 45–55; 76–83.

Price, Beulah M. D'Olive. "The Custom of Providing Shelters for Graves." *Mississippi Folklore Quarterly* 7:1 (1973), pp. 8–10.

Price, Larry W. "Some Results and Implications of a Cemetery Study." *The Professional Geographer* 18:4 (1966), pp. 201–7.

Pitchford, Anita. "The Material Culture of the Traditional East Texas Graveyard." *Southern Folklore Quarterly* 43 (1979), pp. 277–90.

Rauschenberg, Bradford. "A Study of Baroque- and Gothic-Style Gravestones in Davidson County, N.C." *Journal of Early Southern Decorative Arts,* 3 (1977), pp. 24–50.

Ruth, Kent, and Argo, Jim. *Here We Rest: Historic Cemeteries of Oklahoma.* Oklahoma City: Oklahoma Historical Society, 1986.

Slater, James A. *The Colonial Burying Grounds of Eastern Connecticut and the Men Who Made Them.* Hamden, Conn.: Archon Books, 1987.

Tarpley, Fred A. "Southern Cemeteries: Neglected Archives for the Folklorist." *Southern Folklore Quarterly* 27 (1963), pp. 323–33.

Tashjian, Dickran and Ann. *Memorials for Children of Change: The Art of Early New England Stonecarving.* Middletown, Conn.: Wesleyan University Press, 1974.

Wasserman, Emily. *Gravestone Designs: Rubbings and Photographs from Early New York and New Jersey.* New York: Dover Publications, 1972.

Watters, David H. *'With Bodilie Eyes': Eschatological Themes in Puritan Literature and Gravestone Art.* Ann Arbor, Mich.: UMI Reserach Press, 1981.

Welch, Richard F. *Memento Mori: The Gravestones of Early Long Island, 1680–1810.* Syosset, N.Y.: Friends for Long Island's Heritage, 1983.

Weldy, Mary Helen, and Taylor, David L. "Gone But Not Forgotten: The Life and Work of a Traditional Tombstone Carver." *Keystone Folklore* 21:2 (1976), pp. 14–33.

Wust, Klaus. *Folk Art in Stone: Southwest Virginia.* Edinburg, Va: Shenandoah History, 1970.

The Cemetery and Social Values

Ames, Kenneth L. "Ideologies in Stone: Meanings in Victorian Gravestones." *Journal of Popular Culture* 14:4 (1981), pp. 641–56.

Dethlefsen, Edwin S. "The Cemetery and Culture Change: Archaeological Focus and Ethnographic Perspective." In *Modern Material Culture: The Archaeology of Us.* Edited by Richard Gould and Michael Schiffer. New York: Academic Press, 1981, pp. 137–59.

Dethlefsen, Edwin S., and Jensen, Kenneth. "Social Commentary from the Cemetery." *Natural History* 86 (1977), pp. 32–39.

Francaviglia, Richard V. "The Cemetery as an Evolving Cultural Landscape." *Annals, Association of American Geographers* 61:2 (1971), pp. 501–9.

George, Diana Hume, and Nelson, Malcolm A. "Man's Infinite Concern: Graveyards as Fetishes." In *Objects of Special Devotion*. Edited by Ray B. Browne. Bowling Green, Oh: Popular Press, 1982, pp. 136–50.

Higiya, James. "American Gravestones and Attitudes towards Death." *Proceedings of the American Philosophical Society* 127 (1983), pp. 339–63.

Jackson, Kenneth, and Vergara, Camilo. *American Cemeteries*. Princeton, N.J.: Princeton Architectural Press, 1988.

Kephart, William M. "Status after Death." *American Sociological Review* 15:5 (1950), pp. 635–43.

Linden-Ward, Blanche. "Putting the Past under Grass: History as Death and Cemetery Commemoration." *Prospects: An Annual of American Cultural Studies* 10 (1985), pp. 279–314.

Oring, Elliott. "Forest Lawn and the Iconography of American Death." *Southwest Folklore* 6:1 (1982), pp. 62–72.

Ridlen, Susanne S. "Funerary Art in the 1890s: A Reflection of Culture." *Pioneer America Society Transactions* 6 (1983), pp. 27–35.

Smith, Deborah A. "'Safe in the Arms of Jesus': Consolation on Delaware Children's Gravestones, 1840–1899," *Markers* 4 (1987), pp. 85–106.

Smith, James M. "Puritanism: Self-Image Formation Through Gravestone Form, Style, and Symbols," *Daughters of the American Revolution Magazine* 114:4 (1980), pp. 470–85; 569.

Vidutis, Ricardas, and Lowe, Virginia A. P. "The Cemetery as a Cultural Text." *Kentucky Folklore Record* 26:2 (1980), pp. 103–13.

Warner, W. Lloyd. *The Living and the Dead: A Study in the Symbolic Life of Americans*. New Haven, Conn.: Yale University Press, 1959, pp. 280–320.

Wright, Robert A. "Poems in Stone: The Tombs of Louis Henri Sullivan." *Markers* 5 (1988), pp. 168–208.

Young, Frank W. "Graveyards and Social Structure." *Rural Sociology* 25:4 (1960), pp. 446–50.

Zelinsky, Wilbur. "Unearthly Delights: Cemetery Names and the Map of the Changing American Afterworld." In *Geographies of the Mind: Essays in Historical Geosophy*. Edited by David Lowenthal and Martyn J. Bowden. New York: Oxford University Press, 1976, pp. 171–95.

Visual Symbolism

Agosta, Lucien L. "Speaking Stones: New England Grave Carvings and the Emblematic Tradition." *Markers* 3 (1985), pp. 47–70.

Benes, Peter. "The Caricature Hypothesis Re-examined: The Animated Skull as a Puritan Folk Image." In *Puritan Gravestone Art*. Edited by Peter Benes. The Dublin Seminar for New England Folklife Annual Proceedings, 1976. Boston: Boston University Press, 1977, pp. 57–67.

――――. "A Particular Sense of Doom: Skeletal 'Revivals' in Northern Essex County, Massachusetts, 1737–1784." *Markers* 3 (1985), pp. 71–92.

Bergengren, Charles. "Folk Art on Gravestones: The Glorious Contrast." *Markers* 2 (1983), pp. 171–85.

Bronner, Simon J. "The Durlauf Family: Three Generations of Stonecarvers in Southern Indiana." *Pioneer America* 13:1 (1981), pp. 17–26.

――――. *Grasping Things: Folk Material Culture and Mass Society in America*. Lexington, Ky.: University Press of Kentucky, 1986, pp. 93–124.

Clegg, Frances. "Problems of Symbolism in Cemetery Monuments." *Journal of Garden History* 4:3 (1984), pp. 307–15.

Deetz, James, and Dethlefsen, Edwin S. "Death's Head, Cherub, Urn and Willow." *Natural History* 76:3 (1967), pp. 28–37.

Dethlefsen, Edwin, and Deetz, James. "Death's Heads, Cherubs, and Willow Trees: Experimental Archaelogy in Colonial Cemeteries." *American Antiquity* 31:4 (1966), pp. 502–10.

Dewhurst, C. Kurt, MacDowell, Betty, and MacDowell, Marsha. *Religious Folk Art in America: Reflections of Faith.* New York: E. P. Dutton. 1983.

Edison, Carol. "Motorcycles, Guitars, and Bucking Broncs: Twentieth-Century Gravestones in Southeastern Idaho." In *Idaho Folklife: Homesteads to Headstones.* Edited by Louie W. Attebery. Salt Lake City: University of Utah Press, 1985, pp. 184–89.

Gillon, Edmund V., Jr. *Victorian Cemetery Art.* New York: Dover Publications, 1972.

Hall, David D. "The Gravestone Image as a Puritan Cultural Code." In *Puritan Gravestone Art.* Edited by Peter Benes. The Dublin Seminar for New England Folklife Annual Proceedings, 1976. Boston: Boston University Press, 1977, pp. 23–32.

Huber, Leonard V. *Clasped Hands: Symbolism in New Orleans Cemeteries.* Lafayette, La: The Center for Louisiana Studies, 1982.

Jack, Phil R. "Gravestone Symbols of Western Pennsylvania." In *Two Penny Ballads and Four Dollar Whiskey: A Pennsylvania Folklore Miscellany.* Edited by Kenneth S. Goldstein and Robert H. Byington. Hatboro, Pa.: Folklore Associates, 1966, pp. 165–73.

Lindahl, Carl. "Transition Symbolism on Tombstones." *Western Folklore* 45:3 (1986), pp. 165–85.

Linden, Blanche M. G. "The Willow Tree and Urn Motif: Changing Ideas about Death and Nature." *Markers* 1 (1980), pp. 148–55.

Ludwig, Allan I. "Eros and Agape: Classical and Early Christian Survivals in New England Stonecarving." In *Puritan Gravestone Art.* Edited by Peter Benes. The Dublin Seminar for New England Folklife Annual Proceedings, 1976. Boston: Boston University Press, 1977, pp. 41–56.

McDannell, Colleen. "The Religious Symbolism of Laurel Hill Cemetery." *The Pennsylvania Magazine of History and Biography* 111:3 (1987), pp. 275–303.

Murphy, Buck P. "Victorian Cemetery Art." *Design* 75:2 (1974), pp. 6–9.

Prestiano, Robert. "The Example of D. Aldo Pitassi: Evolutionary Thought and Practice in Contemporary Memorial Design." *Markers* 2 (1983), pp. 203–20.

Price, Beulah M. D'Olive. "The Custom of Using Portrait Statues as Gravestones." *Mississippi Folklore Register* 3 (1969), pp. 58–64; 112–20.

Roberts, Warren E. "Investigating the Tree-Stump Tombstone in Indiana." In *American Material Culture and Folklife: A Prologue and Dialogue.* Edited by Simon J. Bronner. Ann Arbor, Mich.: UMI Research Press, 1985, pp. 135–43.

――――. "The Sincerest Form of Flattery: Originals and Imitations in 'Rustic Monuments' of the Limestone Belt of Indiana." In *Viewpoints on Folklife: Looking at the Overlooked.* Ann Arbor, Mich.: UMI Research Press, 1988, pp. 145–61.

――――. "Tombstones in Scotland and Indiana." *Folk-Life: A Journal of Ethnological Studies* 23 (1984–85), pp. 97–104.

――――. "Tools on Tombstones: Some Indiana Examples." *Pioneer America* 10:1 (1978), pp. 106–11.

――――. "Traditional Tools as Symbols: Some Examples from Indiana Tombstones." *Pioneer America* 12:1 (1980), pp. 54–63.

Watters, David. "The Park and Whiting Family Stones Revisited: The Iconography of the Church Covenant." *Canadian Review of American Studies* 9:1 (1978), pp. 1–15.

Epitaphs

Childers, William C. "Some Themes and Variations in Georgia Cemetery Epitaphs." *Southern Folklore Quarterly* 20:2 (1956), pp. 97–107.

Downs, Virginia. "Folk Poetry in Gravestone Verse." *Kentucky Folklore Record* 25:1 (1979), pp. 28–36.

George, Diana Hume and Nelson, Malcolm A. "Resurrecting the Epitaph." *Markers* 1 (1980), pp. 84–95.

———. "Resurrecting the Epitaph: A Holistic Approach." *Kentucky Folklore Record* 26:2 (1980), pp. 83–94.

Mann, Thomas C. and Greene, Janet. *Over Their Dead Bodies: Yankee Epitaphs & History.* Brattleboro, Vt.: The Stephen Greene Press, 1962.

———. *Sudden & Awful: American Epitaphs and the Finger of God.* Brattleboro, Vt.: The Stephen Greene Press, 1968.

Penhallow, D. P. "Epitaphal Inscriptions." *Journal of American Folk-Lore* 5:4 (1892), pp. 305–17.

Vovelle, Michel. "A Century and One-Half of American Epitaphs (1660–1813): Toward the Study of Collective Attitudes about Death." *Comparative Studies in Society and History* 22:4 (1980), pp. 534–47.

Wallis, Charles L. *Stories on Stone: A Book of American Epitaphs.* New York: Oxford University Press, 1954.

Ethnicity

Adams, Robert H. "Markers Cut by Hand." *The American West* 4:3 (1967), pp. 59–64.

Babba, Preston A. *Pennsylvania German Tombstones: A Study in Folk Art.* Allentown, Pa.: Schlecters, 1954.

Bolton, H. Carrington. "Decorating of Graves of Negroes in South Carolina." *Journal of American Folk-Lore* 4 (1891), p. 214.

Clark, Sara. "The Decoration of Graves in Central Texas with Seashells." In *Diamond Bessie and the Shepherds.* Edited by Wilson M. Hudson. Publications of the Texas Folklore Society, no. 36. Austin: Encino Press, 1972, pp. 33–43.

Combes, John D. "Ethnography, Archaeology and Burial Practices among Coastal South Carolina Blacks." *Conference on Historic Site Archaeology, Papers* 7 (1972), pp. 52–61.

Cozzens, Arthur B. "A Cherokee Graveyard." *Pioneer America* 4:1 (1972), p. 8.

Erwin, Paul F. "Scottish Gypsies and Their Burial Customs: Facts and Folklore." *Urban Resources* 4:3 (1987), pp. C1-C4.

Graves, Thomas. "Liebster Kinder und Verwandten: Death and Ethnicity." *Keystone Folklore* (New Series) 2:1–2 (1983), pp. 6–14.

Grider, Sylvia Ann, and Jones, Sarah Jarvis. "The Cultural Legacy of Texas Cemeteries." *Texas Humanist* 6:5 (1984), pp. 34–39.

Ingersoll, Ernest. "Decoration of Negro Graves." *Journal of American Folk-Lore* 5 (1892), pp. 68–69.

Knapp, Ronald G. "The Changing Landscape of the Chinese Cemetery." *The China Geographer* 8 (1977), pp. 1–14.

Lai, Chuen-Yan David. "A Feng Shui Model as a Location Index." *Annals of the Association of American Geographers* 27 (1974), pp. 506–13.

Levy, B. H. "Savannah's Old Jewish Community Cemeteries." *The Georgia Historical Quarterly* 66:1 (1982), pp. 1–20.

Marquardt, Lewis R. "Metal Grave Markers in German-Russian Cemeteries of Emmons County, North Dakota." *Journal of the American Historical Society of Germans from Russia* 2:2 (1979), pp. 18–26.

McDonald, Frank E. "Pennsylvania German Tombstone Art of Lebanon County, Pennsylvania." *Pennsylvania Folklife* 25:1 (1975), pp 2–19.

Mathias, Elizabeth. "The Italian-American Funeral: Persistence Through Change." *Western Folklore* 33:1 (1974), pp. 35–50.

Milspaw, Yvonne J. "Segregation in Life, Segregation in Death: Landscape of an Ethnic Cemetery." *Pennsylvania Folklife* 30:1 (1980), pp. 36–40.

Vlach, John Michael. *The Afro-American Tradition in Decorative Arts.* Cleveland: Cleveland Museum of Art, 1978, pp. 139–47.

Vrooman, Nicholas Curchin, and Marvin, Patrice Avon, eds. *Iron Spirits.* Fargo, N.D.: North Dakota Council on the Arts, 1982.

Warren, Nancy Hunter. "New Mexico Village Camposantos." *Markers* 4 (1987), pp. 115–29.

Weiser, Frederick S. "Baptismal Certificate and Gravemarker: Folk Art at the Beginning and the End of Life." In *Perspectives on American Folk Art.* Edited by Ian M. G. Quimby and Scott T. Swank. New York: Norton, 1980, pp. 134–61.

West, John O. "Folk Grave Decoration along the Rio Grande." In *Folk Art in Texas.* Edited by Francis Edward Abernethy. Publications of the Texas Folklore Society, no. 45. Dallas: Southern Methodist University Press, 1985, pp. 47–51.

Winkler, Louis. "Pennsylvania German Astronomy and Astrology IV: Tombstones." *Pennsylvania Folklife* 22:2 (1972), pp. 42–45.

The Cemetery as Landscape

Blaney, Herbert, "The Modern Park Cemetery." In *Passing: The Vision of Death in America.* Edited by Charles O. Jackson. Westport, Conn.: Greenwood Press, 1977, pp. 219–26.

Howett, Catherine. "Living Landscapes for the Dead." *Landscape* 21:3 (1977), pp. 9–17.

Jackson, J. B. "The Vanishing Epitaph: From Monument to Place." *Landscape* 17:2 (1967), pp. 22–26.

Kniffen, Fred. "Necrogeography in the United States." *The Geographical Review* 57 (1967), pp. 426–27.

Pattison, William D. "The Cemeteries of Chicago: A Phase of Land Utilizaton." *Annals, Association of American Geographers* 45 (1955), pp. 245–57.

Stilgoe, John R. "Folklore and Graveyard Design." *Landscape* 22:3 (1978), pp. 22–28.

Thomas, Jack Ward, and Dixon, Ronald A. "Cemetery Ecology." *Natural History* 82:3 (1973), pp. 60–67.

Walsh, Edward R. "Cemeteries: Recreation's New Space Frontier." *Parks and Recreation* 10:6 (1975), pp. 28–29; 53–54.

The "Rural" Cemetery Movement

Bender, Thomas. "The 'Rural' Cemetery Movement: Urban Travail and the Appeal of Nature." *The New England Quarterly* 47 (1974), pp. 196–211.

Darnall, Margaretta J. "The American Cemetery as Picturesque Landscape: Bellefontaine Cemetery, St. Louis." *Winterthur Portfolio: A Journal of American Material Culture* 18:4 (1983), pp. 249–69.

French, Stanley. "The Cemetery as Cultural Institution: The Establishment of Mount Auburn and the 'Rural Cemetery' Movement." *American Quarterly* 26 (1974), pp. 37–59. Reprinted in *Death in America* Edited by David E. Stannard. Philadelphia: University of Pennsylvania Press, 1975, pp. 69–91.

Harris, Neil. "The Cemetery Beautiful." In *Passing: The Vision of Death in America* Edited by Charles O. Jackson. Westport, Conn: Greenwood Press, 1977, pp. 103–11.

Linden-Ward, Blanche. "Nature by Design: The Art and Landscape of Cincinnati's Spring Grove." Documentary Video (28.5 minutes). Cincinnati: Center for Neighborhood and Community Studies, 1987.

———. "Putting the Past in Place: The Making of Mount Auburn Cemetery." *Proceedings of the Cambridge Historical Society* 44 (1985), pp. 171–96.

———. *Silent City on a Hill: Landscapes of Memory and Boston's Mount Auburn Cemetery.* Columbus, Oh.: Ohio State University Press, 1988.

———, and Sloane, David C. "Spring Grove: The Founding of Cincinnati's Rural Cemetery, 1845–1855." *Queen City Heritage: The Journal of the Cincinnati Historical Society* 43:1 (1985), pp. 17–32.

———, and Ward, Alan. "Spring Grove: The Role of the Rural Cemetery in American Landscape Design." *Landscape Architect* 75:5 (1985), pp. 126–31; 140.

Lockwood, Charles, and Newman, Marvin. "Green-Wood: Fashionable Cemetery with a View." *Smithsonian* 7:4 (1976), pp. 56–63.

Morgan, Keith N. "The Emergence of the American Landscape Professional: John Notman and the Design of Rural Cemeteries." *Journal of Garden History* 4:3 (1984), pp. 269–89.

Remes, Naomi R. "The Rural Cemetery." *Nineteenth Century* 5:4 (1979), pp. 52–55.

Rotundo, Barbara. "Mount Auburn Cemetery: A Proper Boston Institution." *Harvard Library Bulletin* 22:3 (1974), pp. 268–79.

———. . "Mount Auburn: Fortunate Coincidence and an Ideal Solution." *Journal of Garden History* 4:3 (1984), pp. 255–67.

———. . "The Rural Cemetery Movement." *Essex Institute Historical Collections* 109 (1973), pp. 231–40.

Schuyler, David. "The Evolution of the Anglo-American Rural Cemetery: Landscape Architecture as Social and Cultural History." *Journal of Garden History* 4:3 (1984), pp. 291–304.

Sharf, Frederic A. "The Garden Cemetery and American Sculpture." *Art Quarterly* 34:2 (1961), pp. 80–88.

Simon, Donald E. "The Worldly Side of Paradise: Green-Wood Cemetery." In *A Time to Mourn: Expressions of Grief in Nineteenth-Century America* Edited by Martha V. Pike and Janice Gray Armstrong. Stony Brook, N.Y.: The Museums at Stony Brook, 1980, pp. 51–66.

Stannard, David E. "Calm Dwellings: The Brief, Sentimental Age of the Rural Cemetery." *American Heritage* 30 (1979), pp. 42–46; 54–60.

Zanger, Jules. "Mount Auburn Cemetery: The Silent Suburb." *Landscape* 24:2 (1980), pp. 23–28.

Non-American Materials

Adams, John D., ed. *Heritage Cemeteries in British Columbia: Collected Papers.* Victoria, B.C.: Victoria Branch, B.C. Historical Federation, 1985.

Brears, P. C. D. "Heart Gravestones in the Calder Valley." *Folk-Life: A Journal of Ethnological Studies* 19 (1981), pp. 84–93.

Brown, Frederick. *Père Lachaise: Elysium as Real Estate.* New York: Viking, 1979.

Burgess, Frederick. *English Churchyard Memorials.* London: Lutterworth Press, 1963.

Burgess, Pamela. *Churchyards.* London: SPCK, 1980.

Curl, James Stevens. *A Celebration of Death: An Introduction to Some of the Buildings,*

Monuments, and Settings of Funerary Architecture in the Western European Tradition. New York: Charles Scribner's Sons, 1980.

———. "The Design of the Early British Cemeteries." *Journal of Garden History* 4:3 (1984), pp. 223–54.

———. *The Victorian Celebration of Death.* Detroit: The Partridge Press, 1972.

deBrunhoff, Anne. *Souls in Stone: European Graveyard Sculpture.* New York: Alfred A. Knopf, 1978.

Etlin, Richard A. *The Architecture of Death: The Transformation of the Cemetery in Eighteenth-Century Paris.* Cambridge, Mass.: The MIT Press, 1984.

Hanks, Carole. *Early Ontario Gravestones.* Toronto: McGraw-Ryerson, 1974.

Hawker, Ronald W. "Monuments in the Nineteenth-Century Cemeteries of Victoria, British Columbia." *Material History Bulletin* 26 (1987), pp. 19–26.

Kemp, B. *English Church Monuments.* London: Batsford, 1980.

Lindley, Kenneth. *Graves and Graveyards.* London: Routledge & Kegan Paul, 1972.

———. *Of Graves and Epitaphs.* London: Hutchinson, 1965.

Osborne, Brian S. "The Cemeteries of the Midland District of Upper Canada: A Note on Mortality in a Frontier Society." *Pioneer America* 6:1 (1974), pp. 46–55.

Penny, Nicholas. *Church Monuments in Romantic England.* New Haven, Conn.: Yale University Press, 1977.

Ragon, Michel. *The Space of Death: A Study of Funerary Architecture, Decoration, and Urbanism.* Trans. Alan Sheridan. Charlottesville: University Press of Virginia, 1983.

Trask, Deborah. *Life How Short, Eternity How Long: Gravestone Carving and Carvers in Nova Scotia.* Halifax, N.S.: The Nova Scotia Museum, 1978.

Wallace, Robert. "The Elegies and Enigmas of Romantic Père Lachaise." *Smithsonian* 9:11 (1978), pp. 108–17.

Willshire, Betty. "Scottish Gravestones and the New England Winged Skull." *Markers* 2 (1983), pp. 105–14.

———, and Hunter, Doreen. *Stones: A Gude to Some Remarkable Eighteenth Century Gravestones.* New York: Taplinger Publishing Company, 1978.

Guidebooks

Arbeiter, Jean, and Cirino, Linda D. *Permanent Addresses: A Guide to the Resting Places of Famous Americans.* New York: M. Evans and Company, 1983.

Barker, Felix and Gay, John. *Highgate Cemetery: Victorian Valhalla.* Salem, N.H.: Salem House, 1984.

Culbertson, Judi, and Randall, Tom. *Permanent New Yorkers: A Biographical Guide to the Cemeteries of New York.* Chelsea, Vt.: Chelsea Green Publishing Company, 1987.

———. *Permanent Parisians: An Illustrated Guide to the Cemeteries of Paris.* Chelsea, Vt: Chelsea Green Publishing Company, 1986.

Dickerson, Robert B., Jr. *Final Placement: A Guide to the Deaths, Funerals, and Burials of Notable Americans.* Algonac, Mich.: Reference Publications, 1982.

Ellis, Nancy, and Hayden, Parker. *Here Lies America: A Collection of Notable Graves.* New York: Hawthorn Books, 1978.

George, Diana Hume, and Nelson, Malcolm A. *Epitaph and Icon: A Field Guide to the Old Burying Grounds of Cape Cod, Martha's Vineyard, and Nantucket.* Orleans, Mass.: Parnassus Imprints, 1983.

Koykka, Arthur S. *Project Remember: A National Index of Gravesites of Notable Americans.* Algonac, Mich.: Reference Publications, 1986.

Kull, Andrew. *New England Cemeteries: A Collector's Guide.* Brattleboro, Vt: The Stephen Greene Press, 1975.

Marion, John Francis. *Famous and Curious Cemeteries.* New York: Crown Publishers, 1977.

Meller, Hugh. *London Cemeteries: An Illustrated Guide and Gazetteer.* Amersham, England: Avebury Publishing Company, 1981.

Peters, James Edward. *Arlington National Cemetery: Shrine to America's Heroes.* Kensington, Md.: Woodbine House, 1986.

General/Correlative Works on Death and Culture

Ariès, Philippe. *The Hour of Our Death.* Trans. Helen Weaver. New York: Alfred A. Knopf, 1981.

———. *Images of Man and Death.* Trans. Janet Lloyd. Cambridge, Mass.: Harvard University Press, 1985.

———. *Western Attitudes toward Death from the Middle Ages to the Present.* Trans. Patricia M. Ranum. Baltimore: Johns Hopkins University Press, 1974.

Cornish, Vaughn. *The Churchyard Yew and Immortality.* London: Frederick Miller, 1946.

Douglas, Ann. *The Feminization of American Culture.* New York: Alfred A. Knopf, 1977.

———. "Heaven Our Home: Consolation Literature in the Northern United States, 1830–1880." In *Death in America.* Edited by David E. Stannard. Philadelphia: University of Pennsylvania Press, 1975, pp. 49–68.

Farrell, James J. *Inventing the American Way of Death, 1830–1920.* Philadelphia: Temple University Press, 1980.

Habenstein, Robert W., and Lamers, William M. *The History of American Funeral Directing.* Milwaukee: Bulfin Printers, 1962.

Huntington, Richard, and Metcalf, Peter. *Celebrations of Death: The Anthropology of Mortuary Ritual.* Cambridge: Cambridge University Press, 1979.

s'Jacob, Henriette. *Idealism and Realism: A Study of Sepulchral Symbolism.* Leiden: E. J. Brill, 1954.

Meyers, Mary Ann. "Gates Ajar: Death in Mormon Thought and Practice." In *Death in America.* Edited by David E. Stannard. Philadelphia: Unviersity of Pennsylvania Press, 1975, pp. 112–33.

Mitford, Jessica. *The American Way of Death.* New York: Simon and Schuster, 1963.

Montell, William Lynwood. *Ghosts along the Cumberland: Deathlore in the Kentucky Foothills.* Knoxville, Tenn.: University of Tennessee Press, 1975.

Morley, John. *Death, Heaven and the Victorians.* Pittsburgh: University of Pittsburgh Press, 1971.

Panofsky, Erwin. *Tomb Sculpture: Four Lectures on Its Changing Aspects from Ancient Egypt to Bernini.* New York: Abrams, 1924.

Pike, Martha. "In Memory Of: Artifacts Relating to Mourning in Nineteenth-Century America." In *American Material Culture: The Shape of Things Around Us.* Edited by Edith Mayo. Bowling Green, Oh.: Popular Press, 1984, pp. 48–65.

———, and Armstrong, Janice Gray, eds. *A Time to Mourn: Expressions of Grief in Nineteenth Century America.* Stony Brook, N.Y.: The Museums at Stony Brook, 1980.

Sandler, Richard L. "Mourning Delivery: An Examination of Newspaper Memorials." *Journal of Popular Culture* 14:4 (1981), pp. 690–700.

Saum, Lewis O. "Death in the Popular Mind of Pre-Civil War America." In *Death in America.* Edited by David E. Stannard. Philadelphia: University of Pennsylvania Press, 1975, pp. 30–48.

Schorsch, Anita. "A Key to the Kingdom: The Iconography of a Mourning Picture." *Winterthur Portfolio: A Journal of American Material Culture* 14:1 (1979), pp. 41–71.

Stannard, David E. *The Puritan Way of Death: A Study in Religion, Culture, and Social Change.* New York: Oxford University Press, 1977.

Contributors

EDWARD W. CLARK, a member of the English faculty at Winthrop College, Rock Hill, S.C., has focused his interests upon the interdisciplinary study of eighteenth- and nineteenth-century American culture. He is the editor of *The Redeemed Captive* (Amherst: University of Massachusetts Press, 1976) and coeditor of *Puritans among the Indians: Accounts of Captivity and Redemption, 1676–1724* (Cambridge: Harvard University Press, 1981).

KEITH CUNNINGHAM teaches English and Folklore at Northern Arizona University. For many years editor of the journal *Southwest Folklore,* his primary areas of scholarly interest, in addition to gravemarker and cemetery studies, have been American urban legends and other forms of folk narrative.

J. JOSEPH EDGETTE is a folklorist with both teaching and administrative responsibilities at Widener University, Chester, Pa. His long-standing interest in gravemarkers as cultural artifacts has resulted in several published articles and museum exhibitions on various aspects of this area of study.

LYNN GOSNELL, a graduate student in Folklore and Anthropology at the University of Texas, Austin, has concentrated her research interests upon the relationships between folk and popular material culture forms.

SUZANNE GOTT is a doctoral candidate in the Folklore program at Indiana University, where she is primarily concerned with the cross-cultural study of aesthetics, with a particular interest in performance studies.

THOMAS J. HANNON teaches within the Department of Geography and Environmental Studies at Slippery Rock University, Slippery Rock, Pa. His research has focused upon the geography of religion, with special emphasis upon religious landscapes such as the cemetery, and he is currently conducting research for a book on Pennsylvania cemeteries.

D. GREGORY JEANE, a cultural/historical geographer with primary research interests in the areas of necrogeography (the geographical study of death) and the geography of grist milling, is a member of the Geography faculty at Auburn University, Auburn, Ala. Author of a number of articles and monographs, he is presently at work upon a book-length study of rural Southern cemeteries.

BLANCHE LINDEN-WARD is Coordinator of the American Culture and Communication Program at Emerson College, Boston, Mass. She has authored *Silent City on a Hill: Landscapes of Memory and Boston's Mount Auburn Cemetery* (Columbus: Ohio State University Press, 1988) and a number of articles on the cultural history of American cemeteries.

PEGGY MCDOWELL is both an art historian and a practicing studio artist (sculpture). A member of the faculty in the Department of Fine Arts at the University of New Orleans, she is a coauthor of the book *New Orleans Architecture, III: The Cemeteries* (Gretna, La.: Pelican Publishing Co., 1974).

RICHARD E. MEYER is a folklorist and member of the English faculty at Western Oregon State College, Monmouth, Ore. His publications include articles in both Folklore and English and American literature, and he has served for several years as chair of the Cemeteries and Gravemarkers section of the American Culture Association.

BARBARA ROTUNDO, who teaches in the English Department of the State University of New York at Albany, has published a number of scholarly articles on nineteenth-century American cemeteries and is a long-time enthusiastic supporter of the Association for Gravestone Studies.

ELLEN MARIE SNYDER, a specialist in various aspects of Victorian material culture, is presently Chief Curator at the Brooklyn Historical Society, Brooklyn, N.Y.

DICKRAN AND ANN TASHJIAN are the authors of the highly acclaimed *Memorials for Children of Change: The Art of Early New England Stonecarving* (Middletown, Conn.: Wesleyan University Press, 1974). Dickran Tashjian is a member of the faculty of the Program in Comparative Culture at the University of California, Irvine.

Index